A LIFE IN MUSIC

A LIFE
IN
MUSIC

CONVERSATIONS WITH
SIR DAVID WILLCOCKS
AND FRIENDS

EDITED BY
WILLIAM OWEN

MUSIC DEPARTMENT

OXFORD
UNIVERSITY PRESS

OXFORD
UNIVERSITY PRESS

Great Clarendon Street, Oxford OX2 6DP, UK
198 Madison Avenue, New York, NY 10016, USA

Oxford University Press is a department of the University of Oxford.
It furthers the University's objective of excellence in research, scholarship, and education by publishing
worldwide in

Oxford New York

Auckland Bangkok Buenos Aires Cape Town Chennai
Dar es Salaam Delhi Hong Kong Istanbul Karachi Kolkata
Kuala Lumpur Madrid Melbourne Mexico City Mumbai Nairobi
São Paulo Shanghai Taipei Tokyo Toronto

Oxford is a registered trade mark of Oxford University Press in the UK and in certain other countries

© Oxford University Press 2008

The moral rights of the author have been asserted
Database right Oxford University Press (maker)

First published 2008

British Library Cataloguing in Publication Data
Data available

Library of Congress Cataloguing in Publication Data
Data available

1 3 5 7 9 10 8 6 4 2

ISBN 978–0–19–336063–1

Typeset by Refinecatch Limited, Bungay, Suffolk
Printed in Great Britain on acid-free paper by
CPI Antony Rowe, Chippenham, Wiltshire

Contents

I first met David in the early 1970's when I was an undergraduate at Trinity College, Cambridge. He already had a worldwide reputation as Director of the magnificent King's College Choir, but what I remember was his sense of humour and lightness of touch, as well as his perfectionism.

As President of The Bach Choir, I later saw on numerous occasions his extraordinary command of a large choir and orchestra and his ability to draw musicality out of everyone involved. David has always taken as much pride in bringing the best out of amateur musicians as working with world-class professionals. He has brought a love of choral music to countless people here in Britain, in America and elsewhere.

Christmas has always been associated for me with David's music – first with carols from King's College Chapel and then Family Carols from The Bach Choir, as well as his many wonderful carol arrangements published by Oxford University Press.

One should not forget his fine military record, which was recognized with a Military Cross. He has always been modest about his achievements. It is important to acknowledge what he and so many others did for our country in the Second World War – and especially in Normandy and Holland.

I am delighted that Yale University has brought together many people's recollections of David's life, as well as his own fascinating reminiscences. This book represents a wonderful tribute to a remarkable man.

Introduction

This book has developed from an oral history project about the life and work of Sir David Willcocks. It has been a privilege to work with David on this project, and throughout he has been patient, helpful, and inspiring in telling the story of his fascinating life. Over fifty people have generously taken the time to reflect on their experiences with David, and between them have covered the most pertinent aspects of his life and musical contributions. Remarkably, not a single person has refused to be interviewed. Many were emotional: all of them have laughed; some have wept. If there was one connecting thread throughout all the interviews, it has been David's infectious enthusiasm.

The premise of oral history is simple: there are living individuals who either made history or witnessed it, and it is important to have their recollections recorded. Even today, the field is still in its infancy. Of course one encounters discrepancies: any two people who witness an event will remember it differently; from this, perhaps, the truth emerges. I first experienced oral history as a graduate student at Yale University in the late 1970s, when I had the good fortune to work with Vivian Perlis, the Founder and Director of Yale's *Oral History American Music*, on projects devoted to Charles Ives and Aaron Copland. My interest in the field was keen, but I pursued a career in church music. Over twenty-five years later, on a sabbatical from my post as organist and choirmaster, I have been able to attempt my own project. David agreed to an initial round of interviews, and we have been working at it ever since.

A copy of the final tapes and transcripts will reside in the Yale oral history archive and another set with David's papers in the United Kingdom. The material will be open, by permission, to scholars and students on both sides of the Atlantic, and should prove an important resource for research on twentieth-century choral music. I encourage people to *listen* to the actual interviews. Transcriptions can only give the verbal content, and the interviews reveal the emotion, voice inflections, and the many times people—including David—have burst into song or rushed to a piano to demonstrate musically what they are describing. These are the exciting aspects of oral history that bring it to life.

This book has been structured around a central narrative recounting David's story in nine chapters. To accommodate the many other contributions from family and friends, each main chapter is followed by an interlude chapter, containing a selection of reflections and anecdotes from the same period. These are amusing, sad, and generous in spirit, and round out a portrait of a modest yet highly gifted musician. The book is completed, firstly with a selection of wonderful photographs from David's life, and secondly with a CD containing extracts from some of the many seminal and important recordings from David's career.

It is dangerous to begin thanking individuals, but all those who consented to be subjected to my tape recorder and questions are due sincere thanks. Maggie Heywood, our Assistant Director in England, spent countless hours transcribing interviews and helping me with corrections and additions, as well as tracking down people, material, and photographs. Sandra Anderson carefully transcribed David's interviews and several others. Vivian Perlis and Libby Van Cleve from Yale's *Oral History American Music* offered encouragement and advice and agreed to house the project at Yale. I am grateful to the former Rector, the Rev. Dr John Martiner, and current Rector, the Rev. Ruth Lawson Kirk, of Christ Church Christiana Hundred, Wilmington, Delaware USA, for their encouragement and support, and for allowing me to devote time and energy to this project. Sherry Lawton-Fasic and Millie Miller from the church staff helped me in many ways and were patient with my frequent computer issues. Leopold de Rothschild and Philippa Dutton helped with The Bach Choir and Royal College of Music chapters and contributions. Sir Philip Ledger and John Rutter have been constant advisors and read the entire book in manuscript, making countless invaluable suggestions. I am also most grateful to John Rutter for all his help in assembling the CD. David Blackwell and his colleagues in the Music Department at Oxford University Press have been supportive, and aided in all aspects of the book's production. Finally Rachel Willcocks, Sir David's wife, has been unfailingly patient and helpful, and has offered regular counsel; her cheerful, supportive spirit and generous hospitality helped make this project possible.

A last word of thanks is due to the family of Alletta Laird Downs. The enclosed CD of excerpts has been generously supported by funds donated in her memory by some of her relatives. Mrs Downs (1913–2005) was a lifelong parishioner at Christ Church Christiana Hundred. She served as Chair of the Church's Music Committee from 1977 to 2003, and through her joyous and longstanding contributions, many outstanding musicians, including Sir David and John Rutter, have been able to compose and perform under the auspices of the Christ Church Musician-in-?esidence Program.

The book, and the oral history from which it is drawn, is intended as a fair and honest testament of David's life. Of course, his real legacy lies in his music-making, the students he has influenced, and the many amateur musicians he has inspired. In the words of John Rutter, David 'set new standards in choral music in the United Kingdom and beyond. He shook up the dusty profession of cathedral organist, giving it a new professionalism, energy, and stature. In an iconic series of recordings with the King's College Choir, he opened the ears of millions of listeners world-wide to the beauty of choral singing. He revived little-known music of the English golden age and brought new music into the choral repertoire. He almost single-handedly transformed our musical celebration of Christmas. He trained and encouraged generations of musicians. And he led one of our great musical conservatories towards the twenty-first century.'

To me, David's career represents the climax of, and one of the last links to, the Golden Years of English choral music—from Elgar to Vaughan Williams, Britten, and Howells. It is fascinating to see his students and colleagues, many of them represented here, building on the foundations that he has laid so splendidly.

WILLIAM OWEN
April 2008

Selected List of Works by David Willcocks

Below is a selection of the works by David Willcocks published by Oxford University Press. A full list, including details of scoring for the orchestral arrangements, is available from the Publishers.

Anthems and Sacred Works

In addition to the works listed below, David Willcocks was also for many years General Editor of three Oxford series: Oxford Church Services, Oxford Anthems, and Oxford Easy Anthems.

All people that on earth do dwell (Old Hundredth), SATB, congregation, and organ or orchestra

Ceremony of Psalms, baritone solo, SATB, and small orchestra: O sing unto the Lord a new song (Ps. 98); Out of the deep* (Ps. 130); O praise God in his holiness (Ps. 150); The Lord is my shepherd* (Ps. 23); Thou, O God, art praised in Sion (Ps. 65).

Christ the Lord is risen again!, SATB and organ or brass, percussion, and organ

Lift up your heads, you gates, SATB and organ, or brass a8 and organ, or orchestra

Love divine, all loves excelling, SATB and organ

Magnificat and Nunc Dimittis, SATB and organ

My heart is fixed, O God, SATB and organ, with optional brass a7, timpani, and percussion

O Praise God in his holiness, SSAATTBB and organ

O sing unto the Lord a new song, SATB and organ or orchestra

Psalm 150, SSAA and organ

* for baritone solo.

Rejoice today with one accord, SATB and organ or brass and organ

Sing!, SATB and organ or organ and orchestra

Six Hymns of Praise, SATB, congregation, and organ or orchestra: All people that on earth do dwell (Old Hundredth); Christ is made the sure foundation; O praise ye the Lord; Holy, Holy, Holy; Let all the world; The day thou gavest

Thou, O God, art praised in Sion, SATB and organ or orchestra

Two Benedictions, SATB *a cappella*: The peace of God; O God, who hast prepared

Carols

Carols for Choirs, book 1, co-edited with Reginald Jacques

Carols for Choirs, books 2, 3, and 4, and *100 Carols for Choirs*, co-edited with John Rutter

There are numerous carols and carol arrangements by David Willcocks published in the *Carols for Choirs* series, many of which are also available separately. Most of the carols with organ accompaniment are also available arranged for orchestra or brass and percussion.

Two pieces for organ based on carols are published in *The Oxford Book of Christmas Organ Music*: Postlude on 'Hark! the herald-angels sing' and Prelude on 'Irby' ('Once in Royal David's city').

Partsongs and Secular Works

Advance Australia Fair, SATB and organ or orchestra

Five Folk Songs, SATB *a cappella*: The Lass of Richmond Hill; Barbara Allen; Drink to me only; Early one morning; Bobby Shaftoe

National Anthem, SATB, brass, organ, and percussion or brass fanfare and orchestra

O mistress mine, SATB *a cappella*

The Glories of Shakespeare, SSA and piano or orchestra: Fear no more the heat o' the sun; Full Fathom Five; It was a lover and his lass; Under the greenwood tree; Who is Silvia?

CD Track Listing

The CD that accompanies this book includes both spoken tracks (shown in light type in the list below) and musical tracks (shown in **bold** type). The spoken tracks of David Willcocks were recorded at David's home in Cambridge by John Rutter in June 2008. The musical tracks have been selected from David's many fine professional recordings, copyright in which is owned by Decca Music Group Ltd and EMI Records Limited, as detailed below. The Publishers are most grateful to these companies for permission to include these extracts, and also to John Rutter for all his help in assembling this recording.

1. Memories of King George V and Queen Mary at Westminster Abbey.
2. **Handel: 'Zadok the Priest'.** The World of King's: King's College Choir, Cambridge, English Chamber Orchestra, conducted by Sir David Willcocks, ℗ 1963.*
3. Memories of Vaughan Williams and Howells at Westminster Abbey.
4. **Howells: Magnificat from King's College (Collegium Regale) service.** Herbert Howells Church Music: King's College Choir, Cambridge, Andrew Davis, organ, conducted by Sir David Willcocks, ℗ 1967.*
5. Further memories of Howells.
6. **Howells: *Hymnus Paradisi*, Preludio.** The Bach Choir, Choir of King's College, Cambridge, New Philharmonia Orchestra, conducted by Sir David Willcocks, ℗ 1971.†
7. Memories of Vaughan Williams conducting *Hodie*.
8. **Vaughan Williams: *Hodie*, first movement.** The Bach Choir, London Symphony Orchestra, conducted by Sir David Willcocks, ℗ 1965.†
9. On the first performances and recording of the *War Requiem*.
10. **Britten: 'Dies Irae' from the *War Requiem* (excerpt).** The Bach Choir and London Symphony Orchestra Chorus, Highgate School Choir, Melos Ensemble, London Symphony Orchestra, conducted by Benjamin Britten, ℗ 1963, 1999.*
11. Memories of World War II evoked by the recording of the *War Requiem*.
12. Tribute to Peter Pears.

13. **Britten: 'Agnus Dei' from the** *War Requiem*. Peter Pears, tenor, The Bach Choir and London Symphony Orchestra Chorus, Highgate School Choir, Melos Ensemble, London Symphony Orchestra, conducted by Benjamin Britten, ℗1963, 1999.*

14. On performing and recording Tudor music.

15. **Byrd: 'Justorum animae'.** Byrd and his Contemporaries: King's College Choir, Cambridge, conducted by Sir David Willcocks, ℗ 1965.†

16. On performing the psalms in King's College Chapel.

17. **Psalm 23.** The Psalms of David: King's College Choir, Cambridge, Sir David Willcocks, organ, ℗ 1972.†

18. On playing the organ at King's.

19. **Howells: Psalm Prelude No. 1 (excerpt)**. Herbert Howells Church Music: David Willcocks, organ.*

20. On recording the Allegri *Miserere*.

21. **Allegri: *Miserere* (abridged).** The World of King's: King's College Choir, Cambridge, Roy Goodman, solo treble, conducted by Sir David Willcocks, ℗ 1963.*

22. Memories of Roy Goodman, and on choosing soloists.

23. **Gauntlett/Mann: 'Once in Royal David's city'.** Noël – Christmas at King's: King's College Choir, Cambridge, conducted by Sir David Willcocks, ℗ 1964.*

24. Boris Ord gives the note for 'Once in Royal David's city'; on the genesis of *Carols for Choirs*.

25. **Wade/Willcocks: 'O come, all ye faithful' (descant verse).** On Christmas Night: King's College Choir, Cambridge, conducted by Sir David Willcocks, ℗ 1962.*

26. Reflections on descants; letters of appreciation received for Festival of Nine Lessons and Carols.

27. **Darke: 'In the bleak midwinter'.** Noël – Christmas at King's: King's College Choir, Cambridge, Simon Preston, organ, conducted by Sir David Willcocks, ℗ 1962.*

28. On the genesis of *Carols for Choirs 2*.

29. **English trad./Willcocks: 'Tomorrow shall be my dancing day'.** Carols from King's College, Cambridge: King's College Choir, Cambridge, conducted by Sir David Willcocks, ℗ 1969.†

30. On the *St Matthew Passion*.

31. **Bach: *St Matthew Passion*, opening chorus (excerpt).** The Bach Choir, the Boys of St Paul's Cathedral Choir, Thames Chamber Orchestra, conducted by Sir David Willcocks, ℗ 1979.*

32. On 'I was glad'.

33. **Parry: 'I was glad'.** Anthems from King's: King's College Choir, Cambridge, James Lancelot, organ, conducted by Sir David Willcocks.†

* Recordings licensed courtesy of the Decca Music Group Ltd

† Recordings licensed courtesy of EMI Classics

I

Childhood and Westminster Abbey

1919–1934

W.   I'm told that I was born on the 30th of December 1919, the youngest of three boys. My elder brother is eight years older than I am, and the second brother is six years older. Both were born before World War I. I was a sort of follow-up after the war ended. My middle name is Valentine, because I was christened on the 14th of February, the feast day of St Valentine, in St Jude's Church in Englefield Green (Surrey). My mother's name was Dorothy Eleanor Harding. Her father was a country rector in Essex, England. She was one of seven sisters and two brothers. They weren't a wealthy family, and I just cannot think how a country parson was able to bring up a family of nine children in that way. They always seemed very happy and did well in their various ways. One of the two boys, William (known as 'Tam'), died in his thirties from pneumonia, and the other one, Jack, lived to be in his nineties. Three of my aunts were married, and I got to know them all. They were lovely people and were very kind to their little nephew whenever he went to stay.

O.   Where did your mother grow up?

W.   In Essex, in the vicarage. Her family used to rent a house down in Cornwall, a place called Porth, very near to Newquay on the north coast. It was on one of those visits, I think, that my father met my mother, who was down there with some of her family celebrating a holiday. My father, whose name was Theophilus Herbert Willcocks, was a bank manager in Newquay, which in those days was a relatively small town. I suppose there might have been a population of about three to four thousand.

O.   So, did he grow up in Newquay?

W.   No, my father grew up first of all on a farm named Tregorden, near Wadebridge, which is a nice little market town about sixteen miles north of Newquay. His family had farmed Tregorden for two or three hundred years. In those days the elder boy always inherited the farm, so my father, being one of the younger sons, was not eligible. He went into banking, first of all in Wadebridge and then in Plymouth. He then moved to Newquay as bank manager, and was at Newquay for about twenty years before he retired, at the age of fifty-eight. He lived to be ninety-three. He spent more time in retirement than he did working! My mother lived to be in her eighties. She had one of the very first hip operations, carried out when she was in her seventies. Such operations were considered quite risky in those days, particularly for people of her age. She had suffered from bad arthritis, which was very painful, so she was delighted when she found the pain was removed with the artificial hip. She learned to walk again, and she enjoyed life very much during her last years.

O.   Was your father musical?

W.   My father sang in the local choir in Newquay. He had no musical training whatsoever, but he had a very deep bass voice. He sang by ear and probably did not know the names of the notes. He could always harmonize very accurately. Once he had heard a hymn he would sing the bass part correctly. I think he would have done very well if he had had any training, because he had quite a nice voice. I used to play for him when he sang two party pieces. One was 'Asleep in the deep'; the other was 'Crossing the bar', to Tennyson's words, set to music by Sir Hubert Parry. One of them had a bottom C, which he sang with great relish. In those days we didn't have television or gramophone records, so a few friends used to make music in the home. Occasionally someone would bring his or her party piece to sing. Looking back now they were dreadful perform-ances, but they seemed to give pleasure. Sometimes people would recite poetry. It seems inconceivable today that people had to find their own amusements in the evenings.

O.   When were your parents married?

W.   In 1907.

O.   Tell me about the house in Newquay. Was it right in the town?

W.   I was actually born over the bank, because one of the perks of being the bank manager was having accommodation above the bank. So one would actually go in through the main entrance to the bank and instead of turning right to where the counters were, one would go straight upstairs. I can remember very little about the bank, as I was only five years old when my father retired, and the family moved from the bank to a much nicer position up on a hill called Mount Wise. I can remember helping to carry jam-jars up the hill, because my mother saved every jam-jar. We carried lots of other small items because we would save money if the movers did not have to take them.

O.   What do you remember about those years?

W.   I have only slender memories of my life before the age of seven, though I remember being a happy child. I can just recall being introduced to radio. One of my earliest recollections was listening to a weekly radio programme called *The Foundations of Music*, featuring Sir Walford Davies, who was Master of the King's Musick. He was quite entertaining in his way, particularly for young people. I remember him talking about semiquavers [sixteenth notes]. He said something like, 'Now I want today to talk about semiquavers. Those are the jolly little fellows that run up and down the piano like this.' Then he would play some scales. Another week he would talk about Bach. It was as a result of those talks that I first met him. My mother taught me at home to read and write and to do elementary arithmetic, so I didn't go to school until I was about eight or nine years old. My mother wasn't an academic, but she had high standards for grammar. She always used to make me write letters. If they weren't good, I would have to rewrite them. She would try to invent games, so that a lot of my learning was not through formal lessons. I was taught card games when I was quite young. Through these card games I learned to add and subtract and to play cribbage and whist and other games. I didn't learn bridge until I was about eight, I suppose. I just love cards, and I still play bridge.

O.   You must have had a lot of attention from your brothers.

W.   Yes, they were very kind to me. When they went for their long walks—and in Cornwall there are many beautiful coastal walks—it must have been inhibiting for them to have had a little brother trailing along behind them. We used to play ball games on the beach and climb cliffs. At an early age I took up golf, because somebody gave me a club. I used to play along with my brothers on golf courses, and even on the beach.

Figure 1.1. David at home in Cornwall, *c.*1928

Music never featured in my life until I was, I suppose, about six. I was taken to church where I enjoyed the hymns, but criticized the organist! We had an old piano in the house. I don't know why it was there, but I started to strum and teach myself to play the hymns we heard in church, first of all with one finger. I worked out that with some tunes it was easier if I started and ended with C—I discovered that before I ever had a lesson. And then I can remember experimenting with putting in the harmony. It must have been pretty awful, but I had a go at it long before I could ever write anything down. I think I had my first piano lessons at the age of six or seven.

O.   Did your mother play or sing?

W.   No, not at all. But she thought that her little boy—as he was so keen on strumming—ought to have some piano lessons. I suppose that it was after I had been learning for about six months that the piano tuner came to tune the piano. I was playing with cards on the floor, when I noticed that he struggled with one note. I said to him, 'I don't think you've got that B flat quite in tune yet.' He said, 'How did you know it was B flat?' I said, 'I know it is.' So he said, 'What note is this then?' And when he played a note, I said, 'That's F', because I knew the names of the notes. I was over at the other side of the room, and he couldn't understand how I could name the notes. He'd never met anybody with perfect pitch. Well, of course, a lot of people have it, but it is not always discovered so early. He then played two notes together and three notes together, and he was amazed that I could name them correctly. He went out to speak to my mother who was in the kitchen, and I think he said, 'You ought to do something about your little boy, because he's got a very good ear.' So, my mother thought, having heard Sir Walford Davies giving his radio talks, that she'd like to ask him what she ought to do about getting me a musical education. My mother wrote to Sir Walford, who replied, 'I'm so glad he enjoyed my talks. Bring your little boy to Broadcasting House to hear me give the next one. He can sit by me.' My mother thanked him very much, and we journeyed all the way from Newquay, down in Cornwall, right up to London.

O.   How long a journey was that?

W.   Well, in those days it would have been six or seven hours. We duly went to the BBC and were ushered in. Sir Walford spoke to me just before the talk and said, 'You must promise not to make a noise of any sort, because if you do, everybody will hear it right around the world! Once the red light is on, you must be very, very, quiet.' So I was. I can't remember what he said in the talk for I was so interested in watching the people—the producers and sound engineers—that I hardly listened. But afterwards he said, 'Now I would like to give you some ear tests.' So he gave me some, starting with very easy ones and then more difficult ones. He didn't tell me if I had got them right or wrong, but I knew perfectly well that I had got them right! Then he said, 'I'd like to hear you sing something', and he played a little melody and I sang it back. Then he said, 'I'd like to play you something', and he played me a piece of Bach. I think it was the *Chromatic Fantasia*. He watched me and said, 'Did you enjoy that?' 'Oh yes, sir, very much', I replied. I thought that that was all he was going to do; but he turned to me and said, 'I'm going to play something on the piano.' He played a short phrase with the pedal down, and he looked at me and said, 'Can you hear God speaking to you when I played that phrase?' I knew I had a good ear, but I just couldn't. I did listen really hard. I said, 'I think I can, sir, I think I can.' So he said, 'Then you are a *true* musician.' Now to this day, I don't know whether he was joking or whether he was just testing whether I was honest or not. But he never remarked about it again, and when I came out of the so-called audition, my mother was waiting in the next room. She said, 'Well, how did you get on?' I said, 'I liked him very much; he's a nice old man.' I said, 'He gave me some ear tests which I got right, and then he played to me. He played quite well; I didn't hear any mistakes. Then he asked me if I could hear God speaking, when he played.' She said, 'What did you say?' I said, 'I thought I could.' And she said, 'Could you?' I said, 'No, I couldn't; but I didn't want to let you down.' She said, 'I think you were rather naughty to tell a lie.' So then we went back home the next day. My mother must have been thinking what a long way to go and what an expensive trip, just to have some ear tests and to be asked if I could hear God. But she didn't say anything. About a week later there was a letter from Sir Walford in his own handwriting saying, 'Dear Mrs Willcocks, I enjoyed meeting your little boy and you asked for advice. My advice would be that he ought to carry on with piano lessons and also learn a stringed instrument. When he is eight, he ought to go to Westminster Abbey for an audition, to see if he can get into the Westminster Abbey Choir. Meanwhile, I've just written a little line to Dr Ernest Bullock who is the Organist there, to say that I have recommended that your little boy go there in two years' time for an audition.' So we were pleased. I started having cello lessons soon afterwards. I didn't like the cello as much as the piano because I couldn't play any chords on the cello. It was also quite heavy to carry, even though it was a quarter-sized one, I think.

O.   Was there a teacher in Newquay?

W.   Well, she came over from a place called Portscatho on the south coast of Cornwall. She must have come thirty-five to forty miles each way just to teach me. She was very patient, even though I didn't practise regularly. I think that I played reasonably well in tune, but I am sure that my bowing technique was very poor.

Figure 1.2. David playing the cello, *c.*1925

O.   So did your mother contact Dr Bullock?

W.   Yes. When I was eight, my mother wrote to Dr Bullock and asked if I could have an audition. He very kindly arranged to hear me in the Song School of Westminster Abbey. When I met him, he seemed a rather fierce man. He said, 'Well, my boy, have you come from Cornwall?' And I said, 'Yes sir'. He said, 'I'd like to hear you sing something.' So I said, 'I've got a piece called "The Keeper".' It was a little piece every child sang in those days. He said, 'Right, give me the copy and I'll accompany you.' I replied, 'Oh no, sir, . . . do you mind if I play for myself, because the accompaniment is a bit tricky?' He looked at me and said, 'Yes, by all means, my boy.' It never occurred to me that the Organist of Westminster Abbey could sight-read a piece that had two sharps and had a chord with

Figure 1.3. David as a chorister at Westminster Abbey, *c.*1932 (The Wykeham Studios, Ltd.)

four notes in it. I didn't think he could possibly manage that. So I staggered through it, and I think I hesitated quite a time when I came to the difficult chord. But at the end of it, he said, 'Yes, I enjoyed that, my boy.' He didn't laugh at me for having tried the accompaniment. He never made me feel that I'd been conceited or above myself. He chatted and said, 'I think you're a little bit too young to come yet, but I'd like you to join the choir in a year's time. I think you would be happy here.'

O.   And this was at age eight?

W.   Yes. I was aged nine when I actually started in 1929.

O.   Did your parents visit you in London?

W.   No. Neither my father nor mother ever came to Westminster Abbey during the years I was there. Travel was very expensive and my parents only had modest means. They were very careful with money. Sometimes I inherited my elder brothers' clothes. I didn't mind that, because I never felt the need to keep up with others.

O.   Your mother must have delivered you to London.

W.   No, I think I was met at Paddington by one of my aunts.

O.   Really, so they just put you on the train?

W.   Yes, and I remember on one of the train journeys being in a carriage with five sailors who were very jolly and chatted to me all the way up to London. In those days, there was no risk about letting a little boy travel alone with men.

O.   So you lived in the Choir School?

W.   Yes. At the Westminster Abbey Choir School, nearly all of us were boarders. It was a long, long way from home. That first night I stayed awake all night because I had never been away from home. Big Ben is within earshot of the Choir School, and I just waited for the chime of the next quarter of an hour. I was very sad that first night; I think I probably cried under the pillow.

O.   Your mother was probably crying too.

W.   Very probably! But from that day onwards I was very, very happy.

O.   Do you remember your first day?

W.   Not in detail, but I remember an average day. We were called and got up at half past seven. Breakfast would be at eight, after which you would go over to the Abbey for practice if you were in the choir that would be singing the morning service. Members of the other choir would have ordinary lessons. The reverse was true in the afternoon. If you sang on a Monday morning, you would sing on a Tuesday afternoon. If you did Monday afternoon, you would sing Tuesday morning so that the choirs each got experience of matins and evensong, which were sung daily in those days. So the boys were divided into the A choir and B choir which were of equal standard. Then on Fridays, and on Sundays, the services would be sung by C choir, composed of the senior boys from A choir and B choir. I think that Friday was chosen as the day for the senior choir, partly because some of the Sunday music could be rehearsed then, and partly because the music at evensong on Fridays was generally unaccompanied and therefore more demanding. And of course we sang the psalms for the day in full—nowadays they abbreviate them.

O.   How many boys were in the choir then?

W.   I think that in those days there were fifty boys in the choir. About
       thirty to thirty-five were boarders, and the others lived in London
       and came to the school each day. I've got many memories of those
       days. Ernest Bullock was quite imaginative, and he made us feel, right
       from the very beginning, that we were part of a long chain which
       had existed for eight hundred years and that we were continuing a
       great tradition. When we sang any music by organists like Gibbons,
       Blow, or Purcell, he would tell us of the great contribution that they
       made to the music of Westminster Abbey. If we sang music by
       Handel, he would remind us that Handel himself conducted at the
       coronation of King George II and Queen Caroline in 1727, and that
       there was a statue of Handel in the south transept. If there was an
       anthem where the words were by one of the poets who were com-
       memorated in Westminster Abbey, he'd encourage us to look for the
       memorial. We were made to feel that the Abbey wasn't something
       that was built yesterday; it was an enduring monument to previous
       generations. We were told that each one of us was responsible for
       maintaining a standard which we handed on to the choristers of the
       next generation. In turn, they would hand it on to the next genera-
       tion. So we had pride instilled in us from a very early age.

O.   Were there many royal occasions while you were there?

W.   During my time, we had no coronation or royal wedding, but the
       King and Queen did come once or twice each year. One such
       occasion was the Maundy Thursday service at which the Royal
       Maundy was distributed. At this service the King gave sets of
       Maundy money to the poor—a very old custom. If the King were
       forty-five years of age, then forty-five sets of money would be
       minted specially, and given away to poor people from the parish of
       Westminster. How they were chosen I don't know. I think initially
       their feet were washed, but that custom was discontinued. The
       monarch just gave them a little bag containing a silver fourpence
       piece, a silver threepence, a silver twopence, and a silver penny.

       Extra sets were minted for the boys in the choir. I got two sets
       of Maundy money. In one of the sets, I lost the little tiny penny. I
       don't know how; maybe it was stolen.

O.   You still have them?

W.   Yes, I still have them, and treasure them. I'll pass them on to one
       of my children. Of course, the younger the monarch is, the more

valuable are the coins. There would be people outside the Abbey after the service, wanting to buy them off you. I think some of the boys did sell their Maundy money.

O.   I'm glad you didn't. Did you hear from your parents often?

W.   Well, I had a little scheme for keeping in touch with my mother, because she always expected me to write regularly to say how I was getting on. I was rather lazy with letter-writing, so I said to her, 'I hope that you can listen to the radio on Tuesday afternoon, as we shall be broadcasting evensong.' In those days, evensong was broadcast every week from Westminster Abbey. Nowadays, the broadcast is from a different cathedral each week. I said, 'If you listen carefully, after the Dean has said, "Here endeth the second lesson", you'll hear a cough. That will be me coughing and you'll know that I'm well and happy.' So we had that little wireless communication for some time and nobody seemed to notice anything amiss. I think that I must one day ask if the BBC have got any tapes of the Westminster Abbey broadcasts, so that I can see if I can identify that little cough.

O.   Was there a special anthem or a special composer that you remember really enjoying singing when you were a chorister?

W.   Several. I think that I loved 'Zadok the Priest' of Handel, because I associated that with the visits of the King and Queen. They would pass between the choir stalls, side by side, so if the Queen was on my side of the choir, I could have stretched out my hand and touched her. They were as close as that. Of course you never forget that sort of thing and occasionally, after the service, they would talk to one or two of us. To a small boy, it is a great thing to have spoken to the King and the Queen.

O.   What other memories do you have of life at the Abbey?

W.   I still have a number of memories of those happy years. I think it was the first week that I was there that we were playing cricket in a little enclosed area just behind the Choir School. It was the only recreational place there was, except for the grass of Dean's Yard—in the front—where we didn't normally play, because it was used by Westminster School. We had this one little place where there were music practice rooms and this open area, where you could just throw a ball and swing a bat. One of the boys knocked the ball over a wire fence and—because I was the youngest—they all said,

'Willcocks, you go and fetch that ball!' Well, I didn't dare refuse, being the youngest boy there. So I climbed up this wire netting; I suppose it was a good six feet high. It was difficult to get a grip, but I could get my fingers in the mesh and swing my leg over. It was quite difficult to do, so when I got to the top, I just had to jump down on to a dusty stone ledge to collect the ball—I could see it there. I jumped down on to the stone ledge, but it wasn't stone—it was glass. It was a skylight! I fell through this skylight down into the boiler room of the Choir School and landed in a washing basket. It was an absolute miracle. I wasn't even cut. The boys, of course, were absolutely terrified! They were waiting on the other side of the fence, and heard the noise of shattering glass, followed by silence.

O.   So I guess your shoes hit the glass first and broke it.

W.   Yes. I went down feet first. My arms must have been out, I suppose, trying to save myself as I went down. The boys were frightened. They thought I was dead. They went immediately into the school saying, 'There's been an accident.' The porter came down and said, 'Are you all right?' So I said, 'Yes, I think so . . . where am I?' I didn't know—I had no idea at all. He said, 'Are you sure you can move?' I said, 'Yes', so I was taken upstairs. The matron couldn't believe I hadn't been cut to pieces. The boys were told they must never again play games down there. Of course they did—it was allowed after a bit. I was sent up to the sick bay for the rest of that day and overnight, because it was thought that I would have delayed shock. It was legendary for some years—the little boy who fell through the skylight.

Another memory I have is of being caught smoking with other boys. Our pocket money amounted to about a shilling a week, with which we could buy very little . . . perhaps a postcard and stamp, or some sweets. The daring thing was to buy a packet of Woodbines, the cheapest brand of cigarettes, and to try smoking. The only place that seemed safe was in the toilets off the dormitory. We did not enjoy the taste of cigarettes, but it was the 'thing to do' to say that you'd had a cigarette. We used to buy the cigarettes from a little shop by Westminster Bridge, which was not far away. I got caught! The matron came and smelled smoke and asked who had been smoking. We all owned up. We were paraded before the headmaster who said we must never smoke again. So we said,

'No, sir'. Our memories were short. I suppose that it was a year later that I was caught again.

O. A second time?

W. A second time. The headmaster was rash enough to say that if I was caught a third time, I'd be sent home. And meanwhile he'd have to tell my parents. I was terrified. I thought, 'What would my mother say, if I arrived home saying that I had been thrown out of the Westminster Abbey Choir?' Well, about a year later (I think by this time I was eleven and getting quite useful in the choir), I was caught a third time! After we were all asleep, the matron came walking through the dormitory, as she very often did, and she thought she smelled smoke. She went into the toilet and verified that there had been some smoking there. We were all asleep by this time, and she went and felt in our clothes. In my coat she found a packet of Woodbines containing only three (a packet had five). I was summoned to the headmaster, who had already told me the previous time, that I would be thrown out of the school. He said, 'Have you got anything to say?' So I said, 'No, sir'. He said, 'This is very serious. I gave you a final warning. I am going to make you go to see the Dean as soon as he can see you. He will decide when you should be sent home.' I was kept for some days with nothing happening. It was the worst week of my life.

O. That was part of the punishment, I'm sure.

W. The great day came, when I was told that the Dean wished to see me. Why the other boys weren't asked to go I don't know—I wasn't the only boy who had been smoking. Perhaps it was because I was the only one who'd been caught twice before and I was considered to be the ringleader. I was shown into the Dean's study, and he said, 'Is it true that you were smoking in the lavatory?' I said, 'Yes, sir'. So he said, 'Is it true also that the headmaster has twice cautioned you?' I said, 'Yes, sir'. He said, 'Do you realize that God gave you a voice, and that smoking is very bad for the voice and therefore you are sinning against God when you smoke?' I said, 'Yes, sir, I'm very sorry, sir.' There was another pause, and he said, 'Have you got any reason to suggest why I should not send you home now?' I said, 'Well, one thing, sir, I thought it was unfair that the matron, without my permission, should search my pockets while I was asleep, because she was in a position of trust. I think that it was not very kind of her to do that.' Another pause, and he said, 'You know, I rather agree with you on that point. Will you promise me you will never smoke again until you are grown up?' I looked him in the eyes and said, 'I promise, sir'. He said, 'I'll give you one more chance, then.' I went back to school and nothing was said at all, but the matron was terribly nice to me thereafter! I think it must have got back to her what my excuse was, for she never went feeling in people's pockets after that. That was the nearest thing to disaster for me. If I'd been thrown out, the whole course of my life might well have been different. I don't know what would have happened. It was a miracle that I just happened to think of that excuse at that moment.

O. Well, that was two close calls. Who was the Dean?

W. The Dean was called [William] Foxley Norris. He was rather a big man, portly. I always used to laugh when we were singing the psalm verse, 'Whoso hath also a proud look and a high stomach: I will not suffer him' [Psalm 101, vs. 7, *1662 Book of Common Prayer*]. I couldn't make out why God suffered Foxley Norris, because he had a high stomach and had a proud look as he walked along in procession. I remember he taught me a card game, patience, at a party which was given for the boys at Christmas time.

O. It sounds as if the Dean was a very wise man.

W. Well, he was. I wished I could have thanked him later. I would have loved to have gone back to him and said, 'Thank you very much for letting me off that time with the smoking.'

O. Did you attend any concerts?

W. Of course. When I was a little boy at Westminster Abbey, I was once taken to the Queen's Hall, which was bombed later, to hear the *St Matthew Passion* and that made a great impression on me. I suppose I'd have been perhaps twelve then.

O. And who was conducting?

W. Adrian Boult. I had two aunts singing in the choir, and they were very proud to take their little nephew along to hear the performance. That was the first time I ever heard Keith Falkner, who was one of England's leading baritones, sing. He sang the Christus part with great character. I never thought that I would see him later in life. Of course, he became Director of the Royal College of Music after Ernest Bullock. Some forty years later I succeeded Falkner,*

* See Chapter 8.

and I greatly enjoyed his friendship. It's a small world. When you're twelve, these people are absolute heroes. I suppose Keith Falkner would have been about thirty-two then; and Vaughan Williams, of course, was exactly forty-seven years older than I was. He seemed a very old man when I was a boy, and yet later the gap of years narrowed, and I almost forgot that he was older than I was.

O.   Did you have favourite pieces of music that you enjoyed singing?

W.   I can remember that I enjoyed Balfour Gardiner's 'Te lucis ante terminum' because I loved the sound of the organ. I used to look up at the organ pipes and wonder if I would ever get a chance to play the organ, and particularly the organ in Westminster Abbey. My good fortune was that my voice changed when I was about twelve.

O.   You said your 'good fortune'?

W.   I was very sad when I felt that my voice was beginning to go, but Ernest Bullock said to me, 'My boy, this could be the best thing in the world for you. You can't go to your next school until you're thirteen and a half and we've got to keep you until then. I shall miss you in the choir, but from your point of view it is a good thing, because I'm going to let you practise the piano and cello, while the other boys are singing. And what's more, I'll give you some organ lessons.' He never charged my parents anything for those lessons which I had, I suppose, every two or three weeks. I was able to practise a great deal.

O.   On the Abbey organ?

W.   Well, very occasionally on the Abbey organ, but mostly at a church near the Abbey. I was allowed to sit in the organ loft for many of the services and to turn the pages for Ernest Bullock, or the sub-Organist Osborne Peasgood. I was also allowed to pull out the Great to Pedal stop when they nodded. I was allowed later to play the chords for unaccompanied anthems when Ernest Bullock went down to conduct. He told me what chord to play and gradually I was permitted to do a little bit more, and then I was allowed to play for a bit of a rehearsal, when it was an easy accompaniment. Later, I was allowed to play a hymn—I think it was at matins, because there was nobody in the congregation! Once I played an easy voluntary, one of the J. S. Bach *Eight Short Preludes and Fugues*. So I couldn't have had a better last year under any circumstances. I was made to feel that I was a real help, up in the organ loft. Ernest Bullock might say, 'I don't think I can get through this anthem unless you turn over for me; and I'll need you to pull out the Great to Pedal when we get to page three, line four. It is very difficult for me to manage that.' I'm sure it wasn't, but he used to make me feel wanted. That experience was helpful when I competed for a music scholarship at my next school.

O.   You hadn't played the organ until you went to the Abbey, had you?

W.   No, I wouldn't have been tall enough anyway—I wouldn't have been able to reach the pedals. I suppose I started the organ when I was twelve and was sufficiently advanced with my piano studies under Dr G. F. Bullivant. Dr Bullock was a busy man, but he always fitted me in somehow, and gave me something to work at. I did the usual pedal-only exercises, and then the ones where it was left hand and pedal only, which I found more difficult than right hand and pedal. He was a good teacher, and he didn't discourage me from improvising. At that stage it was probably rather crude, but it gave me the confidence to try to experiment with colours and registration.

O.   Did you keep your cello lessons going at all?

W.   Yes, until I started the organ. But I have always been grateful that I studied the cello for some years, because it has given me some confidence in bowing string parts. Indeed, some experience of string playing is very valuable to singers, keyboard players, and other instrumentalists. You must learn to judge intervals more accurately than you do if you are playing the piano. With a stringed instrument you learn which notes must be sharpened and in what context they need to be sharpened. F sharp isn't always the same note—it depends on what happens next and what the chords underneath are. You must learn to adjust and use your ears.

O.   So you always enjoyed ensemble playing?

W.   Yes. Even with the organ I used to practise rather reluctantly on my own, sometimes for two or three hours, but I never got the same satisfaction as if I had been playing duets or making music with somebody else.

O.   Did you sing under any famous conductors or composers at the Abbey?

W.   Yes. Of course, the Abbey has had its great history of big occasions. As I said, I wasn't present for a coronation or a royal wedding, but the King (George V) was very seriously ill, I think in 1932 or 1933.

He went down to Bognor, on the south coast, to convalesce, and when he came back to London there was a thanksgiving service in Westminster Abbey for his recovery. Another highlight for me was in 1932 when the choirs of Westminster Abbey and the Chapel Royal combined to sing near St James's Park for the dedication of a memorial to Queen Alexandra, who was the widow of Edward VII. For that occasion, Sir Edward Elgar, Master of the King's Musick, wrote a special anthem, 'Memorial Ode' (with words by John Masefield), and conducted it. What I remember was Elgar's charisma. He was in court dress and had a sword by his side and the red and blue ribbon going up over his shoulder, which was the Order of Merit, the senior decoration in England. There are only twenty-four people who have the Order of Merit at any one time. He was certainly experienced as a conductor, for he knew how to make us all watch. At the end of the service I said to one of the boys who was at the other end of the choir, 'I don't know why Elgar kept looking at me the whole time.' The boy said, 'Funny, I thought he was looking at me.' Elgar was one of those people who could embrace a whole choir in his gaze and you were fascinated just by watching him. He shook hands with many of us afterwards. This was less than two years before he died. I am very glad to have actually seen him, because he was the great man in music of that day.

O. What music did Dr Bullock programme at that time?

W. The music of Stanford, Parry, Charles Wood, Vaughan Williams, Bairstow, and composers of the next generation like Herbert Howells featured strongly in the music lists. We sang very little Tudor music, even though E. H. Fellowes and C. S. Terry had been undertaking important editorial work for several years. We sang Byrd's 'Bow thine ear' and Gibbons' 'This is the record of John' down in F major. In those days the solo was normally sung by a tenor in the original pitch, because people hadn't realized that the F major of the sixteenth century is roughly A flat or A major today.

O. Did you sing Dr Bullock's own music?

W. Yes. He was quite modest about that. We sang his anthems 'Give us the wings of faith' and 'Christ, the fair glory of the holy angels', as well as a setting of the Magnificat and Nunc dimittis. Ernest Bullock never pushed his own music. He wrote fanfares for big occasions, including the coronation of King George VI and Queen

Elizabeth. He was essentially a shy man, but he could be severe, because he was very anxious that things should go well. I remember being impressed that on the day when he was to conduct a shortened version of the Bach *St Matthew Passion* (I think it was boiled down to about an hour and a half) he said to me, 'I'm going to sleep all this afternoon, because it's nerve-racking conducting a work like the *St Matthew Passion*.' I made a note that I should always lie down for all the afternoon, if I were ever to conduct a concert! I can't say that I've ever felt the need to follow his advice. I am not sure if he was really apprehensive, or whether he didn't want to be talking to people before a concert. I've never found any other conductor who has felt it necessary to lie down for two or three hours before conducting a familiar work.

O.   What was Bullock like as a conductor?

W.   Ernest Bullock wasn't an emotional man. He never worked us up to great degrees of excitement. I would describe him as 'safe' and 'conventional'. Osborne Peasgood (known affectionately as Ozzie) found it difficult to keep us in order, so we were rather naughty with him and played him up. He was a very able organist but sometimes terribly careless—the sort of person who would play the Reubke *Sonata on the 94th Psalm* by heart, but not without some mistakes.

O.   And didn't he fret about it?

W.   No. I remember that on one occasion he left the tuba out by mistake, something that Ernest Bullock would never do. When we went up to the organ loft to turn the pages for him after a service, he would often have a motoring magazine up on the desk and read it while he was playing. I am sure that he did it to amuse us. He would say, 'OK . . . turn over' and you would turn over the next page of the motor magazine! I remember one occasion when he dropped a book by mistake. It went down all the five manuals of the Abbey organ: bump, bump, bump, bump, bump. These are things which one will never forget.

O.   Were there, other than Elgar, any other famous musicians who visited—for instance, Vaughan Williams?

W.   He came occasionally when we were singing an anthem of his, and Herbert Howells also came once. They would come to the rehearsal in the Song School, just to have a word with us and tell us that we were doing well.

O.   But they didn't take a rehearsal?

W.   No. Rehearsals in those days were terribly short. The men generally came in just for the last quarter of an hour. Nowadays choirs generally rehearse for some time in the building, in order to get the balance right with the organ. We never rehearsed in the Abbey. We rehearsed with piano in the Song School. In some ways, it must have been hit and miss. I think that the standards cannot have been anything like as high as they are now, because choirs today are ashamed if they are not good enough to record and to go abroad and tour. So many people come now to the Abbey services that I think the Organist would be embarrassed if the music had not been adequately rehearsed. It isn't enough to have the men a few minutes before a service if the repertoire is to be extended. Considering the very small amount of rehearsal time that we had, I think we did quite well.

O.   Did the choir feel under-rehearsed?

W.   Sometimes we felt unprepared, but I think we became good guessers. The music, much of it Victorian, was much simpler in those days. We did not have to cope with the difficult intervals and rhythms which confront cathedral choirs today. Many of the anthems we sang were slow-moving and chordal. I can't remember singing 'O clap your hands' of Gibbons, or other anthems of that difficulty. It would be interesting to look at the music lists and see just what we did sing. It was later when I went to King's College, Cambridge that I discovered the full beauty of Tudor music. Having lay clerks (or lay vicars as they are called at Westminster Abbey), we sang several verse anthems. These were perhaps better performed there than in places where there were no soloistic singers.

O.   It must have been sad to leave such a place.

W.   When the time came for me to leave the Abbey, I thought I would call at Ernest Bullock's house, which was 8, Little Cloister. I can see it now with the little fountain in the cloisters outside the front door. I said, 'I've just called to say goodbye and to thank you very much for all that you've done for me, particularly this last year when I've been learning the organ.' He said, 'It's quite all right, my boy, I've only done for you what Edward Bairstow did for me. All I ask you to do is to try and find the opportunity to help the next generation whenever you can. That's the thanks I would like.' I thought, 'What a lovely man.'

O.   A great tradition.

W.   Yes, looking back on those Abbey days, I realize that we learned
       quite a lot of history. We saw in the north choir aisle the graves of
       many musicians and learned in which centuries they lived. In the
       north transept we could look at the statues of great prime minis-
       ters, which made us aware of what was happening beyond the
       realm of church music. It was a wonderful experience to be
       steeped in music and to be part of a professional choir singing in
       such an historic building. When I left the Abbey, I didn't fully
       realize there was another world besides church music. I hadn't
       heard a string quartet. I hadn't heard or been to an opera. There
       were enormous gaps in my general knowledge of music. And that
       would be a significant factor in the next part of my education.

Interlude 1

Reflections on Childhood

Theophilus Willcocks is the eldest of the three Willcocks brothers—eight years older than Sir David. He worked in the Bank of England in Bristol and was interviewed on 10 November 2005 at his home near Cambridge.

TW.   When I was young we used to go down to the beach almost every day and play cricket, bathe, and build sandcastles and such. We were always taken down because we had a nanny who was extremely good. I didn't see so much of my mother, because she was busy cooking and making bread—during the war everything was very scarce. We had a very pleasant time.

O.   What do you remember about David's coming into your life?

TW.   Well, I hadn't been expecting it. They didn't tell me there was another child coming, but we got on extremely well. He was always very good at running and could outrun me. He loved bathing or playing on the beach, that sort of thing.

O.   Both of your parents lived nice long lives.

TW.   Yes, they did. My mother was a strong-willed person, and she would never give way to anything. She had very definite views on various things. She was a more dominant personality than my father. He was rather different, and was what I call 'easy-going'. I don't think I ever saw him angry or upset. Of course, his activities were limited because he was lame—that was a great handicap, but he never complained. When he was in his teens he got TB in a form that doesn't affect the lungs; in fact I think it may protect you from the other sort. In a sense I think he was lucky because some of the other family members died of TB. It was very prevalent in those days. It did, however, affect his legs, leaving him with one leg considerably shorter than the other. He had a rather unusual built-up shoe. It had a sort of iron contraption on the bottom, difficult to describe, really, because it wasn't a solid thing at all. What he found rather difficult was walking on sand. I think his easy-going temperament kept him going a long time—he didn't worry.

Wilfrid Willcocks is the middle Willcocks brother—six years older than Sir David. He was a stockbroker and financial adviser and lived in London. He was interviewed on 10 June 2003 in Cambridge.

WW. Our mother's family were professional middle class. They lived in the home counties—the counties around London in the southeast of England. My grandfather went to Wadham College, Oxford. In those days, most of the clergy in the Church of England were Oxbridge people, and their social status was much better then than it is now. My grandfather and great-grandfather were vicars in a place called Hockley, in Essex, about fifty miles from London, only in those days it was complete country. My mother's family were almost entirely clergy or in the legal profession. At that time there were a lot of spinsters, for some reason or other. It's rather surprising that more of them didn't marry, because they were a very good-looking family, but it seemed to be the rule rather than the exception. I think people had to move in their own caste, and if you didn't have the opportunity of meeting people, the marriage market was very narrow. I think that applied to both our families, on my mother's side and my father's side. When mother married my father they went straight to this bank house, which was on the central square of Newquay. It was really rather like an opera set. Everything went on around this square. It was surprisingly quiet. Cars were very thin on the ground, most of the traffic was buggies or horses and carts, so there wasn't a lot of noise.

O. The age gap between you and David must have seemed enormous when you were growing up.

WW.   It was. As a lark, I used to sit on the piano—the result being a tremendous discord. He could invariably tell me every note I was sitting on. I suppose that meant that he could tell the notes at either end of the range covered by one's bottom—the notes in between would be no problem!

O.   Was bathing a large part of life in Newquay?

WW.   Life was very leisurely in those days. My father always stopped work before four o'clock in the afternoon, and all through the summer we were taken to the beach and joined friends. Our respective nannies sat in deck chairs and were supposed to watch us and see we did not fall into any mischief. You could hire a bathing machine where the ladies undressed and we hired one of these for the season. A man was employed the whole summer to take them—drawn by a horse, as the tide went out, every fifty yards—down to the sea, so the ladies when they wanted to bathe wouldn't have to walk across the beach. We kept all our gear there, surfboards and that sort of thing, and we'd go down every day in the summer holidays. My mother, although she was perfectly fit in those days, only used to bathe about twice a year, when it was very hot.

O.   Your mother was obviously a big influence.

WW.   We're all good on spelling in our family through Mother. She was a very good teacher. Even now David will always go through every programme thoroughly to check it. David's very competitive, you see—he's highly competitive. We're all hopeless with our hands. We ruin everything we touch. Rachel, David's wife, does everything like that in this house. She's very practical but David's hopeless in that way, as I am. My mother used to do puzzles every day. David's a great man on puzzles; he spends hours and hours. That's his chief hobby, difficult puzzles. We're all mathematical, our family.

Sarah de Rougemont (née Willcocks) is Sir David's eldest daughter. She was interviewed on 14 June 2005 at her home in London.

SR.   My father's parents lived in Newquay until they died. My mother's parents also had a house there, so we used to go and stay with my mother's mother, but visit my father's parents every day. My father's mother was a Victorian lady, very tall and erect with white hair in a bun, and I remember she wore shoes with a strap across and a button. When we got there, we'd have to stand side by side in the sitting room. Our eyes would be swivelling to the left, to the bottom of the sideboard, where the sweet jar was. We weren't allowed to have a sweet until we'd told her what we'd done the day before. She made us separate the various different papers around the sweets. In those days it was cellophane on the outside, and then there was silver paper inside, but the silver paper also had a greaseproof paper backing. So you had to peel the cellophane off, and that went in the bin. Then you peeled the silver paper off the greaseproof paper, and the silver paper, which she was collecting, would go in the silver paper container. I think this is the sort of upbringing Dad had, which probably made him very frugal and careful. He is just the sort of person who would separate silver paper from greaseproof paper before eating the sweet, and keep very small bits of string.

My grandfather was quite a lot older than my grandmother—he died when I was about eight. He looked very much like Dad looks now actually, quite twinkly eyes, just like Dad's, but with a walrus moustache. He was short, and my grandmother was tall. He had a broad Cornish accent, which my grandmother didn't have. She brought up her three sons not to have a Cornish accent either. I liked him a lot. He was quite quiet. He'd just be sitting in a chair, and my grandmother would hold forth, but then he would occasionally pipe up and say something. Grandmother didn't really encourage girlfriends, to put it mildly. Phil and Wilf have never got married. I don't know whether it was the war that made Dad able to have a bit of independence for four years, and pluck up the courage to bring a girl home. Grandmother was so anxious for grandchildren that she was quite pleased to have a daughter-in-law at last. My mother always had a very formal relationship with her. I was the first grandchild. She was quite severe to us as children and really quite formal.

2

From Clifton College to King's College

1934 – 1940

O.   You next went to Clifton College in Bristol?

W.   Yes. I went on my own for an interview, having applied for a music
scholarship. I was introduced to the Director of Music, a man
called Douglas Fox. I'd heard what a wonderful person he was.
When he was eighteen he won a senior scholarship at the Royal
College of Music as a pianist. While there, he won all the prizes
and was extremely talented, as both a pianist and an organist. He
also had an Organ Scholarship at Keble College, Oxford. Here he
came under the influence of Sir Hugh Allen, who was both the
Professor of Music at Oxford and also the Director of the Royal
College of Music in London. While Douglas Fox was at the RCM,
people forecast a brilliant career for him. Then he went off to
World War I, and in 1917 he was severely wounded in his right
arm. The army doctor had to make an agonizing decision—
whether he should amputate the arm or not. If he didn't amputate
the arm, Fox might die of gangrene. I do not know if the doctor
knew that Douglas Fox was a pianist, but he decided that he must
amputate the arm. Fox returned home absolutely bereft. His hopes
of a successful career in music were dashed. What made the situation worse was hearing later that another doctor doubted whether
it had really been necessary to amputate the arm. When he got
home, almost everybody whom he knew wrote to him to offer
sympathy. Many organists wrote to him; many pianists wrote to
him. The only person who didn't write to him immediately was
Sir Hugh Allen, the one man Douglas most hoped would write.

Eventually he received a letter in which Sir Hugh said that, before writing to Douglas, he felt that he would like to have something that he could say which would give hope for the future, rather than express regrets at what had happened. He related how, during the previous week, he had carried out an experiment. He had tied his right arm up in a sling, and had played for evensong in New College, Oxford, every day. Nobody had noticed anything different from the usual. He told Fox that if that were possible without any practice, he must realize what could be done after diligent practice. He assured him that he would have a great future.

O.   That's an incredible story.

W.   Isn't it? Well, that's documented in Douglas Fox's obituary. He did in fact have a successful but limited career as a pianist, performing the Ravel Piano Concerto for the Left Hand, not only in England but abroad as well. He also gave some organ recitals, carefully selecting pieces that he could manage. He adapted the organ at Clifton so that he could just press a little button and all the pedal stops would go in. That device enabled him to play passages for manuals only, using double pedalling. He could play many of the Bach preludes and fugues without anybody detecting any omissions.

O.   That's amazing.

W.   It is as a brilliant, but demanding, teacher that Douglas Fox will be affectionately remembered by his many pupils. It is probable that he wouldn't have devoted his life to teaching, had it not been for the loss of his right arm. He was a great character, terribly nervous, very diffident, but a real taskmaster. I was frightened of him because he always judged exactly how much (or how little!) I had practised. At Westminster Abbey, I had managed to deceive my piano teacher, Dr Bullivant, who always thought that I had practised hard before lessons. Fox expected his pupils to devote every bit of spare time to music, but he realized that I was quite keen on sporting activities, such as cross-country running and squash racquets. He was the sort of person whom everybody respected for his courage. When he conducted a choir or orchestra, he had to temporarily stop conducting to turn over the pages. Everybody watched him very carefully and we never felt any interruption of the music. It was not unusual for him to go to the Headmaster the day before a concert, and say that the choir and orchestra would not be able to undertake the concert unless an extra hour of rehearsal was granted. If the Headmaster refused the request, Fox would say, 'All right, we'll cancel the concert then.' Eventually the Headmaster would say, 'All right, you can have half an hour.' It was difficult to refuse any request made by Fox because he was held in such affection. On one occasion a little boy called Charles (his surname), who was a good pianist, played at a school concert and the audience applauded wildly because they thought the performance was very good. Douglas Fox came on to the stage and said, 'I don't know why you're clapping, it was disgraceful! Charles will now play the piece properly.' Poor Charles had a nervous breakdown after it.

O.   Really?

W.   Douglas didn't mean to upset Charles, but he was determined that he shouldn't get away with it and think that he'd done well. Fox insisted that things must be absolutely right. If you were doing score-reading exercises, he wouldn't let any error pass. If you filled in a chord, or if you didn't hold a note for exactly the right length, he would upbraid you, even if it sounded all right. He insisted on good fingering technique. Despite his own handicap, he always knew the best fingering for right-hand passages. Fox quickly discovered that I was steeped in church music. If he had said to me, 'Wesley in E', I could sit down and play it straight off. If he had said, 'Thou wilt keep him in perfect peace', I could remember it and play it. I knew all the church music that we'd sung, and it is still with me today. He realized the immense gaps in my musical experience, and he made me listen to symphonies, chamber music, and to a lesser extent, operas. He felt that every musician must know the nine Beethoven symphonies, the Mozart symphonies 39, 40, and 41, and the four symphonies of Brahms. From that base he made us explore many later examples of the symphonic repertoire. He opened many musical doors for us all. At the Colston Hall in Bristol I heard many great musicians, like Schnabel, Moiseiwitsch, Horowitz, Rubinstein, and Cortot. I especially remember Rachmaninov. Douglas Fox took me in his car to Oxford to hear Toscanini conduct the BBC Symphony Orchestra, and Furtwängler conduct the Berlin Philharmonic Orchestra. He wanted all his pupils to be intellectually curious and to widen their knowledge of music. I realize how much I owe to him.

O.   How did you happen to go to Clifton?

W.   It was one of the very few schools that offered a music scholarship.
        My parents wouldn't have been able to afford the fees for a private
        school. The very first school to offer a music scholarship each year
        was Rugby. Clifton followed suit, I think, some years later. One such
        scholarship was offered each year, and I was fortunate in being
        awarded one in 1934. Clifton College had always attracted musical
        people. In fact, Fox himself was a boy there. I was particularly
        attracted because it was in the West Country, nearer to Cornwall
        than London, where I had been when I was a little boy.

O.   How long a journey was it?

W.   I suppose about 150 miles from my home in Cornwall. The
        countryside was much more attractive. In London we were very
        circumscribed, with limited places where we could play football or
        cricket perhaps twice a week. At Clifton College we had playing
        fields on the doorstep and we had the beautiful downs where you
        could walk and take part in cross-country running, which I en-
        joyed. It was the one sport where I could represent the school and
        it was something very different from music-making.

Figure 2.1. David (*left*) with his father, mother, brother Wilfrid, and Dan the
dog, at Kelsey Head near Newquay, *c.* 1935

Figure 2.2. Clifton College Running VIII, c.1937; David, third from right and insert

O.   Was there a chapel and an organ?

W.   Yes, and we had daily services which many schools don't have
         now. The service lasted about twenty minutes, and consisted of one
         or two hymns and bible readings. It was a wonderful opportunity
         for those learning the organ to play hymns and voluntaries, to
         accompany anthems, and to improvise before the service.

O.   Did you do most of that playing or did Douglas Fox?

W.   Fox played until he had pupils who were capable. By the time I was
         fourteen or fifteen I was able to take my turn in playing for the
         school services. I wasn't the only one who could play, of course;
         there were often two or three others who were also learning the
         organ. Douglas Fox was always very critical and he'd make sure that
         everything was absolutely right. The singing by the whole school
         was lusty, but not very well polished. The singing of the school
         choir, which included members of staff, was of a reasonable stan-
         dard. I suppose about a third of the boys at Clifton learned one or
         more musical instruments, so the school could give pupils experi-
         ence in orchestral work. I got a chance to play continuo in various
         works, on the piano or organ.

O.   Did you have a weekly lesson with Dr Fox?

W.   Yes, on both the piano and the organ, each for about an hour a
         week. Piano was his speciality because he had a wonderful touch,
         and with his left hand he could demonstrate the tone, phrasing,
         and *rubato* demanded in each piece. He had a remarkable ability
         to 'thumb' out a tune at the top, preserving good balance of the
         supporting harmonies. You would never know, if you just walked
         into a room, that this was a man with only one arm. He could play
         many types of music that you wouldn't think possible for a person
         with his disability. On the organ, for instance, he could play
         trumpet voluntaries. He had a very big hand so his thumb would
         be playing the tune on the lower of two manuals and the other
         fingers would provide the accompaniment on the upper manual.

O.   That's amazing. Were there any special musical events there that
         you remember?

W.   I think that the main things were the school concerts at the end of
         each term. I was able to perform several solo items and the
         Beethoven Fourth Piano Concerto.

O.   You were the soloist?

TOP ROW. – D.F. CALLANDER, G.R.DUNN, R.G.M. BAGGOTT, J.L.BRAITHWAITE, C.P. LEWIS-SMITH, W.R.COLE, D.V.WILLCOCKS, P.F.MIDDLETON.
2ND ROW. – K.R.WENGER, A.I.POTTER, D.I.PIPER, E.C.DE CHAZAL, L.W.POBSON, A.E.COMER, J.WAY, D.H.FORSTER, A.M.E.TROWER, J.R.HETLEY, F.M.COUSINS, B.V.JACOB, R.E.H.CHARLCO-
SEATED. – A.I.MACLEOD, W.F.PALMER Esq, F.B.ARTER Esq, N.AMBACHE, M. ALEXANDER Esq, D.G.A.FOX Esq, M.H.HARDY Esq, G.S.MOWAT, Y.P.LIDELL Esq, W.H.OLDAKER Esq, L.J.PAGE.

Figure 2.3. Clifton College Orchestra, December 1935; David, back row, second from right; Douglas Fox,
front row, centre

W.   Yes. I think that my proudest moment was winning a silver cup for a performance of *Jeux d'eau* by Ravel. So that was good experience.

O.   What other activities were you involved in at Clifton, apart from music-making?

W.   I enjoyed very much being a Rover Scout and camping under supervision. We climbed the cliffs in the gorge at Clifton and we went pot-holing in the Mendip Hills in Somerset, where there are underground caves, some of which can only be explored with ropes. Pot-holing could be quite dangerous because if it had been raining you could be flooded out, with potentially fatal results, but the scoutmasters were always careful that we didn't get into trouble. My main concern, however, was preparing for an Organ Scholarship to Cambridge. With that in mind, Douglas Fox made me take my ARCO [the examination for Associateship of the Royal College of Organists] when I was sixteen, and my FRCO [Fellowship exams] when I was seventeen.

Figure 2.4. David wearing FRCO gown and mortarboard, June 1938

O.   That's quite early, isn't it?

W.   Yes, very early. But there was another boy at Christ's Hospital School called Ivor Keys, who was about the same age as I was. Our teachers, who knew each other well, were determined that we shouldn't compete against each other. So I was earmarked for King's College, Cambridge, and Ivor was earmarked for Christ Church, Oxford. We became good friends but we never went head-to-head in competition. The Director of Music at Christ's Hospital, C. S. ('Robin') Lang, who was a great friend of Douglas Fox and a Cliftonian himself, took Ivor Keys and me to the Three Choirs Festival in 1936 and 1937. We attended a party after a concert in John [Herbert, known as John] Sumsion's home and Vaughan Williams was present. Unfortunately, there were not enough chairs, so juniors sat on the floor. I sat at Vaughan Williams' feet—I had never seen such large feet in my life!

O.   Did Keys end up at Christ Church, Oxford?

W.   Yes, he did, and subsequently became Professor of Music successively at Belfast, Nottingham, and Birmingham universities. I enjoyed his friendship until his death.

O.   What about your academic studies?

W.   While at Clifton, I was doing all the normal subjects, like French and German. The only thing I missed there was science. I never went into a laboratory and I've never studied chemistry or physics because I was allowed to miss those subjects in order to concentrate on music.

O.   Were there any special events during this year?

W.   I remember one rather special occasion—it was Empire Day, which was the 24th of May 1938, when there was a Command Concert at the Royal Albert Hall attended by the King and Queen. Every now and again there would be a Command Concert to mark some great event, and on this occasion their Majesties expressed a hope that as many people as possible from different parts of the United Kingdom could take part. Many schools from all over the country were invited to send a representative. I was selected by Clifton to take part in this concert. There were about seven or eight different conductors, of whom I remember particularly Sir Malcolm Sargent, Sir Hugh Roberton (who conducted a group performing Scottish music), and Sir Adrian Boult. The two young Princesses

(Elizabeth, our present Queen, and Margaret, her younger sister) attended the rehearsal on the concert day, and the King and Queen came to the concert. I remember particularly being high up among the basses in the tiered Royal Albert Hall, looking out on the sea of faces, and wondering if I would ever conduct in that hall or maybe play the organ. I don't think that I had prepared the music very carefully because there was no chance of attending an organized rehearsal before the concert day. I was immensely impressed by the efficiency of the rehearsals. I think the Royal Choral Society acted as a sort of core choir, but the rest of us sang along as best we could. I was impressed by Malcolm Sargent's clarity of beat and the way in which he conducted the rehearsal. It was beautifully timed, for he didn't waste a second. Afterwards I got a letter, which I still possess, signed by Sir Walford Davies, who had been so kind to me when I was a small boy. He wrote to everybody in the chorus, saying that he had been asked by the King and Queen to convey to all who took part in the concert the great pleasure the King and Queen had by the singing and playing at that concert. I never thought I would see Walford Davies again, but I got occasional opportunities later to thank him for what he did for me when I was a little child.

O. What happened to you after leaving Clifton?

W. I had what is nowadays described as a 'gap' year between school and university. This was very valuable for me. I had three main objectives during this year: (1) to become an ARCM (piano playing), (2) to obtain the newly instituted Archbishop of Canterbury's Diploma in Church Music, and (3) most importantly, to compete for the Organ Scholarship of King's College, Cambridge.

O. How did you go about achieving the ARCM?

W. During the year I studied at the Royal College of Music [RCM], where I had weekly organ lessons from Ernest Bullock. He had said that he would like to teach me, because he had started me off on the organ five years before at Westminster Abbey. He allowed me to play at the Abbey sometimes, which was always exciting. I had piano lessons from a fine pianist and teacher named Frank Merrick, and harmony and counterpoint tuition from R. O. Morris, author of the then standard book on counterpoint. At the RCM I was able to sit in at rehearsals of the college orchestras at a time when Malcolm Sargent was conducting the first orchestra and Constant Lambert was conducting the second orchestra. At the rehearsals I would follow the music with a miniature score and observe their every gesture, noting too their rehearsal technique. Malcolm Sargent was a very competent and elegant conductor. Not all professional players liked him because he was considered to be conceited, but he was invariably kind to me. His stick technique was absolutely wonderful. You were never in a moment's doubt what he wanted. I found that year was very good because I was able to concentrate on music only.

O.   Where did you live while you were studying at the RCM?

W.   I lived at the Royal School of Church Music which was then at Chislehurst in Kent. While there, I was able to travel to London to spend two days each week at the RCM. At Chislehurst I was able to practise to my heart's content to prepare for the forthcoming trial for the King's College, Cambridge Organ Scholarship in December 1938. Ernest Bullock encouraged me to learn the major works of Bach by heart. He said that, if I did that, I would never forget them and they would be 'there for life'. So I learned twelve of the major works by heart, which proved to be useful later when, for a few years, I gave regular organ recitals. Concurrently I was able to study for the Archbishop of Canterbury's Diploma in Church Music. This was a relatively new examination devised to make sure that cathedral organists weren't just good players. It was a sort of accredited certificate which assured any Dean and Chapter that a holder of the Archbishop's Diploma was a competent player, a competent choir trainer, had studied liturgiology, and knew about the place of music in worship. I think you had to be an FRCO and you had to have taken the Choir Training Diploma before you could enter this examination. It was a sort of 'top layer' to two exams, and anybody who wanted to get a cathedral post was recommended to get this qualification. In preparation for the examination, I learned about liturgiology and the history of hymns and psalms. So it was back to church music again after four and a half years! The choir at the College of St Nicolas, Chislehurst was small. Over the years there were a few students from Canada and the United States. I think that there were twelve of us altogether specializing in church music.

O.   Did you have any choral training at Chislehurst?

W.   We had a daily service and gained experience in choir training. I have always felt that you learn choir training best by watching others, and then by personal experience.

O.   What about your third objective for the gap year?

W.   I took my scholarship examination for King's in December 1938, never having been to Cambridge before. None of my family had been to a university, so it was a bit intimidating as a young person to go to a place with such a great reputation for learning. I presented myself at King's for my trial and met the Organist, Boris Ord, and the other candidates for the examination. Only one of those was an FRCO, so I started with some advantage. Another possible advantage was that Boris Ord had also been at Clifton, although that could have made for some difficulty, because he wouldn't want to be accused of favouring somebody who had been to the same school as he had, lest people feel that it had all been fixed. In fact it had been all but fixed, because Douglas Fox was determined that I should go to King's, and he'd been telling Ord for some years how I was getting on. It was evident that I had been 'groomed', and he knew that Ernest Bullock was also hoping that I would get to King's. At the actual test, we first of all had to play the organ. Boris Ord said, 'What would you like to play?' I said, 'I would like to play from memory any one of twelve Bach preludes and fugues (which I specified). Will you choose?' I think that he chose the B minor [BWV544], which I got through all right. Douglas Guest, who was my predecessor as Organ Scholar of King's, was up in the organ loft with me, prepared to turn the pages. I think he was quite surprised that I didn't have a copy for such an important examination. Then I was given a sight-reading test, which was of roughly the same standard as for the FRCO, followed by some transposition, and then some improvisation. Boris Ord said, 'I'd like you to start a piece in A flat minor and when I tell you to do so, you must modulate to B minor. I want you to get there in a skilful manner without the modulation being too abrupt, and I'd like you to do that in about ten seconds.' So I'd be playing away in A flat minor and he'd say, 'Right, to B minor', and I'd have to continue in the same style and end up gracefully in B minor. Then I had to accompany the choir in an anthem. He warned me that I would have to play 'ahead' because of the Chapel acoustics. 'You'll hear the choir late, and I don't want you to drag.' I had never had to do that before. I don't know whether I did it well or badly, but he seemed satisfied. Then the most difficult task for me was having to conduct a short rehearsal of the choir, because I'd had little experience of conducting. He said, 'I want you to rehearse the choir. You have ten minutes with them, and I want it to be better when you finish.' He gave me a short anthem called 'If ye love me' by Tallis. Well, I stood out in front of the choir and conducted as they sang it through. The performance seemed to me to be absolutely perfect. I had never heard singing like it. For a moment I didn't know what to do. I felt that I could not say, 'That's perfect' because I had been given ten minutes to rehearse. In near desperation I asked, 'Can any boy tell me what was wrong with that?' There was a little pause during which I feared that no-body was going to speak. To my great relief one boy said, 'I think that it could be a little bit quicker, sir.' I said, 'Very good. Any other suggestions?' Another boy said, 'I think the tenors were a bit too loud, sir.' So I said, 'We'll sing the anthem again and see if they're better next time. Any others?' And one by one the boys put up their hands and mentioned things that they thought could be bet-ter. So I said, 'Right, we'll have another go, and I want everybody to correct the things that have been pointed out.' So they sang it again, but in exactly the same way as before! So I thought, 'Oh dear, what can I do now?' I asked the boys whether the second performance was better and they all agreed that it was. I still had a few minutes left, so I said, 'Now I'm going to do something as an experiment. I'm going to put it up half a step, to see if it's better in F sharp rather than in F.' I said, because it sounded brighter, 'Does everybody agree it was better in that key?' And they said, 'Yes, it was'. Afterwards, the Provost, an old man with white hair who wasn't very musical, came up to me and said, 'I so enjoyed that rehearsal. It was wonderful how you involved them all in it. It was a learning experience for them all, and it sounded quite different the last time.' I heard later that day that I'd been elected to the Organ Scholarship, which gave me great joy.

O.   What were your first impressions of King's College Chapel? You said this audition was the first time you had been to King's.

W.   Yes. I'm not conscious of ever having heard any music from King's
       before that. I don't think I'd even heard the carol service, but I had
       heard the choir at evensong the night before the trial. They were
       singing a piece of Tallis, and I thought, 'What beautiful music'.
       The whole atmosphere made an enormous impression on me as I
       entered the Chapel and looked up at the painted glass windows,
       the beautiful fan vaulting, and the great organ case. I was very
       moved by the beauty of it. It was winter when I took the Organ
       Scholarship examination. There was just the candlelight in the
       Chapel—no electric light of any sort. Nowadays there are imita-
       tion candles, because the old candle-grease used to make the
       Chapel dirty with the smoke. At that time, the panelling went all
       the way round the choir stalls, but now it's been removed in order
       to accommodate the Rubens painting. I'm sorry that's happened,
       because I loved the Chapel as it was. You went up some steps to
       the high altar. Now it's all on the same level, because it was neces-
       sary to lower the floor at the east end in order to fit the picture
       under the great east window.

O.   Did Boris Ord offer any suggestions for your gap year?

W.   Yes, he said, 'Go to as many concerts as you can while you are near
       London, because you won't get much chance when you're at
       Cambridge.' I did go to London occasionally for concerts. The first
       time I ever heard Walton's *Belshazzar's Feast* and *The Hymn of Jesus*
       by Holst was during that year.

O.   Were they conducted by Malcolm Sargent?

W.   Yes, he was conducting the Royal Choral Society. He always con-
       ducted *The Dream of Gerontius* on Ash Wednesday and *Messiah* on
       Good Friday. I was very impressed by his assurance. Adrian Boult
       was always considered more academic, but I found him rather dull,
       because he conveyed little emotion in his conducting. I thought
       the conductor ought to enthuse the audience. I was beginning to
       make up my mind as to what was important and what was less
       important. I think that I've changed in one respect in that I now
       think a conductor's main task is in rehearsal. People who rehearse
       well almost always perform well in concert.

O.   What other playing did you do that year?

W.   I played for the BBC Daily Service a few times, when George
       Thalben-Ball was responsible for the planning and presentation of

those services with the BBC Singers. I remember also playing for Harold Darke at one of his concerts with his St Michael's Singers at St Michael's, Cornhill. Included in the programme, which was broadcast, was Britten's *Te Deum in C*, which we performed with strings and organ. All those engagements provided me with valuable experience during my gap year between Clifton and Cambridge.

O.   And then it was off to King's?

W.   Yes, in September I went up to King's and I was given a room in college. I unpacked all my organ music and left it in the Chapel. On the morning of the 3rd of September, I followed the instructions from the Provost to listen to the radio as the Prime Minister, Neville Chamberlain, was going to address the nation. In the course of this speech, he informed us: 'This morning the British Ambassador in Berlin handed the German Government a final note stating that, unless we hear from them by 11 a.m. that they were prepared at once to withdraw their troops from Poland, a state of war would exist between us. I have to tell you now that no such undertaking has been received, and that consequently this country is at war with Germany.' We were told that it was likely that first-year students would not have to join the forces until the completion of their first year. This proved to be one of the most important turning points of my life.

O.   So you were able to begin your studies. Do you remember where your room was?

W.   Yes, it was by the river. An advantage was that, in those days, we had to be in by half-past ten or eleven, but anybody who was out late could get into my room from the river by climbing up from a punt, which is one of those flat-bottomed boats. I could let a little rope down from my room and people could clamber up.

O.   What were your duties as Organ Scholar?

W.   My duties were to assist Boris Ord in a number of ways: (1) by taking about half of the daily morning rehearsals of the boys at the Choir School, (2) by accompanying at the rehearsals of the full choir which preceded every service in the Chapel, and (3) by taking over full responsibility for the choir whenever Boris Ord was away from Cambridge. Nowadays there are two Organ Scholars, senior and junior. The junior one learns much from the senior one. I was all on my own, and of course in one's first term the first big service is the carol service on Advent Sunday. Boris Ord always went down to conduct the choir on that sort of occasion. At that service the Chapel is completely filled for the first time in the academic year. The acoustic of the Chapel is different when it is full, so I had to learn to accompany the big hymns in a different way. The first broadcast service for which I played at King's was the Christmas Eve Service of Nine Lessons and Carols in 1939.

O. Do you remember much about your first carol service?

W. I can remember only a few details. It had for some years been customary for the service to begin with the singing of the hymn 'Once in royal David's city', the first verse being assigned to a solo boy, singing unaccompanied beneath the organ screen. It had become traditional for there to be one or two minutes of complete silence in the Chapel while the choir slowly moved from the choir vestries to form up in the antechapel, in readiness for the processional hymn. It was truly a magical moment when the silence was broken by the lone treble singer.

O. After such a long silence, how did the solo boy know what note to begin on?

W. Boris Ord plucked a tuning fork, leaned toward the solo boy, and hummed an indeterminate note into his ear. Sometimes this note was readily accepted by the boy, but on some occasions the boy would look appealingly at Boris Ord, as if to say, 'Please hum it again!' In recent years, the Organ Scholar has played quietly until a few seconds before the solo boy has started to sing, never straying far from G major.

O. How did it work for your first carol service?

W. Boris Ord instructed me to leave the first two verses of 'Once in royal David's city' unaccompanied, and then to 'creep in' quietly during verse 3, with a *crescendo* through that verse and verse 4 to prepare for the congregational singing in verses 5 and 6. That was the pattern which Ord inherited from his predecessor, Dr Mann (always known affectionately as 'Daddy' Mann) and which I then inherited from Ord. The Dean of King's in 1939 was Eric Milner-White, who had composed the original bidding prayer and selected the nine lessons, a form of service that has been adopted widely throughout the English-speaking world. It had always been intended that the hymns and carols should, where possible, be relevant to the words that have just been read.

O.   What about the acoustics of King's College Chapel?

W.   There are difficulties in that music in the Chapel has to be more detached; otherwise, it sounds blurred in fast-moving music. There is little advantage in singing very loudly because you can hear a very quiet sound clearly right throughout the Chapel. I think the general range of dynamics in there should be from *ppp* up to *forte* rather than *piano* to *fff*. The choir can somehow ride over the full organ in certain cases. It's a wonderful acoustical environment in which to sing. The reverberation period is about five seconds. There is a downside, in that any chord that is not in tune goes on for a while! Most visiting choirs have found it difficult to sing in King's College Chapel. Some assume that it's going to be easy, but it's really very difficult because the singers cannot easily hear each other. The time lag between the organ and the choir can also be very perplexing. In fact, if it's right when you're sitting downstairs, it sounds wrong when you're up in the organ loft because you think that the organist is hurrying. In order to be with the choir, the organist has to anticipate.

O.   Can you recall your first impressions of Boris Ord as a choir trainer?

W.   I was amazed that a person with such a gravelly, rasping voice could produce a choir with such a beautiful, blended tone— both from the boys and from the choral scholars. I was astonished too that he could control the choir during a service using only the index finger of his right hand, lightly placed on a desk. This was a method of direction that he inherited from Dr Mann. Even in works requiring some *rubato*, this minimalist beat sufficed to ensure good ensemble. He was insistent upon good tuning and punctilious over words, especially getting final consonants absolutely together. He required all final consonants to be on the beat.

O.   On the beat?

W.   Yes, always. I no longer adhere to that strict rule. There are occasions when I like final consonants 'cleared' before the beat where there is a change of chord, or an entry in another voice. There are occasions too when final consonants can effectively be delayed. One other feature of Boris Ord's choir training was inherited from Dr Mann. Whenever a boy or choral scholar made a mistake in rehearsal, he was expected to acknowledge it by raising his hand. This made it unnecessary to spend precious time correcting it. If, rarely, a mistake was made at a service, the offender would be expected to stay behind after the service to make apology.

O.   Boris Ord was obviously a major influence. Was he a good organist?

W.   He wasn't a particularly good organist, but he was a very good harpsichord player. He rarely practised and I'm afraid I've got bad habits myself about practising. A person who can sight-read reasonably well can manage with less practice. I did, however, increase my organ repertoire at King's because I had to give recitals there. I was able to fire off all the pieces I'd learned at the Royal College under Bullock. I never had any more organ lessons—Boris Ord never wanted to teach the organ at all. I just taught myself, really, after that. I found the best incentive for practice was to programme a piece three weeks ahead. Then you had to learn it.

O.   Were there other teachers at Cambridge who had a special influence on you?

W.   I went for a weekly lesson with Hubert Middleton, Organist of Trinity, for composition, but I did not attend harmony and counterpoint classes, as I had covered the syllabus requirements in preparing for the FRCO examination. I attended some history classes and lectures on acoustics.

O.   Did you participate in any musical activity other than your work at King's College?

W.   I accompanied the University Chorus. Boris Ord was the conductor of the Cambridge University Musical Society (CUMS) which consisted of a chorus of about two hundred and fifty and a symphony orchestra. Playing the piano for those rehearsals was good experience. I also conducted a little choir called the Granta Singers, which was an amateur mixed-voice group in Cambridge. It had nothing to do with the university.

O.   Did you have to take any further examinations?

W.   As I had completed my FRCO examination and had studied harmony and counterpoint at the RCM with R. O. Morris, I was allowed by special permission to take Part One of the Bachelor of Music (MusB) examination at the end of my first term, which is normally a one-year course. I was lucky enough to be awarded a first class in this examination. Later, when it was known that I would be going off to serve in the war, I was allowed by special grace of the university to take Part Two of the MusB, which is normally a further two-year course, at the end of my first year in May of 1940. I managed to get a first class in that examination too. During that year I was also awarded a John Stewart of Rannoch scholarship in sacred music. On the strength of having got a first class in both Parts One and Two of the MusB degree and having been awarded a Stewart of Rannoch scholarship, King's College gave me an open foundation scholarship in addition to the Organ Scholarship. That was a very satisfactory first year for me.

O. So you completed a three-year course in one year.

W. Yes. I think that they may have thought that, as I was going off to the war, I might be killed or wounded. I was very lucky in being allowed to take those exams at that age and at that seniority. Nowadays the MusB is a postgraduate degree. Those enrolling for the MusB course get a BA first, after three years. In their fourth year, they must have distinguished themselves in the previous three-year music tripos course, leading to a BA (Music). Although I had passed the MusB examination, I was not allowed to have the degree conferred upon me until I had been in residence for nine terms. All I had to do after the war when I came back to Cambridge was just to *be there*. I had to behave myself and be within, I think, three miles of Great St Mary's Church—such are the ancient rules. But it sent me away with a sort of confidence. I don't think I was conceited, but I just felt thankful to have got all those requirements out of the way. I felt glad that I had no more essays to write, and that I did not need to compose ever again under examination conditions.

O. During your first terms at Cambridge, what were your thoughts about the war that had started?

W. It seemed a phony war. Soon after the declaration of war in 1939 the British sent an expeditionary force to France. Nothing much happened during that first winter, as the Germans sheltered behind their very highly fortified Siegfried Line, while the French and British forces felt secure behind the supposedly impregnable Maginot Line. It seemed to be a stalemate.

O.   So when you were at King's, things were very quiet?

W.   Shall I say, relatively quiet? We realized that we were at war and that both sides were engaged in reconnaissance, both in the air and on the ground. On the home front there was rationing of petrol, food, and clothing. Urgent steps were being taken to strengthen civil defence—gas masks were introduced, and many homes were provided with Anderson shelters for protection against anticipated air raids. I think that some men engaged in postgraduate work may have enlisted in 1939, but, being a first-year undergraduate, I knew that I would not be called up until the end of May 1940. It was in May 1940 that the Germans outflanked the Maginot Line by invading Holland and Belgium. This brilliant surprise attack was known as the Blitzkrieg. The German army poured into France, trapping the British army at Dunkirk. The evacuation from Dunkirk took place in late May and early June of 1940. It was a major victory for the Germans. We were alarmed then, because there appeared to be little to prevent the Germans invading England. It was a desperate situation, but Britain and the Commonwealth under Churchill's resolute leadership were not prepared to contemplate defeat. During the summer of 1940 it seemed likely that Hitler would invade, but first it would be necessary for him to achieve air supremacy. In September 1940 a sustained air battle, known as the Battle of Britain, took place in which British pilots, though outnumbered, emerged victorious. Hitler decided not to invade England. And, much to our good fortune, having signed a non-aggression pact with Russia, Hitler soon reneged on the agreement and invaded Russia. This relieved the pressure on England. We could not understand why he did that. There was nothing to stop him from walking into England. Our only defences were our remaining army, navy, and air force, and the English Channel.

Interlude 2

Reflections on Clifton

Professor Sir Brian Pippard was a student at Clifton College with Sir David. He was interviewed on 8 March 2007 at his home in Cambridge.

BP.   David and I are more or less parallel as far as our time at Clifton was concerned. He had a lot of experience in music and was a shade older, but we moved up together and we left school together. However, at a very early stage when David had just arrived, it became well known that he was an outstanding musician.

O.   Did you study with Douglas Fox?

BP.   From the age of eleven to eighteen I was taught the piano by Fox, and that was a revelation. He was definitely an eccentric man. He lived on his nerves. He was capable of sudden rages and equally sudden repentances for his rages. I remember one choir rehearsal when one of the small boys had been misbehaving. Douglas rushed up from the piano, seized him with his left hand by the hair and tugged, and the boy shrieked and burst into tears. Douglas said to him, 'I shouldn't have done that—here, pull mine.' He leant down and the little boy took his hair in both his hands and Fox immediately cried, 'Oh, not as hard as that!' He did have a wonderful gift for transmitting musicality. When he died, I wrote a short obituary for the college magazine, and one of his pupils, who was after my time, wrote a longer one. I remember he told of the horror of being taught by Douglas and how he would sit at the piano in tears unable to do what Douglas expected of him—simply mortified by his failure and how frightened he was and all the rest of it. He finished up his obituary—'He was the greatest man I ever knew.'

That sums him up extremely well. Years later, I went to Clare College, Cambridge which is next door to King's. David said to me about that time, 'Until I came to Cambridge I never really appreciated how great a teacher Douglas was.'

O.   Did you and David ever perform together?

BP.   I think the only time we did was a very strange occasion. A group of boys from South African schools had turned up, and some of us senior boys were recruited to show them around Clifton. They broke up into small groups and each of us took a group and showed them around the school. Towards the end of the afternoon, I'd more or less run out of anything to do, and I ran across David and his group who were clearly in the same state. So David said to me, 'Come along, let's play to them.' We took our boys along to the Big School where there was an organ and a grand piano. David sat at the organ and I sat at the grand piano and we improvised on popular tunes. I have to say that David was quite clearly the leader—I followed him and simply decorated what he was doing. The boys were enormously impressed, and one or two of the masters dropped in to see what was happening. They'd never seen a performance like that before—two people actually improvising together.

O.   Did you see much of David as your separate careers progressed?

BP.   We've always done our jobs separately, and hardly ever impinged. But there is one thing I must tell you. When I was fourteen I had taken my school certificate. It was necessary then to start being selective in what I ought to learn, and my housemaster, who was a scholar, was very keen that I should carry on doing classics. The science master was equally keen that I should become a scientist, and Douglas was very keen that I should become a musician. Certainly in those days at the age of fourteen I had no independent will of my own; I was under the power of my parents and my teachers. My father was an engineer and wanted me to be a scientist. I was very happy to be a scientist, and I've never regretted that for a moment, but as far as I was concerned the important thing was having known, even at that age, someone like David, who was a real musician. Looking back, I never had the slightest regret about not taking up music professionally. I was a useful pianist, that's all. I would never have been a top-class musicologist or musician of any sort, and it is knowing David that has made me cease to regret what happened to me. You can do science and music together; you can't do music and science. So I have that continuing gratitude to David, but he doesn't know it.

3
David's War
1940 - 1945

O.   I think your war service lasted about five years.

W.   Yes, from May 1940 to early November of 1945. I was having a very
peaceful year in Cambridge and was then ordered to go for an
interview where they decided what form of national service I
should do. I thought that I would probably be best employed in sub-
marines, because I believed that submarine detection was done very
much by sound. I thought that one could tell by pitch how big a
vessel was. I asked at my interview, 'Would that be a good thing to
do?' and was told, 'Oh no, it's all done automatically now through
radar and sonar, not human ears.' So my little dreams of being in the
navy and in submarine service disappeared immediately. At the
interview they said, 'Where do you come from?' and I said,
'Cornwall'. I then had a medical test to see if I was fit. I remember
I was sitting with my legs crossed. A doctor came up with a hammer
and started hammering my knee, not very hard; and I thought he
was testing me to see if I would flinch in danger, so I gripped the
side of the chair and kept absolutely still. He tapped away, but nothing happened at all. It was only years later that I discovered that
he was trying to test my reflexes. What he wrote down in his little
book I never have discovered. He must have thought that I was an
absolute idiot, for I had no response at all! Well, I was pronounced
medically fit anyway and was told that I ought to be in the infantry.
I think it was because I wasn't clever enough to be in anything else.
They said, 'We would like you to report to Northampton [in the
middle of England] and get preliminary training there.' I duly
reported at the barracks there. I had never heard such language as on
that first night. I learned more words than I ever learned at school!

The same four-letter word would be used as an adjective, adverb, noun, and verb. It could be used five or six times in a single sentence. I met all sorts of people there, chaps who could neither read nor write. There was one chap who played cribbage brilliantly but couldn't sign his name. Yet he had a marvellous card sense. He could look at a hand of cards and say, 'That is worth seventeen.' In the barracks with me were people from all walks of life: some were obviously quite wealthy and arrived in grand cars, while others were from very poor circumstances. We were there for about a month before they started selecting people for officer training. I had done my marching up and down the parade ground and polishing my boots—not only the top of the boots but the bottom part of the boots was polished as well. There were brass things too, which we had to polish. We were inspected every day. You had to have your kit folded out on your bed. It was inspected to make sure that you had folded your socks in a particular way. It was all to instil discipline in

Figure 3.1. Lance-Corporal Willcocks, 1940

us, I suppose. I thought, 'What an awful waste of time.' But I enjoyed it, because I have always enjoyed meeting people from different walks of life.

It was decided then that I was suitable material for officer training and after, I think, three months in Northampton I was sent to North Wales, to a place called Barmouth, for officer training. We again got some drill, but time was devoted to the study of army history, training in the use of weapons, and tactical exercises. We had map reading—you were given a map and told you've got to report to various places. We had to go on night marches and to experience twenty-four hours without food, and then we had exercises where we had to climb up a mountain called Cader Idris in full battle gear. We had initiative tests, where you might have to devise ways of crossing a river. We had instruction in driving and vehicle maintenance, extending to cars, motorcycles, three-ton lorries, and Bren gun carriers. We were taught how to conduct a pay parade, where the non-commissioned officers and other ranks come forward to receive the money due to them. We learned how an officer must never eat until the troops under his command have been fed and how to go around when they're eating and say, 'Has anybody got any complaints?' Every aspect of man management was taught. There were lectures on military and civilian law, aircraft recognition, and cooperation with other branches of the army, for example, artillery, engineers, signallers. It was altogether a well-structured four-month course. I felt well prepared, and after that I got my commission as a second lieutenant and received my first posting. This was to my county regiment—the Duke of Cornwall's Light Infantry. Its 5th battalion, to which I was assigned, was then stationed at Welwyn Garden City, which is between Cambridge and London. There we were trained as a battalion. We had mock exercises where you surrounded and attacked a village, with or without air support, artillery, and so on. We did not use live ammunition in these exercises, but used blank cartridges. We carried on with our drill. Marching, involving the quick response to orders, was considered to be an important element in the inculcation of discipline. Attention was paid to physical training and to the maintenance of good health. We underwent endurance tests to toughen us up, ready for the battles which we feared lay ahead. As an invasion of Great

Britain was expected after the retreat from Dunkirk in June 1940, we were not surprised to be moved to Frinton, which is on the east coast near the important port of Harwich. It was thought one of the invasion places the Germans would choose would be a port, so Harwich was considered quite a target for them. At that stage of the war, we still thought we were going to be invaded. There were red alerts and yellow alerts, which required different states of preparedness. Particularly, we were conscious of the tides. The Germans were more likely to invade when the tide was high. Night and day we patrolled the beaches at Frinton. They were all mined, and there were also concrete beach defences. There were frequent rumours that the Germans were among us, dressed as civilians. We were always on the lookout for the German 'Fifth Column', the term for people who might be spies. We became friendly with the girls in the Royal Navy. They were called Wrens (short for Women's Royal Navy Service) and many of them served at Harwich and Dovercourt nearby. It was discovered that I could play the organ, so occasionally I used to play for church services and for dances in the officers' mess. Luckily, I knew all the popular dance tunes of the 1930s, so I could 'oblige' on pianos of all sorts.

O. Tell me about your senior officers.

W. My commanding officer was a fine man, Sir John Carew-Pole, a member of a very famous old Cornish family dating back generations. He was later to become Lord Lieutenant of Cornwall. He was very well connected and owned one of the most beautiful houses in Cornwall, called Antony House. He wasn't an academic, but we all recognized his ability to train us civilians to be a unit ready for battle. He was from a Guards battalion, always impeccably turned out, so he insisted that all his officers and men had uniform haircuts and acquired a military bearing. It was not long before Sir John appointed me intelligence officer of the battalion, a post which I held until I was demobilized in November 1945, some four years later. An intelligence officer is responsible for map-reading and for informing the commanding officer in a battle where our troops are, where the enemy troops are, how strong the enemy is, and, if possible, what regiment they are from, for example, whether they are infantry or tank crews. An intelligence officer had to report to his battalion commander and to brigade headquarters daily.

(At brigade headquarters I reported to John Denison, staff captain of the brigade. Since the war I have kept in close touch with him.) He would seek a report from each company in the battalion as to where they were, what they were doing, what their needs were with regard to food and ammunition, and what casualties they had suffered. So the intelligence officer would regularly send a battalion report back to brigade headquarters, who would pass this information to division headquarters. All this training in England was going to prove very useful when we eventually got to the Continent in the summer of 1944. At various times our battalion was inspected by senior officers. They would come around to see how we were faring. We had an Air Ministry Experimental Station in our battalion area. I don't know what its purpose was, but I think that it was to do with radar or something. A general came around one day and said to my commanding officer, 'Tell me, what do you think of the new AMES', and there was a little silence for a moment, after which my commanding officer said, 'Oh, he is a splendid chap, sir; I like him very much.' He hadn't realized the General meant the Air Ministry Experimental Station! I thought, 'Oh God, how can I save him?' I whispered in his ear and Sir John quickly said, 'I'm so sorry, you meant the Air Ministry Station, didn't you?' I got him out of it a bit. After we had been on beach defences in Essex, we moved to other places. We went up to Northumberland to Bamburgh Castle, where we were stationed for a bit. It was unlikely that the Germans would invade there. We did some assault training up in Scotland at Loch Fyne, where we had to run up and down mountains with mortars and other equipment. We had mock invasions, using landing craft. We only realized later that we were training for a sudden attack on the Azores, which are Portuguese. Portugal was neutral, supposedly, but the Azores are in the middle of the Atlantic and our intelligence sources knew perfectly well that the Germans were using them as a base for their U-boats. Churchill realized that we could not afford to lose any more shipping. He decided that we must capture the Azores even though Portugal was neutral. So we were all geared up to go. We didn't know exactly where we were going, but we had maps of the landing places selected. Shortly before we were about to go south to embark, word came through that the Azores had been 'bought'. I believe that Churchill made an arrangement whereby we could go there and occupy the islands, thereby preventing the Germans from using them as a base.

O. Where did you go next?

W. Then we went to the Isle of Wight. I think the Azores expedition would have been in 1943, because the Battle of the Atlantic had been going on and we had been losing an enormous number of ships. Every gallon of petrol had to be brought to England. We had petrol rationing, of course. The Battle of the Atlantic was terribly important. If we hadn't overcome the German U-boat menace, the Americans would have never been able to come over with their convoys, first of all to North Africa, Sicily, and Italy, and then to England. At this stage Russia was getting very worried that the Allies were doing little to relieve the pressure on the eastern front. We had been driven out of France in 1940 when most of France had surrendered. Many French soldiers had escaped to England, where they formed the Free French Army. It became known that Russia, which had been attacked by the Germans, was getting desperate. Stalingrad was an epic battle. As had been the case with Napoleon in 1812, the German lines were over-extended. Both the Russians and the Germans were losing thousands. The Russians were pleading with us to open a second front and to invade France. At long last we did, on the 6th of June 1944. That was D-Day. By that stage the Americans had entered the war because of the Japanese attack on Pearl Harbor in December 1941. It was known then that we were all in the war together—Japan, Germany, and Italy against the United States, the United Kingdom, and the other Allies. It was Churchill's happiest day when Pearl Harbor was attacked. He realized then that the Americans were actually going to declare war on the Axis powers. Of course that made all the difference when it came to June 1944, when the vast numbers of American troops came to our assistance with the invasion of France. In 1944 our battalion was one of those planned for the advance, but not the initial advance.

O. Where were you stationed?

W. We moved to several locations. We went down to Cornwall for a little bit. Then we went to Kent for quite a long time, where we did further preparatory exercises. Then we moved to Sussex and Hampshire in readiness for the invasion, which we realized was imminent. We were in huts concealed in some forest so that we could not be seen from the air by German reconnaissance planes. An enormous army was built up—partly Americans and Canadians, partly us—waiting to cross the Channel from different ports. Our families and friends did not know where we were. When I wrote home, I couldn't say where I was. King George VI visited many fighting units during the weeks before the June invasion to boost our confidence. I remember presenting one of our officers called George King to His Majesty. I just couldn't resist! I said, 'Your Majesty, I beg leave to present George King . . . King George.'

O. When did you actually cross?

W. We crossed about the 20th of June. We sailed from somewhere near Southampton, probably from Exbury. I remember seeing the Isle of Wight as we went by it. Then the most terrific sight . . . I shall never forget the mass of planes and the great armada of vessels, battleships, cruisers, destroyers, small boats, and landing craft going across.

O. This was all going by the Isle of Wight?

W. Yes, across to Arromanches, which is on the Normandy coast. We knew by this time where the invasion had taken place, but still there was some doubt as to whether some units might be sent to Calais as a diversionary attack. There was in fact a deception plan to make the Germans think that the main allied attack would be in the Pas de Calais area, which would have involved the shortest Channel crossing. It was very important that the Allies had some troops actually appearing in Dover with war equipment on, so that the German spies should suspect that there was going to be something there. In fact, that was a bluff. Our planners even had Montgomery, or somebody looking like Montgomery, with field glasses, looking across from Dover. All those ruses were there. Historians tell us that Hitler kept strong forces in the Calais area. He thought for some days that Normandy might be just a feint attack. When we got to Arromanches, the beaches had already been cleared. Of course we had to be careful, as all the beaches had been very carefully mined. The engineers had cleared paths and marked them, so that tanks and infantry could go through safely. The roads also had to be cleared of mines. When we landed, the bridgehead was perhaps three or four miles deep. During the first days we were fully aware of the stench of dead cattle and sheep. The first night we were in a wood and we could hear the distant rumble of fighting. It was two days before we moved up to the front line. Though we were shelled, we had air superiority. It was a comforting fact that we rarely saw a German plane. Our Spitfires and Hurricanes were constantly overhead. We could call on their support if we ran into enemy opposition. When we moved up to the front line near the little village of Cheux, we relieved some men of a Scottish battalion, the 9th Cameronians, who had been in the line for about a week. They were unshaven and looked very tired and weary. The second day we were there the Germans attacked and we lost Jack Atherton, our commanding officer, and two other senior officers, Percival Coode and Basil Aimers. The commanding officer was loading an anti-tank gun. I was very near him. I knew him very well and he was a wonderful man. It was quite a rude start, on the first day in action, to lose your commanding officer, signal officer (Basil Aimers), and about twenty other men. Percival Coode was a great friend of mine and popular with everyone, but there was no time for emotion. I had never seen a dead body before I arrived in Normandy, but here corpses were lying everywhere you looked. When we could, we'd dig a grave and mark the spot with a wooden cross. You would make a mental note to write to the widow or mother when you got the chance. To counter that, some of our men managed to put five German tanks out of action, an extraordinary feat. It made us realize that the Germans were not invincible. The German armour was much better than ours. If we put an English Sherman tank opposite a German Tiger tank, the Germans could always win. The German tanks easily penetrated our armour, whereas our guns couldn't penetrate the Tiger, except in the turret and possibly the tracks. However, people in tanks have to get out to eat and rest, so that is when they are vulnerable. Also, if their tracks get stuck in mud, they are vulnerable. There is a place therefore for the infantry. We were being very heavily shelled by day and by night at that time, because the Germans realized that these first days were terribly important. If they could drive us back into the sea that would solve all their problems. Once we had established a bridgehead and more and more supplies were being delivered, they were really worried. There was a precious delay because Hitler couldn't quite make up his mind whether to blow up the bridges or whether to leave them there for a counterattack. There was hesitation and he was arguing with his generals over tactics. It is very interesting to hear the Germans' account of this stage of the war—how, if only he had allowed them to do this or that, they could have pushed us back. I can remember the sound of those mortars which were called 'moaning minnies'. You always thought that they were coming straight for you. We had many casualties every day. My job as an intelligence officer was to visit each of the companies each day with our commanding officer and to gather intelligence about our own troops and those of the enemy, including information about enemy morale. Every little scrap of information we gleaned was very important. If we took prisoners, they were officially required to give only their name and number. But if you could wheedle more information out of them by offering cigarettes or chocolate, it was fair game. We were told exactly how to interview people, and also, if we were captured, exactly what we should do. We were told that the Germans would stick to the Geneva Convention, which indeed they did, and I believe we did as well. I was never aware of our ever mistreating a prisoner. In fact we always found it paid to treat them well, because you got more information out of them that way. I spoke enough German to undertake a preliminary interview and make them feel welcome. After that they would be escorted back to Brigade Headquarters.

O.   What was the next encounter?

W.   Our second major encounter was in July 1944. This was after we had been in Normandy for three or four weeks. On the 10th of July we got orders to move up to a village called Fontaine Étoupefour. There we were told that our battalion would be required to attack and capture an important area of high ground, known as Hill 112— anybody who was in possession of Hill 112 had a wonderful view of the country in every direction. It was especially important too, because it had already been captured by the British, but they had not been able to withstand the German counterattack. The Germans had accordingly reinforced their hold on the hill. When our new commanding officer, 'Dick' James, received the orders for our attack, he was told that we would be given very heavy artillery and air support. We were to advance under the cover of smoke. We attacked and sustained heavy casualties. During the night it became apparent that our forward companies had captured the little wood at the top of the hill, but they were being very heavily shelled by German tanks and infantry. James climbed a tree to get a better view in order to be able to direct artillery fire. To our great dismay he was killed. He was an exceptionally brave young man, aged twenty-six. It was a great blow to lose our second commanding officer. I was then with the adjutant of the battalion and we took temporary command of the battalion, as we didn't know who was alive and who was dead. During the night I got as much information as I could, and informed our brigade headquarters of the serious situation. We were told that we had to hold the line at all costs, because it was important that the Germans should not break through. Our casualties grew. I think that about three hundred of our seven hundred men were killed or wounded that night, just in that small area. It became apparent in the end that we wouldn't be able to hold the hill. Some of our chaps came streaming back. The adjutant and I, with the commanding officer of the 5th Somersets, Lieutenant-Colonel C. G. Lipscombe, persuaded many of our troops to return to the top of the hill and to continue the fight until we got more assistance. They had every justification for coming back, because their position in the sheltered wood was absolutely untenable. Hill 112 became known as 'Cornwall Hill' after that dreadful night, and a memorial was later erected on the site. Several months later, General Montgomery held a ceremony in which several of our officers received awards for their fighting in Normandy. I was honoured myself to receive the Military Cross. I was sorry that there were not more posthumous awards to many of those who had been killed or badly wounded, for they had borne the heat of the battle.

O.   Who was your next commanding officer?

W.   It was Lieutenant-Colonel George Taylor, who had been second in command of the 1st Worcestershire Regiment, also in our division. We all took an immediate liking to our new commanding officer. Then we had some skirmishes; the front was gradually being enlarged. The battle was really for the city of Caen, that was the pivot. Many roads met there. Montgomery's plan was for the British, by attacking Caen, to draw on to their front all the German armoured divisions and so weaken the enemy flanks. The Americans, under the dynamic General George Patton, could then sweep around

Figure 3.2. Field Marshal Montgomery presenting Captain Willcocks with the Military Cross, November 1944 (War Office photograph)

on the west front in a large flanking movement and cut the Germans off. It was a plan which came off brilliantly. Normandy was won by this big encircling movement, and the German Army suffered severe losses of men, tanks, and munitions in the Falaise gap. The Germans were hemmed in, so our fighter planes could destroy them on the roads. One learned so much in those days about people's characters.

I think perhaps I may have been relatively cheerful, because I felt that we all had to make the best of the situation in which we found ourselves. I felt sorry for people like the doctors who had to tend to the wounded, and maybe decide whether to amputate a limb, with possibly devastating effect on somebody's future career, like that of Douglas Fox. I felt sympathy too for the padres (chaplains) who had the responsibility for the burial of the dead. What I found difficult was writing to the widows of my comrades who had been killed in battles which I had survived. It was distressing to find, in the pockets of dead friends, pictures of their loved ones and family letters.

O.   Was that part of your duty, to write to them?

W.   Only the people I knew. Every next of kin received a personal letter. All officers might write if they knew the person. It was such a different life. I didn't miss Cambridge; I didn't think about it because we were absorbed in battle. I never thought of music at all, except when we captured a village and there was a church there. Someone might say, 'Say, Willcocks, does that thing there work?' I would go and see if the organ was playable or not. If there was a piano in a pub or private house, I might play it. I could play all the dance tunes of the day—'Night and day', 'Cheek to cheek', and so on.

O.   This is where you played the piano backwards, with your hands behind your back?

W.   Yes, with the hands the wrong way around. I even made up songs. One was, 'When there's mistletoe above, then it's time to fall in love!' The battalion quickly picked up some of these songs. Sing-songs and variety shows were somewhat rare occasions, but after about a fortnight, generally, we would be taken out of the front line and sent back where we could get clean, shave, and rest. Most commanding officers arranged for a parade where we were inspected; it was good for morale that we were clean, tidy, and shaven.

O.   Where did you move next?

W.   After the fighting in Normandy we advanced through France; we had smaller battles on the way, including the crossing of the River Seine at Vernon. That town was defended, but the Germans were pulling back by that stage. We then proceeded to Belgium and then to the Dutch border. When we got to Holland in September 1944, we learned that Montgomery had devised a daring plan to capture five bridges across successive canals and rivers in Holland.

Figure 3.3. Officers of the 5th Battalion, The Duke of Cornwall's Light Infantry, Normandy, July 1944: David, front row, left; Lieut.-Col. George Taylor, front row, centre

Our corps (30 Corps) would either drive right up through Holland's one major road and then swing to the right to encircle the Ruhr (the industrial heartland where all the German munitions were being manufactured) or swing left to destroy the bombs being unleashed on Britain. Montgomery believed one of these options might bring an end to the war by Christmas. The plan involved the capture of the first four bridges by American airborne troops, and of the fifth (and last) bridge by British airborne forces. The last bridge, the furthest north, was at Arnhem. The Germans at this stage were occupying the whole of Holland, so it was a very daring and imaginative move to cut right through their army and outflank them. Our orders were to advance as quickly as possible along the single road, over the four captured bridges to Arnhem to relieve the British and then possibly advance beyond that to Apeldoorn. It was hoped that this swift advance could be accomplished in a few days. Well, all the paratroops landed, and the first three bridges were captured. We drove along the single narrow road being shelled from the sides. When we got to Nijmegen, which was the fourth bridge, we were held up, because the Germans were in strength in the area between Nijmegen and Arnhem. The delay made us desperately late. We were supposed to be there in forty-eight hours, and the British were being very heavily attacked at Arnhem and to the south. About ten thousand men had landed by parachute or in gliders, but they had suffered heavy casualties, owing to the unanticipated presence of SS Panzer divisions in the Arnhem area, which were being refitted and regrouped following the German retreat from France and Belgium. The Germans recaptured the Arnhem bridge and encircled the remaining British airborne forces in an ever-shrinking area at Oosterbeek, some six miles west of Arnhem on the north bank of the Rhine. It was six days before we were able to establish contact with the beleaguered British airborne forces by reaching the little village of Driel on the south bank of the Rhine, by a circuitous route. There we could look across the river at the area where our airborne forces were surrounded, almost without food and ammunition. It was a desperate situation, for we could not ferry troops, ammunition, food, and medical supplies across the fast-flowing river. At a crucial stage of the battle, our corps commander (Lieutenant-General Horrocks, Commander of 30 Corps) came forward to join us. My battalion commander (Colonel Taylor) and I were with him when we climbed the tower of the little church at Driel to look across the Rhine. It was then that he decided that the British airborne forces and the Poles must be ordered to withdraw through our lines that night. Montgomery's plan (now known as 'A Bridge Too Far', from the title of the well-known film) had failed. More than seven and a half thousand British and Polish soldiers were killed, wounded, or taken prisoner. The Allies had, however, gained substantial territory and inflicted equally heavy casualties on the Germans. That was one of the big battles of the war in which there was nothing that we could do. My battalion sustained heavy casualties in warfare that resembled World War I, but it was a necessary prelude to the crossing of the Rhine and entry to Germany in March. The winter months were spent clearing the area between the rivers Maas and Rhine. This area included the heavily fortified Reichswald Forest, part of the Siegfried Line. The weather for the most part was horrible—wet and very cold. It was a complete surprise to us on the 16th of December 1944 when the full weight of the Fifth and Sixth Panzer Armies plus the Seventh German Army attacked the US VIII Corps in the Ardennes. Though a daring last attempt, this brilliant and bold plan, known as the Battle of the Bulge, was only partially successful. Our brigade was not needed even though we had been sent down to Bilsen to act as a 'long-stop' in case the Americans were over-run. During the first month of 1945, it became more and more evident as we progressed through the remainder of Holland and into Germany towards Bremen that many of the German army were losing heart. Although they still managed to put up spirited resistance, we took increasing numbers of German prisoners.

After the German surrender we ended up opposite the Russians, who had also advanced to the river Elbe at Dannenberg. At first we were not allowed to fraternize with them, but eventually the rules were relaxed. We were allowed to invite a number of Russian officers to cross the river to join us in a celebratory dinner at Dannenberg. We thought we would show them how we lived in the West! We put on a good spread because we had just captured some good china and glass. We got good wines out. We made a seating plan which placed each Russian officer between two British officers. Our commanding officer had the senior Russian officer on his right. When our waiters came around with a plate of hors d'oeuvres containing some portions of ham, fish, potato, cheese, onions, etc., the senior Russian officer helped himself to all the ham, so his neighbouring British officer tactfully took all the cheese. So it went around the table. The Russians clearly didn't realize that they were supposed to take a little bit of each. The last chap had all the onions! Then I played the wrong Russian national anthem. I played the Red Flag one, when it should have been another one. Nobody seemed to mind, as we had consumed a lot of alcohol. We didn't speak a word of Russian between us; the Russians didn't speak any English. So we just bowed to each other!

O.   Did you stay long after the war?

W.   Yes. After the ceasefire, I stayed with my battalion until September or October.

O.   In Dannenberg?

W.   Yes, I think that we were in the same general area, though we moved around a bit. We had to guard certain prisoners, and I watched some of the preliminary trials. We had to be kept occupied, so we engaged in a lot of sport. I remember we were not allowed to fraternize with the Germans at that stage, as we had to be very careful. I did take part in a concert with a German soprano in Dannenberg. I have the actual programme because we managed to print it. Captain Willcocks was the soloist! In those days I could remember several piano pieces which I had learned at school—*Rondo brilliant* by Weber and *Clair de lune* by Debussy and things like that. I found no difficulty in giving a recital even though I had not practised for six years. I remember that while I was in Germany I learned to ride a horse. I had a German groom who came and knocked on my door each morning with a cup of tea, which I drank while my horse neighed outside the door.

O.   Have you been back since?

W.   In 2004 I took my wife and two daughters, Sarah and Anne, back to Arnhem to view the landing grounds. We attended an enormous annual display of wartime British, American, and Polish planes. Included in the celebration was a sacred service in the cemetery at Arnhem. For every person buried there, a Dutch child stepped forward and laid a flower by each gravestone, saying aloud the name of the person buried there. I also gave a talk at Elst and it was immediately translated into Dutch. Another year I took my wife and children to Hill 112, where each year a service is held to remember those who gave their lives or were wounded. Prince Charles attended the services at Elst many times.

Interlude 3

Reflections on David's War

John Denison CBE (1911–2007) served in the same brigade as Sir David during the war and remained a life-long friend. He was Music Director of the Arts Council of Great Britain, General Manager of the Royal Festival Hall, and Director of all the South Bank concert halls. He was interviewed on 12 September 2003.

JD.   I did not meet David personally until we were both in the army. We found ourselves in two different regiments but in the same brigade, which had three battalions. We were on defence duties on the Isle of Wight and used to go on duty an hour before dawn to 'stand to' against landings from the air or from the sea. This little story of that time is an example of what a gentleman David was. The great social event, as the weeks went by, was a dance in Newport, the town in the centre of the island. David found himself there on a Saturday evening where the dance was going on, and there were, I think, ten or twelve Wrens.* They were all very intelligent girls, working as linguists in Ventnor intercepting signals from all the ships that were going up and down the channel. After the dance these girls had to get back to their establishment, which was ten miles away, but for some reason or other the transport that they had arranged disappeared. David, who had got a little truck from his own unit, said, like a gentleman, 'I'll take you home.' They all got in and, blow me down, the truck was stopped halfway between Newport and Ventnor by the military police!

O.   No!

* See p. 52.

JD.   At this time it was automatically a court-martial offence to be found using a military vehicle without an authorization chit. David's colonel, Sir John Carew-Pole, was a great and very influential sort of person. When David reported what had happened, Sir John came immediately up to brigade headquarters (where I, by then, had become the staff captain to the brigadier commanding the whole three units) and said, 'This is all damn nonsense. We can't have a young man like David Willcocks going before a court martial for an offence of this kind.' The brigadier and he conversed urgently. I was sent for and the brigadier told me to draft a special submission to the general officer commanding in Southern Command explaining the circumstances and suggesting, perhaps, that alternative arrangements should be made other than sending him for court martial. Well in the end David, the brigadier, and his colonel went up to Salisbury, which in those days was the headquarters of Southern Command, the largest unit under the War Office with stationary, home defence troops, in England. The outcome of it was that David was given a severe reprimand and avoided a court martial.

O.   Were you with him when you crossed to Normandy?

JD.   Yes, we went to Normandy together. The crossing wasn't at all simple and we sat on that boat for three or four days because of the general congestion in the bay, with the landings of all the different troops. The battles developed. Perhaps the most bitterly fought struggle in taking Normandy was around Hill 112. The Germans hung on to it for a very long time and the battles were very heavy. David, as the intelligence officer, was always at the side of the commanding officer of his battalion. His colonel—Colonel James, borrowed from my regiment—was killed in a matter of hours. One of the few officers right there at the nodal point of the battalion headquarters was David. Even though he was only a lieutenant then, he had to take charge and coordinate the action, such as it was, that had to be taken in the heat of battle. He was very cool under fire and all the rest of it. He was awarded the Military Cross, which is an award given not only for being competent and able, but also for gallantry.

Figure 3.4. David at a war cemetery in Normandy, July 2002

Sarah de Rougemont (née Willcocks) is the eldest of the four Willcocks children. She was interviewed on 14 June 2005 at her home in London.

SR.   When I was thirteen my family took the ferry to Caen from Portsmouth for a holiday in Brittany. My father suddenly thought, 'We're very near Hill 112, shall we go and have a look at it?' It was then twenty years after the war and he hadn't been back. We did a slight detour from Caen and stopped near the hill. I was in a bad mood and I wouldn't get out of the car. It sounded so boring, so I sat in the car in a sulk. The other three children and my parents got out and were gone for a very long time. I was just beginning to wonder whether they were ever coming back, when they re-appeared, and my father had tears in his eyes. I've never seen that before or since. I remember Anne particularly was looking really shocked, and Jonny and James were very quiet. Nobody said anything. They just got back in the car, and we drove on. I knew I had missed something really important. Forty years later, we visited Hill 112 together for the sixtieth anniversary of the battle and we had an incredibly moving few days. I saw a side of my father that I'd never seen before. He was much more introspective. It was extraordinary to think of the extremes of experiences that he'd had. It's partly the ethos of the time. You didn't pour your heart out, you didn't complain. I think that same stoicism probably helped him survive boarding at Westminster Abbey when he was a boy, and also now as he is getting older. He's really not giving in to getting older at all. Presumably he sometimes gets aches and pains, but he just decides not to complain or mention it. So the war really fits into the same pattern, I suppose, as his whole life. He told me one thing that had happened to him when he was a chorister at Westminster Abbey and far from home. His parents never visited him there at all—apparently, they couldn't afford the train fare. He needed to have his tonsils out when he was about nine, and so all by himself he was sent to hospital. He had the operation by himself, and recovered by himself, and went back to school again. I only heard about this when my second daughter, Hannah, had her tonsils out when she was six. My father visited her in hospital every day, even though I was staying in the hospital with her and she was only in for two nights. He'd obviously remembered this terrible pain of being abandoned in hospital when he was little.

4

Return to King's College and Salisbury Cathedral

1945 – 1950

O.   So you returned to Cambridge in the autumn of 1945?

W.   Yes, in early November. I went to King's as soon as I could. I think I may have gone home for a couple of days, to get out of my army clothes. We were each given a demobilization suit and a hat. Before leaving the army, we were all interviewed and asked what we were going to do. I said that I was planning to go back to Cambridge. The senior officer who was conducting the interview said to me, 'Have you considered staying on in the army? You've got a good rank for your age and if you stayed on for five or ten years, you would get a good income and pension. Then you would be able to save enough money to have no worries at all about pursuing your music. Do you really want to go back to writing essays and being an undergraduate again after you've been an officer in the army?' I said, 'I'll have to think about it. May I come to see you in the morning?' I went back the next day and said, 'I've thought about it and I have decided to go back to Cambridge.' He looked at me and said, 'I think you are probably doing the right thing, but I thought I would test you.' I thought that that was a very nice thing to say. Having made that decision, I came back and I was amazed to find Cambridge exactly as it was back in 1939: the busy city, the hundreds of bicycles, and the river flowing peacefully. It was just as though nothing had happened at all. During the war years Dr Harold Darke had looked after the King's College Choir while Boris Ord was away on service. Boris was in the Royal Air Force, not as a pilot, but serving in an administrative role. He had been in the Royal Flying Corps during World War I. He returned to Cambridge at about the same time as I did. He was anxious about the state of the King's choir because of the difficulties faced by Harold Darke during the war years. For example, several students stayed for one year rather than three. Dr Darke did very well, I think, in keeping the choir going at all. He was well liked in the college and was elected to a fellowship of the college.

O.   How did Boris Ord's work with the choir compare with that of Harold Darke?

W.   Boris Ord was a much more disciplined choir trainer; he was punctilious over detail, making everybody sing absolutely in tune, getting words and phrasings together, and planning dynamic levels. My first big service was the Advent carol service. I had hardly played the organ for more than five years. Herbert Howells was in the congregation. I remember he was impressed that I managed to quote from his 'A spotless rose' in my improvisation. That was the beginning of a long friendship with him, which I enjoyed until he died in 1983. I had met him briefly when he came to Westminster Abbey when I was a boy, but he wouldn't have remembered me. He was very keen to help me at that stage. He had spent most of the war as organist of St John's College, Cambridge, in place of Robin Orr who had been away on war duty. I didn't play for the Christmas Eve carol service in 1945, because Boris Ord played and Harold Darke conducted—that was his last service. Then from January onwards Boris Ord began to rebuild the King's College Choir and I, as his sole Organ Scholar, assisted him in that task.

O.   Were some of the choral scholars, like you, also returning from war service?

W.   Yes. Some of them had come up to Cambridge before the war and they were side by side with those just out of school, aged eighteen. I remember that we all got on very well together; it was a happy team. My tasks during that time were again to go to the Choir School to rehearse the boys, three or four times a week. Boris Ord, as before, always took the full rehearsals in the Chapel. I learned a lot during that time, because I attended every rehearsal which Boris Ord took. More and more he entrusted me with the playing of the services and the voluntaries, because he enjoyed being downstairs with the choir. That gave me a great chance to get accustomed to

Figure 4.1. King's College Choir, 1946; David, second row, fourth from left; Boris Ord, second row, third from right

accompanying the psalms, something that I have always enjoyed. It is an interesting challenge to provide varied registration to illustrate the mood of the words. I got to know Boris very well. Before the war I was a little frightened of him, but afterwards I felt we were colleagues. I welcomed his kindness very much.

O.   Were there any recordings and broadcasts from King's in 1946 and 1947?

W.   I don't think that any records were made during those years. Boris Ord had made some records in the 1930s, I think, and 'Daddy' Mann had made some in the 1920s. Those 78 rpm records give an idea of the sound of the choir and an indication of the very slow tempi adopted by Dr Mann.

O.   What else were you doing, outside your duties in the Chapel?

W.   As I had completed my MusB requirements, I was free to study for a BA. It was suggested to me that I should read for a degree in history and economics. There was a special course devised for people coming out of the forces who did not have three years to devote to an honours degree course and yet wanted to complete a degree. I was unusual in having had only one year during which I studied for the MusB degree. I read history and economics and enjoyed them very much indeed. I was lucky to get first class in both of those exams as well and that gave me a BA in addition to the MusB. This broadened my interests beyond music, which I've found valuable. I have always thought it beneficial for Organ Scholars and Choral Scholars to read subjects other than music.

O.   Were you involved in any music-making activities outside King's?

W.   I took part in the Cambridge University Musical Society (CUMS) rehearsals and concerts. Boris Ord was the conductor, but he gave me the opportunity in 1947 to conduct two performances of the Purcell opera, *Dioclesian*, while he played the harpsichord. This was good experience for me. I also played the piano part in *The Rio Grande* of Constant Lambert. I was also President of the Cambridge University Music Club, an organization that mounted weekly chamber concerts. I was able to plan programmes and to conduct some, including the 1947 May Week concert, for which I chose the programme. I played the Bach D Minor Keyboard Concerto. I was very keen in those days to conduct things by heart, because I thought it was good for me and good for prestige.

O.   I believe you conducted the Cambridge Philharmonic Society for a short period.

W.   Yes, from February to June of 1947. This is the 'town' equivalent of the university chorus and orchestra. The members are mainly drawn from the city of Cambridge. Many university people sang in it because the rehearsals were on a different night of the week and it suited them better. They were roughly of the same standard as the university chorus and orchestra. The previous conductor was John Lowe, who had suddenly been invited to become director of the BBC Third Programme, an important classical music programme. He invited me to take over from him, at very short notice, for two concerts, which were being scheduled for Holy Week of 1947. One was a complete performance of *Messiah*; the other was an almost complete performance of the *St Matthew Passion*. It was a wonderful opportunity for me to take, for the first time, some rehearsals of a group where I was in command. I enjoyed these concerts very much, and I think they went well. I conducted the *St Matthew Passion* by heart; that very much impressed Dr Darke because he had conducted it many times at St Michael's, Cornhill in London. He said that he would never dare to do it by heart. The Christus recitatives are much more difficult than the choruses and arias, especially if sung in English. I didn't worry in those days—it's funny how one is more cautious when one gets older. Such opportunities helped with the initial build-up of a reputation.

O.   I believe it was about this time that you met your future wife, Rachel.

W.   When I took over the Cambridge Philharmonic Society for the *St Matthew Passion* we had professional soloists coming to do the main solos—the Christus, the Evangelist, and the arias. We thought we would audition from within the choir for the small roles like first and second maid, and first and second high priest. I suppose for the first and second maid I had about six or seven volunteers who said they would like to stay behind after rehearsal and audition. Among them there was a very nice girl called Rachel Blyth, whom I knew slightly because we had played on the beach together as little children, or at least we were told we did. My parents knew her parents, and I had been to tea with her family.

Rachel sang very prettily at the audition but did not get the role. She happened to be the last one to be auditioned, so I walked home with her and she asked me to tea the following week. I told her she hadn't got the part, but she seemed quite resigned to it. She accepted an invitation from me to be my partner at the King's College May Ball, which is one of the main social events of the college year. We became engaged later that summer, in August 1947, and were married on the 8th of November 1947. I had little spare money at that time, so I arranged to give an organ recital in London before our wedding. I played at Holy Trinity, Sloane Square; it paid for the first night of our honeymoon!

O.   Were you married in King's College Chapel?

W.   No. It was in Selwyn College Chapel. Rachel's father was then Senior Tutor at Selwyn College and it was customary for marriages to be in the bride's church. The King's College Choir came to sing. Boris Ord played the organ and Rachel and I chose the music. It was a lovely occasion.

Figure 4.2. David and Rachel on their wedding day, 1947 (Portman Press Bureau)

O.   Do you remember what music you chose?

W.   I know that Boris Ord played the *Choral Song* of Samuel Sebastian
       Wesley, which is a moderately easy piece. Among the choral music
       was 'Jesu, joy of man's desiring'. Rachel and I had a honeymoon in
       St Helier in Jersey, which was as far south as one could go in those
       days because of restrictions on the purchase of foreign currency.

O.   Had you begun to think of what sort of career might lie ahead
       when your student days were over?

W.   Yes. To stay at Cambridge was an attractive option, as I could con-
       tinue to conduct the Cambridge Philharmonic Society. Further-
       more, I had just been elected to a fellowship of King's for four
       years. This was an unexpected honour which would allow me
       to remain in King's and possibly undertake postgraduate research,
       leading to a higher degree.

O.   That sounds like a wonderful opportunity.

W.   Yes, it certainly was. I was relieved that I need have no financial
       worries for four years. I looked for an interesting subject to form
       the basis of research and fixed on John Blow, the important
       Restoration composer, who had been Organist at Westminster
       Abbey for two periods. After the first period he resigned in order
       that the prodigiously gifted young Henry Purcell could take over.
       Then, on Purcell's death, he was reinstated as Organist. I consulted
       Watkins Shaw, who had written a number of articles on Blow and
       was known to be quite an authority. He was very helpful and gave
       me suggestions. I went to the college library and spent *one day*
       doing research! Then the next day I got an invitation to be Organist
       and Master of the Choristers at Salisbury Cathedral. The invitation
       came out of the blue. I was astonished that I was not asked to make
       formal application for the post and was not required to send a
       CV. It transpired that the Precentor of Salisbury Cathedral, who
       had only recently been appointed, was given the responsibility for
       advising the Chapter about the appointment of a new Organist.
       As neither the Dean nor the residentiary canons at Salisbury were
       musical, the Precentor was given discretion to make the appointment.
       The Precentor, who was called Cyril Jackson, had been a minor
       canon at York Minister, where the Dean was Eric Milner-White,
       who had been Dean of King's during my first year as an undergrad-
       uate before World War II. He was a close friend of Boris Ord. It was

perhaps natural that Cyril Jackson should consult Eric Milner-White before making an appointment, and I believe Eric Milner-White got in touch with Boris Ord to ask him if I was sufficiently experienced for the post. Boris Ord must have reassured him and felt that it was the right move for me. I had no hesitation in accepting the invitation from Salisbury, because it was a very prestigious appointment. It would be an interesting and exciting challenge, not least because Salisbury Cathedral, dating back to the Middle Ages, had a great musical tradition.

O.   Where did you live in Salisbury?

W.   I knew that I would eventually have a lovely house there, but when I arrived it was unsuitable for me. The Dean and Chapter were reluctant to ask Sir Walter and Lady Alcock to move out of the Organist's house, so I stayed with the Bishop of Sherborne and Mrs Key in their lovely house, South Canonry, until such time as I got married. They were very kind to me. Meanwhile, of course, Rachel came down once or twice to see me there.

O.   Who was your predecessor?

W.   The Cathedral Organist, whom I was to succeed upon his retirement, was Sir Walter Alcock, aged eighty-five. He was a greatly respected organist, and certainly one of the best players of his generation. He was knighted in 1933, having served as an Assistant Organist of Westminster Abbey and as Organist of the Chapel Royal in London. He had played for three coronations, the only person ever to have done that (for Edward VII, George V, and George VI). He was asked to play for part of the service for George VI because he had officiated at the other two. The story is that on this third occasion, when he was asked for his security pass on entering the Abbey, he said, 'I don't need these things; I've got a season ticket for these shows!' He was a delightful man. Rachel and I paid our first visit to Salisbury in July to meet the Dean and Chapter; they were very welcoming. I went to call on Sir Walter, who by then was confined to bed. I can see his fine features and white hair now. He was a very good-looking man. Mentally very alert, he was obviously sad to be retiring after thirty years. He died early in August, and my very first service in Salisbury Cathedral was his funeral. At King's, I had learned Sir Walter's *Introduction and Passacaglia* for organ, which is a fine piece, so I was able to play that at his funeral service. The

Cathedral Choir was on holiday during August, so did not sing at the funeral service, Lady Alcock being reluctant to interrupt the boys' holiday. Their place was taken by the 'voluntary choir', an *ad hoc* mixed choir drawn from the Salisbury Musical Society. We sang by special request 'Souls of the righteous' by Tertius Noble, who had been a friend of Walter Alcock. The service went quite well, despite the shortage of rehearsal time. I didn't see the full choir until a few weeks later when they returned from holiday. They were very welcoming. I got the impression that some of the lay clerks, although they were devoted to Sir Walter, felt that he had lost interest in the choir. He retained to the end his great ability as a player, but the standard of the singing had really gone down. The choir had performed little new music. He was very fond of Victorian music, and he had included in the repertory works by early twentieth-century composers such as Parry, Stanford, Charles Wood, Vaughan Williams, Ireland, and Bairstow. The repertoire was somewhat similar to that inherited by Boris Ord from Dr Mann in 1929. He had not explored the music of younger composers.

O. Probably not much early music either?

W. No. Encouraged by Cyril Jackson, the Precentor, I added many new anthems and settings of the canticles by the leading Tudor composers. I always found room for much music by contemporary composers. Among these was Francis Jackson, who has been a life-long friend. Francis is almost exactly my age—about two years older. He was appointed to York Minster the year before I was appointed to Salisbury.

O. He followed Bairstow at York, didn't he?

W. Yes. He is a worshipper of Bairstow and was his student. We are told we look very alike. Very often when I have been up in Yorkshire for something, people have shouted across to me, 'I did enjoy your recital, Dr Jackson.' I've never said, 'I'm David Willcocks, I'm sorry.' I say, 'Thank you so much, I'm so glad you enjoyed it.' It would make them feel foolish. I have often been introduced as Dr Jackson. I sometimes don't say who I am; other times I correct it if it is going to lead to trouble. We both even lost our hair at the same rate over the last seventy years! We have both been President of the Royal College of Organists at various times and we would meet at council meetings.

O.   What music of his did you introduce?

W.   I introduced his setting in G of the Evening Canticles and one or
        two of his anthems. There were several other people who were
        composing music for the church. One was Henry Ley, who had
        been appointed Organist of Christ Church, Oxford at the age of
        twenty-one, but subsequently moved to be Precentor of Eton. He
        used to send me copies of recently published anthems and I would
        add some of them to our repertoire. I was eager to introduce any
        new works by Herbert Howells, as I admired his craftsmanship and
        originality. Before I came, I believe that the Choir only sang the
        early setting of the Evening Canticles in G major. We added other
        settings as they came out.

O.   You made significant changes.

W.   Rachel helped me to clear out the choir library and to dispose of
        much of the old music. It was understandable that Sir Walter
        Alcock, in his eighties, did not feel inclined to clean and catalogue
        the music library. To the end of his life he enjoyed playing for the
        services. I was told that if he was asked by the men if they could
        rehearse a passage from an anthem which they found difficult, he
        would say 'Don't worry, as I shall be at the organ.' He was always
        confident that he would be able to 'steer' the choir through. In
        those days people did rely on the organ more. There was less un-
        accompanied singing. I believe that Sir Walter rarely, if ever, went
        down to the choir stalls to conduct the anthem. He'd leave it to
        the lay vicars.

O.   You mentioned Bairstow—did you know him?

W.   Bairstow I knew more by repute. I met him once or twice. He was
        a hard taskmaster; he loved York Minster and knew everything about
        it. He could be quite rude as an adjudicator at festivals. He had a
        reputation of being asked to a festival *once*, and never again. He had
        a great reputation in the North, because he'd conducted many of
        those famous choirs there. I think he was offered the post at
        Westminster Abbey, but refused because he said he would rather
        reign up in the North than be in hell down in the South. He could
        be brisk, but he was a very fine musician. I love his music now.

O.   Who was the Dean at Salisbury?

W.   The Dean was a man called Robins—the Very Reverend Henry C.
        Robins. He would have been about seventy, I suppose. He was

obviously frail and suffered from a progressive illness, akin to Parkinson's disease. He had a shaky hand, but he tried to hide the fact by holding one hand still with his other hand. He was a great character. I got to know him quite well during the three years that I was at Salisbury. Cyril Jackson was really the person with whom I dealt. In the old cathedrals it is the Precentor who has overall control of the music. Technically the organist is responsible to the Dean and Chapter through the Precentor. That arrangement worked well, and we used to meet over coffee once a week to plan the music for the statutory services and for any additional special services in the coming week. We had in front of us what was done the previous year, and we would consciously each week introduce one or two works which the choir hadn't done. So the change was gradual and I got rid of the anthems and canticles which I thought were of inferior quality and replaced them with others. We had to be careful not to have too many new things, because the lay clerks (or lay vicars) only came twice a week for rehearsal. It wasn't like King's, where we had a rehearsal every day of the full choir in the Chapel.

O.   What was the schedule? Was there daily evensong?

W.   We had sung matins two or three times each week, and evensong was sung on five weekdays. There was one free day when the boys could play cricket or football. There were two services each Sunday, one of which would usually be matins. We had a sung Eucharist about once a month and that enabled us to sing English settings of the communion service by Stanford, Vaughan Williams, and Darke. I also began to introduce Latin Masses, such as those by William Byrd and Palestrina, which were not normally used in England at that time.

O.   Who was your assistant at Salisbury?

W.   It was Ronald Tickner, who had been a fellow student at the Royal School of Church Music in 1938–9. He was a fine organist and later devoted his life to teaching.

O.   Did you only work with the cathedral choir?

W.   No, I was appointed conductor of the Salisbury Musical Society, which was quite a good community choir, numbering about a hundred and fifty voices. The Society could afford to engage a professional orchestra for at least two out of the three concerts

which were given each year. For the third concert we used a local
orchestra or maybe performed *a cappella* works. My first concert
was with the local orchestra, which was quite good. We performed
the Mozart Requiem and we filled up the programme with
another Mozart work and the solo *Exsultate Jubilate*. For one of
the concerts each year we engaged the Bournemouth Municipal
Orchestra,* which gave me an opportunity to do more orchestral
conducting. At that time, the conductor of the Bournemouth
orchestra, Rudolf Schwarz, was often away, as he was being
headhunted for other orchestras. That gave me the chance to conduct them on a freelance basis as a guest conductor. We became
good friends, but it was not long before he moved to Birmingham
to become conductor of the City of Birmingham Symphony
Orchestra, and subsequently to the BBC as Chief Conductor.
He had been in a concentration camp during the war . . . I
think that it was at Belsen. He was a fine musician and a
delightful man.

O.   What was the daily routine at Salisbury?

W.   The daily routine was much as it would be in any cathedral. I rehearsed the boys every morning, but I think that it was rare to
have any afternoon rehearsal before evensong. In all, we had much
less rehearsal than I would have liked.

O.   What was the full complement of the Salisbury choir?

W.   It was a choir of sixteen boys and six men only—two altos, two
tenors, and two basses. One of the tenors, a man called Mr
Stevenson, sang a little bit below the note with a sort of slow
wobble. I didn't know what to do, so I wrote to Boris Ord and
asked his advice. He replied on a postcard, 'Get on your knees and
pray, there is nothing else you can do.' I had not been at Salisbury
very long before Mr Stevenson came to me and asked if I could
possibly do him a favour. He explained that he was thinking of
applying for a job at Worcester Cathedral and he would be grateful
for a letter of support from me, if I felt able to give it. I could not
believe my luck! I told him that I would do my best to help him.
He then asked me to write to Sir Ivor Atkins, who had been
Organist at Worcester for more than fifty years. I wrote along these

* It became the Bournemouth Symphony Orchestra in 1954.

Figure 4.3. David rehearsing Salisbury choristers, including Colin Prince (*far right*), 1947 (Picture Post, photo K. Hutton, © Getty Images)

lines: 'Dear Sir Ivor, I've been asked to write to you on behalf of a Mr Stevenson, who has been a lay vicar in the Choir of Salisbury Cathedral for some years. I must confess that I have only known him for a relatively short time, but during that time he has been very friendly. He seems to get on very well with his colleagues in the choir, and he is always punctual for rehearsals and services. He has often stayed in the Cathedral after a service and offered to put the music copies away. I very much hope that you will be able to grant him an interview and audition, so that you can judge if he would be a satisfactory member of the Worcester Cathedral Choir.' I managed to fill both sides of the piece of notepaper without having mentioned his voice at all. I was satisfied that I had not told any lies in the letter, so I placed it in the mailbox. Some days later I saw Mr Stevenson walking across Salisbury Close with a jaunty step. He told me he had been to Worcester and met Sir Ivor Atkins. I asked if Sir Ivor had asked him to sing. 'Oh no,' came the reply, 'He just chatted to me and asked me about Salisbury. He said he'd like to offer me the job, so I accepted.' I tried not to look too pleased or too surprised! I told him that I hoped that he would be very happy at Worcester. He stayed, I think, for another few weeks and I was able to replace him by a King's Choral Scholar, called Derek Sutton, whom I had known well. That was the first of a number of changes in the membership of the choir. Among the lay vicars there were some experienced singers who could be entrusted with solo work. There was a bass called Claude Norris, who had a very big voice, and a tenor called Tom Tunmore, with a much lighter voice, so problems of blend and balance had to be solved. The lay vicars were a delightful group of men, who never appeared to resent being directed by someone who was junior to them by many years. By the time I left I think that we had six very good men. I had inherited three of them and the other three were appointed by me.

O.   Where did you eventually live?

W.   We lived first in a delightful little cottage at No. 22 The Close, and then in May 1948 we swapped with Lady Alcock and moved into No. 5. All Lady Alcock's furniture and all of our furniture was in the middle of the Close on what was, mercifully, a fine day. Lady Alcock settled quickly into her new home, where one of her daughters came to look after her. We, too, quickly settled into our lovely historic house. For centuries it had been the place where the choristers rehearsed. The boys used to come from their school to rehearse in the song room there. Alas, they no longer do that, because that particular room has been taken over as a diocesan office. It is sad to think that that great tradition has been broken. Being a newcomer to Salisbury, I was glad to meet my fellow residents in the Close. I was taken around by the Precentor's wife, who was very friendly and helpful to me. She thought that I would like to know something about my neighbours. As we were walking towards the Deanery, chatting, she said 'Oh, by the way, have you seen the old medlar?' (because there was, and still is, a rare medlar tree in the Close, just outside the Deanery). I did not realize that she was referring to a tree, so I said, 'No, I haven't met him yet.' That was my first gaffe, but there were others to come.

O.   Were any of them musical?

W.   Yes. On the day before Easter Day, Holy Saturday, I was rehearsing for the Easter services in the Cathedral. We were practising a hymn

Figure 4.4. The Organist's house at Salisbury, No. 5 The Close, with the Song Room to the right

or anthem containing the word 'hallelujah' when the Head Verger came and tapped me on the shoulder and said, 'Mr Willcocks, the Dean wants to see you down in the nave.' I said, 'I can't see him at this moment because I am in the middle of rehearsal. Please tell him I'll come down in a few minutes, or I could come over to his house later.' A few moments later the verger returned and said, 'I'm sorry, Mr Willcocks, but the Dean wants to see you *now* in the nave.' So I went down to see the Dean. He said, 'Mr Willcocks, did I hear the choir singing "hallelujah"?' I said, 'Yes, Mr Dean, we are rehearsing the music for tomorrow.' Back came the Dean's reply: 'Our Lord is still in the tomb: I will not have it! We cannot have "hallelujah" sung in Salisbury Cathedral until the gladsome morn!' I said, 'I'm very sorry Mr Dean. We shall not do that again.' I returned to the choir and said, 'The Dean does not want us to sing the word "hallelujah" until tomorrow morning, so I suggest that in rehearsal we sing 'fa-la-la-la' instead of "hallelujah". I think the Dean will be quite happy.' So we did that. The Dean was a very sincere man. He didn't mean to be interfering or to create difficulties for me. He just felt that I ought to know that Holy Saturday is a day when our thoughts should be directed to the suffering of Christ on the cross. He may have wondered afterwards whether he had upset me, but he hadn't. I ought to have anticipated such a problem, but I was young and anxious that the singing of the choir on Easter Day should be really good.

O.   Did you teach the organ in Salisbury?

W.   Yes. One instance which is implanted in my memory is of the evening when I was giving an organ lesson to a pupil. He was a bachelor—a very nervous sort of chap who lived with his elderly mother. We had to use the Cathedral when it was closed to the public because they didn't like people teaching the organ while tourists were in the building. Suddenly, I realized I ought to call somebody on the telephone so I said to him, 'Just carry on practising while I go home. I've just got a quick call to make and I'll be back in about ten minutes.' I locked the door behind me because of the security and went back home to make my telephone call and absolutely forgot I was in the middle of a lesson! I don't know what distracted me—I don't think we had television or anything in those days. I just chatted with my wife, Rachel. We went to bed, I suppose, at about ten or eleven o'clock, and went to sleep. In the middle of the night, Rachel nudged me and said, 'Did you hear the cathedral bell toll?' I said, 'No' and then we waited a moment and the cathedral bell tolled again. I thought, 'Gosh, I've left him in the cathedral!' I quickly put on a dressing gown and ran across the Close and opened the door. The only light in the Cathedral was from the organ loft. This poor little man had spent an agonizing time.

O.   How old was he?

W.   He was about thirty but was a nervous sort of man. He had first of all played on the full organ—getting out all the couplers, the pedals, and the tuba stop to try and make somebody hear, but nobody came to the rescue. He then walked, feeling his way around the Cathedral, to see if he could find an electric light or anything that would be useful. At night a cathedral is very mysterious with all these tombs. You can put your hand out and find you are touching the nose of some effigy! At long last he found the bell rope, which I think was at the west end of the cathedral. He thought, 'I'd better toll.' He did it once and nothing happened, so he left a space and tried it again, and at long last he heard me coming over. He was so apologetic and said, 'I'm so sorry to have dragged you out of bed. I wouldn't have done it except that my elderly mother would have been so nervous and wondered where I was.' I felt so awful; I didn't know what to do for recompense. I think I gave his mother some flowers. I made a mental note, 'I must never lock anybody in a cathedral!'

O.   The other Salisbury story I wanted to ask you about is the 'Amen'.

W.   Oh, yes! In Salisbury Cathedral the canons were very unmusical, really, apart from the Precentor, Cyril Jackson, who was actually a very well-qualified organist. He was a Fellow of the Royal College of Organists, but went into the church. One of the canons loved to join in singing the responses and the 'Amens'. It annoyed me so much when he would scoop up with 'AAAAAAmen, AAAAAAmen'. I thought, 'I'll teach him a lesson.' I told the choir when it came to the end of a prayer, let him sing it all on his own: 'AAAAAAmen', and after a pause of about two seconds the choir would sing 'Amen'. Nothing was said afterwards but he never did it again. He didn't reproach me, and I didn't say anything to him. I often wondered what he thought of me. It was very unkind, really. Arguably, if a person is joining in a prayer to God, one ought to let him sing. I was just so anxious that things should be good in every respect—that we should all be doing our best. There is no point in performing music unless it is done well. I am afraid I let that sentiment get the better of me and I have always slightly regretted that I never apologized to him.

O.   Now what about the Dean's encounter with Henry Willis?

W.   Oh, yes. Soon after I arrived in Salisbury I received a letter from Henry Willis III, then the senior living member of the distinguished family of organ builders, who had been responsible for building and maintaining what are arguably some of the very best organs since the mid-nineteenth century. Sir Walter Alcock was very proud of the Salisbury organ, and saw that it was kept in beautiful condition; in fact he wouldn't allow Henry Willis to take any of the pipes out of the Cathedral when it was being restored. So I was made conscious of the historic importance of the Salisbury Cathedral organ. When Willis wrote to me saying that the organ was due for cleaning and overhaul, I went and told the Dean. He said, 'It seems only yesterday that the organ was cleaned. I want to see Mr Willis, so that he can explain to us why it needs to be cleaned.' So I wrote to Mr Willis and he duly came down to Salisbury and I accompanied him to the Deanery. The interview started in this way: 'Mr Willis, I understand from Mr Willcocks that the organ needs cleaning. How can this be the case when it's your organ, and your firm is responsible for its maintenance? How is the organ in this state after only twenty-five years?' There was a little pause after which Mr Willis said, 'Mr Dean, I need to ask you a question. What would happen if your study wasn't cleaned for twenty-five years?' The Dean, visibly angry, replied: 'Hold your tongue, Mr Willis. I am not here to be interviewed by you. I will brook your insolence no longer!' That's a lovely old phrase. It shows that the Dean didn't want to be hoodwinked into signing a contract for something which was unnecessary.

O.   Did the organ get cleaned?

W.   Yes, it did, but I think Mr Willis probably reduced the bill.

O.   Do you remember any special musical events while you were there? Any special pieces?

W.   I remember clearly the first time that I conducted Elgar's *The Dream of Gerontius* in 1949, a work of which I have been very fond ever since I first heard it as a schoolboy at Three Choirs Festivals and recognized its dramatic power. Lady Alcock had generously given me the full score which Sir Walter had owned and which had some annotations by Elgar and Sargent in it. She said that she would love to feel that I was going to use it.

O.   Do you still own that score?

W.   Yes, I have treasured that generous gift and Sir Walter's signature and the gracious inscription on the first page: 'To David Willcocks— Wishing you every success in your future musical career—Naomi Alcock'.

O.   What were the forces at that first performance?

W.   The chorus was the Salisbury Musical Society with the Cathedral choristers singing the semi-choruses; the Bournemouth Municipal Orchestra; and three of the leading soloists of the day: Mary Jarred, William Herbert, and Norman Walker.

O.   Were there any special services?

W.   We had the consecration of a new bishop, for which I wrote some fanfares and special hymn arrangements. They were my first compositions, though at school and at Cambridge I had been required to write choral and instrumental pieces in prescribed styles. People seemed to enjoy the fanfares so I thought that I might be able to produce that sort of thing later when the need arose. I had never had the urge, or indeed the time, to compose original music. But if a special arrangement of a hymn seemed desirable, I would immediately undertake the task and then forget about it. I never thought of offering anything for publication.

O.   Were there any special events?

W.   We had the diocesan choral festivals, when we invited choirs from all the villages and towns once every two years, I think it was, to participate in a special service at the cathedral. I tried to go to some of the churches for a preliminary rehearsal. The repertoire would include anthems like 'O thou, the central orb' by Charles Wood. This anthem is not very difficult and is especially suitable for large forces. I believe that the country choirs really appreciated coming to the 'mother church'. It was very exciting for singers from a little village to participate with others in such large-scale music-making.

O.   Were you involved with the Royal School of Church Music at this time?

W.   Yes, I had already become associated with the RSCM and had become a Special Commissioner, which involved visiting a number of affiliated choirs to advise the organist/director and to encourage the clergy and choir members. I also joined the council of the Royal College of Organists. For many years I was by far the youngest member of the council, as most of the members were in their sixties and seventies, and one or two of them in their eighties. I was only twenty-seven then. I sometimes felt that I was the only person who didn't have a nap during council meetings after lunch! I'd see these old men nodding their heads, and I'd think, 'Goodness, I wonder if I will ever get to that age.' I enjoyed meeting them. I was 'Willcocks'—in those days men called each other by their surnames. How things have changed! Nowadays boys and girls often call adults by their first names. There was much more formality at council meetings. I would always wear a suit and I even arrived wearing a trilby hat to be properly attired for a council meeting.

O.   Did you begin doing adjudications at competitive festivals at this time?

W.   Yes. My first was at the invitation of Herbert Howells. He was a very busy adjudicator, popular and experienced. He was a brilliant speaker, and would have something different to say about fifty people who had all sung the same song. All would have some encouraging words on their mark sheet, but he would always suggest things about a performance that could be bettered. He could be quite amusing in his summing up. He rarely talked about individual performances, but would talk about the class as a whole. Each person would get a piece of paper with his signature on it with those little bits of advice. I learned a lot through observing his techniques when dealing with competitors of different ages and from different backgrounds. I suppose he judged as many as twenty festivals a year, which would perhaps occupy fifty days. I often wondered if he weren't spending so much time on adjudication, what works he might have written.

O.   That's always a question.

W.   He always seemed to be short of money. He would often travel home very late at night in order not to have the expense of a hotel. I felt sorry that a man of such distinction should need to watch every penny of his expenditure. He did not have any extravagances, for he didn't drink and he didn't smoke. He could not have earned much from the sale of sheet music, as copies of anthems or songs cost only a few pence. Performing fees were negligible and few records were being issued. Since a great proportion of his original work is church music he received little income, because there has always been an understanding in this country that churches will not be subject to performance fees for music used during divine service. He taught composition for many years at the Royal College of Music, but there again the remuneration was small.

O.   Did you continue adjudicating?

W.   Yes. I soon received invitations from many festivals, many of which I accepted in order to augment my relatively small income from the Cathedral and from organ recitals. During the three years at Salisbury, I learned much about the music profession. I joined the Incorporated Society of Musicians, and attended occasional conferences, where educational policies were discussed and advice was given to young performers.

O.   What about your invitation to move to Worcester?

W.   As Rachel and I had been in Salisbury for only two and a half years, we were somewhat surprised when I received an invitation from

Canon Briggs of Worcester Cathedral to succeed Sir Ivor Atkins as Master of the Choristers and Organist of Worcester Cathedral. Canon Briggs was the father of David Briggs who had been a Choral Scholar at King's College, Cambridge, when I was Organ Scholar. He explained to me that if I came to Worcester Cathedral as Organist, I would also be appointed conductor of the Worcester Festival Choral Society, and therefore be intimately involved in the Three Choirs Festivals, which enjoyed international renown.

O.   Was this Canon Briggs, the hymn composer?

W.   Yes, G. W. Briggs was the author of many hymns, and the editor of many hymnals. Canon Briggs suggested that I should go to Worcester to meet the Dean and to learn more about the post. I agreed, as Rachel and I, though very happy at Salisbury, felt that we should at least consider this offer. Before going we had a chat with Sir Bruce Richmond, a former editor of the *Times Literary Supplement*, with whom we had become friends. He was a well-connected man, very fond of music, and he had been to our concerts in Salisbury Cathedral. He said that he would like to ask Sir Adrian Boult, in confidence, whether we should move or not. Accordingly he contacted Boult, who immediately got in touch with me. He told me that I *must* go to Worcester. The Three Choirs Festival goes back to the 1720s and many famous musicians such as Mendelssohn, Elgar, Vaughan Williams, and Holst had been associated with it. 'It is a great chance for you; you ought to go. Furthermore I believe that there is a vacancy for the conductorship of the City of Birmingham Choir, which again is very important. I can't be sure, but you might be able to combine the two.' So that put a different perspective on our deliberations. I then examined the finances of it all. I was getting five hundred pounds a year from Salisbury plus a house, rent- and rate-free. Worcester offered me five hundred and fifty a year plus a house, rent- and rate-free, plus the prospect of the City of Birmingham Choir, which would probably offer me two hundred pounds. That made Worcester financially more attractive, though at Salisbury I had been able to give many organ recitals for the BBC and in cathedrals, as well as adjudicating at many competitive festivals. In the end, it was really for the musical reasons that we would accept the Worcester offer, which was soon followed by an offer from the City of Birmingham Choir. We knew that it would be a wrench to leave Salisbury, where we were so happy, and where we had made many friends. I loved the choir, and we had that lovely house in the Close with a glorious view of the Cathedral. I had enjoyed a number of concerts with the Bournemouth Municipal Orchestra. I had agonizing moments. I found myself crying on our last evening in Salisbury, as I talked to my great friend Douglas Guest, who was succeeding me. He was very understanding. I thought, 'What on earth have I done? Why are we leaving this beautiful place? What could our friends be thinking of us?' I know what one old lady thought, for she said, 'I can't believe that you are moving to Worcester. It is ecclesiastically inferior to Salisbury.' She was probably quite right, for there is a 'pecking order' of cathedrals. Canterbury is number one, York is number two, Durham is number three; I believe that the Bishop of Salisbury is regarded as being senior to the Bishop of Worcester. The Dean and Chapter had given me this wonderful chance as a relatively unknown young man. I had been preferred to much older, established, musicians such as Harold Darke, who admitted that he would have dearly loved to be Organist of Salisbury Cathedral all his life. Many other organists of Darke's generation had been watching Sir Walter Alcock get older and older, and hoping that they might be chosen to succeed him. It had been customary for a cathedral organist to be appointed at the age of fifty or so, by which time he had gained wide experience. He might then hold the post until he was seventy or eighty. The sudden influx of young men appointed to senior cathedral posts immediately after World War II must have been deeply wounding for qualified organists who were serving in junior positions, awaiting their turn for promotion. The young Francis Jackson enjoyed the same good fortune as I did when he was appointed to succeed Bairstow at York Minster. Gerald Knight was equally fortunate in being appointed Organist of Canterbury Cathedral. All three of us were fortunate to have survived the war, when so many of our contemporaries had been killed or wounded.

Interlude 4

Reflections on Salisbury

Lady Willcocks was interviewed on 18 June 2003 at her home in Cambridge.

RW.　My maiden name was Blyth. My mother incorporated her family name in mine, so I am called Rachel Gordon. My father was Senior Tutor at Selwyn College, Cambridge, and I spent my early days here in Grange Road. I trained as a primary school teacher at the Froebel Educational Institute in London.

O.　When you finished that course, did you come back to Cambridge?

RW.　Yes. My first job teaching was in Cambridge, but I only taught very briefly—for one year. It's been my disappointment that I haven't had an opportunity to teach again. I met David in Cambridge when I was singing in the Cambridge Philharmonic. Our conductor went off to work at the BBC and this young chap came in three weeks before our Easter concert. Our families were acquainted because my grandmother lived in the same town as his mother, and they went to the same church. But there are five years between us, so when we were children playing on the beach, we naturally didn't have anything to do with each other. We met in May, got engaged in August, and married in November.

O.　That's pretty quick!

RW.　It would have been quicker, but David started his first job in Salisbury in September. I was still bound to my teaching job and couldn't be free from that until October. It was very difficult to set a date because he was engrossed in his new job.

O.　How did you feel about the prospect of moving to Salisbury so early in your marriage?

RW.   David has always been very fortunate in being approached about jobs. Rather to my surprise, before we were engaged he said, 'You've got to come. I've been asked to do this job. Let's go and have a look and see what we think.' I thought, 'That's all very well, but I'm not sure I ought to be making decisions for him before we are engaged.' But he said, 'Oh well, I'll think about marriage when you are older.' Then on my birthday he sent me a telegram proposing, which I accepted. I was very much in favour of the Salisbury job; it seemed to have everything: a beautiful place, a house and a very interesting job, and it is high up in the hierarchy of cathedrals.

O.   You said he proposed to you by telegram?

RW.   Yes. At the end of the summer term in 1947 I had a chance to go sailing on the Norfolk Broads with four friends. I said to David, 'Would you like to come too?' He said, 'I'd love to, but I've got to play in the opera.' Of course, that has been the story of my life ever since: he'd love to, but he's got to do this, that, or the other! Anyway I sailed in to Potter Heigham to get supplies of food with one of the men of our party on my birthday, and there was this telegram—reply paid!

O.   That sounds very practical.

RW.   It was a very short telegram. In those days you wrote the thing and the Post Office girl counted the words. It was a penny a word, I think. Of course, she said to David, 'You'll have to come in and tell me what she says.' He went back and said the answer had been favourable. We got married a week before the Queen!

O.   Tell me about the wedding; I think it was in Selwyn College Chapel?

RW.   Yes. We had the best of both worlds, really, because the King's College Choir came and sang for us, which was lovely, and we packed the Chapel with our friends and relations. Actually the most notable thing about that wedding for most of our friends was that my small cousin, who was a bit of a tearaway and around four years old, enticed his cousin, also aged four, to put his head between the bars of the pews; as you know, college pews face each other so everybody was watching this little boy put his head through and get stuck. We were blissfully unaware up at the altar. He managed to get out without actually having to break the pew or burst into tears, so all was well in the end; but it took him practically the whole of the service to do this!

O.   Tell me about your house in Salisbury.

RW. We were very lucky. It was unbelievable just after wartime for a young couple to have a house! At first, lots of rewiring and things had to be done to it, so for the first two months the ground floor was completely up, and we had to live upstairs. Each day a crocodile of boys came up from the Choir School to rehearse at the back of the house. David would quickly gulp his cornflakes and go in and take the ten past eight practice.

O.   That was very convenient. Tell me about life in Salisbury.

RW. I am the daughter of a parson, but there were lots of surprises about the Cathedral. Growing up in wartime, I was used to doing many jobs for myself and was prepared to do the work in the house and the garden. To my surprise and alarm, I inherited a gardener—Mr Rattoo. He was used to bedding out plants and things like that and knew the Latin names for plants. One of his duties was to come and sweep the Song Room every Friday evening, and he would bring a bag of old tea leaves which he scattered on the floor, which apparently kept the dust down. He retired after a year and after that I battled with ground elder, an orchard of fruit trees, and a long flower border, quite happily, but with not very good results.

O.   You were warmly received in Salisbury socially, I think?

RW. It was strange. I was twenty-two and the seventy-three houses in the Close were nearly all lived in by elderly people, including two bishops and a lot of distinguished people. There were also houses for the widows of clergy. So my neighbours tended to be the age of my grandparents. They still practised a charming habit that when a newcomer came, you went and made yourself known to them—to call on them—and then you were acquainted. Luckily, we lived next door to the Deanery, and the Dean's wife, Mrs Robins, was very kind and explained to me that I must get some calling cards for myself and for my husband. So I did this. She said, 'They will come and call on you between three and four in the afternoon and they won't stay more than twenty minutes and if you offer them refreshment, they won't accept.'

O.   So they weren't coming for tea?

RW.   No, next you would call on them. Later they would invite you to
       tea, you would invite them back and after that you are fully
       acquainted and you could go to dinner or whatever. This was quite
       a bit outside my experience. Around they came in hats and gloves,
       usually two together, and they brought their cards; and if I wasn't
       in, they would leave their cards through the letter box, and that
       counted as a call. Then I had to start returning the calls. I was
       taught by Mrs Robins that if it was a couple I was calling on, I
       took two of David's cards, one for the man and one for the
       woman, and one of mine because a woman only calls on a woman,
       not a man. So three cards would usually come through and then,
       if you had an unmarried daughter (which I didn't!), you used your
       own card and turned down the corner. Anyway, this went on and
       it was very nice, though I think they thought I was rather brash
       and odd. One day I was having trouble. We had a coke boiler to
       heat the water and it wasn't working very well, and one of my
       friends told me that if I swept the flue that went from the stove, it
       would help. I thought I would do this, so I put on some old
       trousers of David's and tied my hair in a duster and had a go. Then
       the doorbell rang and I thought it might be the plumber coming
       to help me. So I went to the door and it was two ladies calling on
       me! I took them into the sitting room (which by now had a floor
       down) and I shot upstairs and washed my face and hands. I put on
       something and I came down and said, 'How do you do?' And
       nothing more was said! I suppose the story went around the Close
       but they didn't embarrass me; it was very charming. I went to a lot
       of tea parties and had some rather unusual experiences. David
       opted out: he was much too busy to accompany me. And I did find
       that when there was a funeral on, I could dash around and put my
       cards in rather quickly! But we came to the moment when we
       owed tea parties to about eighty people. We thought we would
       have a sherry party. As we couldn't manage more than forty since
       the rooms were quite small, we planned to have two sherry parties
       and this seemed all right. Then word got about: which party have
       you been asked to, the first or the second?

O.   So it became the 'A' crowd and the 'B' crowd.

RW.   Yes. We asked our friend the Bishop of Sherborne, with whom

David lodged before we were married, to be the star of the second party, because we had the Bishop of Salisbury at the first. We hoped that people were happy with that arrangement.

O.   Did you get involved in David's work at the cathedral?

RW.   Well, we went through the whole of the music library, reorganizing it with splendid help from the Precentor's wife and daughter. There was very little official help for the Organist in those days. David had an Assistant Organist, but not a librarian or secretary. After that I thought we'd have a bit of time off, but actually David doesn't go in for that; he's a workaholic and likes to get on to the next thing. He was paid five hundred pounds, which we thought was pretty good. My salary as a teacher that first year had been two hundred and seventy pounds, I remember. We started married life with a thousand pounds between us, and it took us about three years before we got back to that, because moving into two houses in succession takes quite a lot of money.

O.   How did you feel about the choristers? Did you get involved with them in any way?

RW.   I saw quite a lot of the boys. Before becoming choristers the boys are probationers. I took their practice for a few months, thinking it would give David a bit more time off.

O.   Did you end up going to most of the services?

RW.   Yes, I was free to in those days and also sometimes I would go in the organ loft. I remember one time David was giving an organ recital and, after the tuner had gone, there was a cipher and so I went into the bowels of the organ; it is very difficult for him to play missing out one note. As soon as he played the faulty note, I would hold it shut to stop it sounding. I was absolutely filthy; I can't tell you how dirty the inside of an organ can be.

O.   Did you enjoy living in Salisbury?

RW.   Oh, yes, we were very happy. It was a great shock to move. For David, it was the first choir for which he had full responsibility, and he was getting quite a lot of conducting on the south coast and with the Salisbury Music Society, which blossomed under his leadership. But we never regretted it. David is always so happy at what he is doing at the time; he never has time to say, 'if only'. He's not that sort of person.

Colin Prince was a probationer chorister at Salisbury Cathedral under Sir Walter Alcock and, in 1949–50, Senior Chorister under Sir David. He was interviewed on 21 January 2005 at the Athenaeum Club in London.

CP.   David arrived in Salisbury, and that was like a new planet for us.

O.   Were you there the entire time of David's tenure in Salisbury?

CP.   Yes. I can remember we had moved from rather limited accommodation on one side of the Close into the Bishop's Palace, and we had huge grounds to play in. It was the beginning of the rugby season, and we had a rugby ball and we were kicking it around, and a young man arrived. I think he was coming to see the Head or something like that, but he came and joined us, and the news went around that this was David Willcocks. He took hold of the rugby ball and gave it a massive kick and it disappeared into the distance. For youngsters, he'd made his mark with us in a big way!

O.   Very impressive.

CP.   You knew that he was a great organist and he'd got good traditions from King's, he was decorated and mentioned in dispatches in the war, and now he could kick a rugby ball. I realized that someone had come into our lives who was really worth following. As a child you look for examples of that kind. He could get very angry though, about his music. He was a perfectionist and it must have been very galling for him to have an 'also-ran' choir. In 1947 David was the person who had to take that choir, with all our weaknesses, into the twentieth century. I can remember the men could sing almost anything from the old repertoire you put in front of them— they didn't need the music in many cases—but when David introduced Britten and things like that, that was tough going for all of us, particularly for the men. We needed people like Derek Sutton to come into the choir and give it a little bit of finesse.

O.   How was the choir when David arrived?

CP.   An unusual thing had happened. Before David arrived, eight of the sixteen choirboys left in one year; if the choir is not being very carefully trained, that can leave a big hole. I was suddenly ejected from being a junior to a senior chorister—part of what we called the semi-chorus—which under normal circumstances would take a year or two to happen. A lot was expected of us at rather short notice. Senior habits which ought to be developed by the Organist weren't being developed at all, and if things were being handed down, they were handed down by senior choristers. Some of this was quite crude. If, for example, you hadn't found the right music at the right time, you would be reminded by a quite brutal hack on the shins or something like that. I saw boys reduced to tears because they had not managed it. I wasn't taught much in the way of vocal expertise; you just got on with your singing. When I was a senior chorister with David such behaviour faded away. David moved things on by his input and by his skills, achieving what he wanted by his charm and insistence. In three years he made a huge impact, on the repertoire and on the kind of singing that he wanted out of the choir. In Sir Walter's time we sang a lot of Victorian compositions, pieces from the eighteenth century—dismal stuff on the whole and no early works, apart from Henry Purcell. The Fellowes editions were coming out and editors were bringing to life music which had been silent for two or three hundred years, but Sir Walter wasn't part of that movement. Boris Ord was, and King's was doing a lot of that kind of music, so David fits into that tradition. With Sir Walter we often sang from single parts set out in large print on lovely thick paper in huge great leather-bound books, two feet by a foot-and-a-half. Before the service they were all laid out for the men and boys in the right place. There were eight boys on each side so you had three or four of these tomes to a side. When David came we began to sing much more twentieth-century music, from single copies. Under Sir Walter the repertoire often seemed fairly commonplace. Matins was always a bit of a moth-eaten process. Sometimes the men came and sang with us, but you could never be sure of all four parts. When we come to David's time, we were constantly learning new works and he raised standards considerably.

O. Did you have much contact with his wife, Rachel?

CP. David soon brought his wife with him and we just thought she was the best thing we'd ever met in our lives. Boys aren't supposed to think about girls in that way and she was much older than we were, but she was very sweet with us. I remember one occasion when the clocks changed with the season. We turned up at the right time with the new clock and were waiting for choir practice

but there was no Organist, no sub-Organist, nothing. I can remember the delight in the choir when we sent the senior choristers off to raise David. They had to go and find him and dig him
out of his wife's bed to bring him to choir practice. We thought
that was hilarious, but we weren't quite sure why.

O.   Did David direct the choir or stay in the organ loft?

C.P.   We didn't do very much without him, I think. David would stand
there on the Cantoris side, right next to the Senior Chorister. He
would sort of envelop him with his left hand behind this boy's back,
so that it could be seen by the men on that side. His right hand
could be seen by the rest of the choir, and Decani. He would blow
the pitch pipe and start everything off, and usually it was all right,
but when it got to little bits that were difficult, or where we needed
a lot of concentration and help, there was a tension. When I was
Senior Chorister in this place I could feel David's hand coming into
my back, and then something would go wrong, or the timing and
the two choirs weren't working well together, or a lead was missed
and this had to be put right by a signal or by David singing (which
was a disaster anyway) or by me being nudged and prodded even
harder. I got quite used to this bashing, but it was hidden from most
of the congregation. David was very demure and pulled back and I
thought that was rather nice. The responses were carried by two
men on each side as usual, and David—when up in the organ loft—
would then listen to us. If it went out of tune, he would stand in the
organ loft and hiss and kick the wood and make huge tutting sounds
about how terrible it was.

5

Worcester Cathedral and the City of Birmingham Choir

1950 – 1957

O. So you decided to make the move to Worcester?

W. It was quite a big move and I felt very sad leaving Salisbury, because we had been so happy there. But I had been advised by Sir Adrian Boult and others that the combined opportunities offered in Worcester and in Birmingham would be far greater than I could ever experience in Salisbury, so I decided—with Rachel my wife's agreement—to go to Worcester. To start with, we couldn't move into anything like the sort of house we enjoyed in Salisbury, and we stayed temporarily in an old vicarage, while the Dean and Chapter considered where on earth they were going to put the Organist. The Worcester Cathedral Choir was much the same as the choir at Salisbury: composed of six men although we sometimes had three extra, singing as volunteers at the weekend, and again the same number of boys—sixteen.

O. Who was your predecessor?

W. It was Sir Ivor Atkins, who was aged eighty, whereas Sir Walter Alcock had been aged eighty-five. I was beginning to make quite a speciality of taking over from what seemed to me *then* to be *very* elderly gentlemen; *now*, people of that age seem quite young! Well, Sir Ivor Atkins was very much alive and, like Sir Walter Alcock, somewhat reluctant to have given up because he was very fit physically and mentally. Both he and his wife, who had been a Mayor of Worcester, were very welcoming. Immediately I became aware of his great love of Worcester Cathedral. He had been there for fifty-three years, and his devotion was deep. He had very many memories of Three Choirs Festivals over that long period. He had been a close friend of Edward Elgar and was undoubtedly the greatest living authority on the composer's life and work. He knew exactly how Elgar had conducted all his works. Ivor Atkins received his knighthood in recognition of his part in restoring the Festival, which had been in abeyance during World War I; almost certainly Elgar recommended that he be honoured in that way. He wasn't renowned as a very able conductor, although he was a good scholar. He would go to great trouble to prepare a piece through assiduous rehearsal, yet fail to give an assured performance because of unreliable stick technique. He was more confident with a chorus than with an orchestra. As a young man I believe he had quite a fiery temperament and red hair. But he couldn't have been kinder and more welcoming to me. His son, Wulstan Atkins, who died in 2003 aged ninety-eight, also had very clear memories of Elgar, who was his godfather. Wulstan was named after St Wulstan, for whom there is a shrine in the Cathedral.

O.   So Sir Ivor was very much on the scene when you arrived.

W.   I only saw him occasionally. He came to one or two meetings of the Three Choirs Festival Committee. I showed him, privately, my plans for the 1951 Festival. When I arrived at Worcester, Ivor Atkins said, 'I've got a surprise for you in the organ loft.' It was a list of the Cathedral organists, going right back to the very first. I looked at this plaque, and admired how beautifully it was done—all in gold leaf. He had the names of all the organists listed, but no room for any more at the bottom—his name was the last one on the list! So for seven years I had to sit there and wonder. I've never dared go back and look to see if it still ends with Atkins or not. He was a very nice man—very kind to me. He never once said to me, 'Now Elgar used to do it this way, you did it that way.' No, he said, 'What you did would have pleased Edward Elgar very much. It's nice to find the younger generation "feeling it" as the old man did himself.'

O.   He lived several years after you were appointed, didn't he?

W.   Yes, about three years. Sir Ivor felt he did not wish to participate in the 1950 Three Choirs Festival in Gloucester, even though he was still technically the organist of Worcester Cathedral. 'John' (Herbert) Sumsion, who directed the Gloucester Festival in 1950, felt it would be nice to include me as a gesture to the new Organist of Worcester.

O.   How was the Cathedral Choir?

W.   Now when I arrived I was obviously interested in the state of the Cathedral Choir. They were quite good. The boys sang with a pleasing tone and blend. The men's voices were of variable quality. Among them was my friend Mr Stevenson, whom I had known in Salisbury!

O.   And highly recommended for the post!

W.   To be fair, I think he had improved a bit. He lived for another year or so after I arrived in Worcester. I was genuinely sorry to see him go, because he was such a nice man. He was really an amateur singer—I think he was a baker. The rest of the choir were very keen. There was a man who used to sit at a table in the Cathedral and mend the music copies—his name was Captain Kirkby. He used to swear aloud to the great consternation of people. Visitors, while going around the cathedral would hear 'Bugger! Bugger!' as he talked to himself in a loud voice while mending the music. I felt a bit embarrassed by him. We had the usual daily rehearsals with the boys in the Chapter House every morning. The boys all attended the King's School situated in College Green, adjoining the Cathedral, so no time was wasted in getting to rehearsals and services. The repertoire was much more advanced than what I inherited from Sir Walter Alcock. Atkins was kept up to date by the Three Choirs Festivals where he had a good record of putting on new works or works which were considered avant-garde almost when they were written. Works like the Vaughan Williams *Benedicite* and *Magnificat*, Holst's *The Hymn of Jesus* and the Szymanowski *Stabat Mater* were introduced at the Festival when they were still quite new, and many composers such as Zoltán Kodály, Lennox Berkeley, Arthur Bliss, Benjamin Britten, George Dyson, Gerald Finzi, and Herbert Howells came to conduct or hear their works at the Festivals. Some of the works received their first performance at the Three Choirs Festival, which was held in rotation at the Cathedrals of Gloucester, Worcester, and Hereford.

O.   I believe Herbert Howells wrote the Worcester service for you?

W.   Yes. Anybody who asked him, he would write something for them.

O.   Did he talk to you very much about what you wanted or did you just tell him you wanted a Magnificat and Nunc dimittis?

W.   I said, 'Do give us an evening service. We sing the Howells Evening Service in G, the King's College (Collegium Regale), Gloucester, and St Paul's services, and those are the only four we have. I'm sure you've got more under your belt.' He said, 'Well, I might have. I'll keep you in mind.' And sure enough, along it came! It gave us all great pleasure.

O.   When did you begin work on the Three Choirs Festival?

W.   I was asked on my arrival in 1950 to plan the programme for the Worcester Festival of 1951—my first as principal conductor. Generally the chorus at these Festivals numbered about three hundred, of which a hundred and fifty would be from the home choir and about seventy-five from each of the other two. Each choir rehearsed independently until about a month or two before the Festival, when we would have a joint chorus rehearsal occupying one whole afternoon and early evening. There would be a second joint rehearsal about two weeks before the Festival. Looking back, I find it extraordinary that we ever got through those Festival programmes. There would be one whole day—called Black Monday—when we would rehearse all the works that were going to be performed with orchestra during the Festival week. We had no further rehearsal. There would be three concerts each day on Tuesday, Wednesday, Thursday, and Friday.

I think that it would be revealing for you to know my first experience of the Three Choirs Festival as the Worcester Conductor participating in the Gloucester Festival of 1950. This was in early September when I had just become organist of Worcester Cathedral. Who would ever think it possible in one week on six hours of joint rehearsal to do the whole of Haydn's *Creation*, a new work by Finzi, *Intimations of Immortality* (first performance, to be broadcast), Symphony No. 6 by Vaughan Williams, *The Hymn of Jesus* by Holst, the Elgar Cello Concerto, the Fauré Requiem, the whole of Bach's *St Matthew Passion*, followed by an orchestral concert, consisting of the Beethoven overture *Leonora No. 3*, Brahms Piano Concerto No. 2, then *Fantasia on the Old 104th Psalm Tune* by Vaughan Williams, *Crown Imperial* by Walton, *Hymnus Paradisi* by Howells (which was a new major work of great difficulty, also to be broadcast), the *Hundredth Psalm* of Vaughan Williams, *Missa Brevis* by Kodály, the Fifth Symphony of Sibelius, *The Dream of Gerontius* by Elgar, and *Messiah*. All of the choral works were rehearsed in one day!

O.   In six hours?

W.   Yes, in six hours, less the usual mid-rehearsal breaks!

O.   You couldn't even play it all through.

W.   No, indeed we couldn't! I think that *Messiah* was allocated five minutes' rehearsal. The chorus and orchestra were all expected to know it—some had probably sung it for forty years under different conductors. I remember on one occasion that Dr Sumsion said, 'The following will be the cuts in *Messiah*: no cuts in Part One, no cuts in Part Two, but we will omit the following movements in Part Three. Any questions?' After a moment's pause a brave tenor put his hand up and said, 'Dr Sumsion, "And with his stripes" . . . is it loud or soft?' Dr Sumsion said, 'What do you do at Worcester, David?' I said, 'I think we would start it *forte* because there is nothing in Handel's score, and if he doesn't write anything, you presume it's *forte*.' 'What do you do at Hereford, Meredith?' And Meredith Davies, who was the Organist at Hereford, said, 'I think we start it quietly and then get gradually louder through that movement.' Sumsion said, 'Well, that settles it. We will sing it *mezzo forte*.' I thought, 'What a wonderful man—what pragmatism!' He said, 'Just watch me and it will go all right.' Some years later I decided to sing bass in the Festival chorus, and I was absolutely amazed at how ragged it all was. I had heard the rehearsal before and the chorus really sounded quite good, out in the Cathedral; so it just shows what awful things can happen within a chorus, and yet they're not immediately apparent to the listeners. Well that was my introduction to the Festival at Gloucester. I ought to say that Herbert Sumsion, known affectionately to his friends as John, was the sort of 'grandfather' of the Festival at that stage. For many years he had been the 'grandchild', because he had been the junior member when Sir Ivor Atkins at Worcester and Sir Percy Hull at Hereford were much older, but overnight he became the 'grandfather', when I was appointed to Worcester and Meredith Davies to Hereford. We looked to him for guidance and we found in him a great friend. He was a keen golfer, so when he and I discussed future programmes I used to go to meet him on a course at Minchinhampton, near Gloucester. I thought it much more sensible than sitting around a table.

O.   What were your duties at the 1950 Gloucester Festival?

W.   My main assignments were to conduct two works, one of which was *The Dream of Gerontius* by Elgar, which I think John Sumsion

knew that I liked very much. He thought it would be a wonderful piece with which to 'launch' me. I thought it was very generous of him, because I am sure he would have enjoyed conducting
it himself. He knew the work inside out. I had comparatively little
rehearsal with soloists, choir, and orchestra together, probably half
an hour. It is a work that lasts for an hour and forty minutes. If I
hadn't known it well beforehand and performed it at Salisbury, I
am sure that I would have been in trouble. He also allotted me
another Elgar work, the Cello Concerto, which I had never conducted before. He gave me a little bit more rehearsal time with
that, and I had a very experienced soloist in Anthony Pini.
Sumsion was equally kind to Meredith Davies. We both felt it was
a wonderful introduction into a new life.

O.   Did you get to know Vaughan Williams at this time?

W.   Yes. I'd met him at the Festivals of 1936 and 1937. He had succeeded
Elgar as being the 'master' of the Three Choirs Festival. He was the
senior person—very much loved by everybody because of his
modesty and great ability. He attended all the concerts and would
listen with his earphone because he was beginning to get deaf. He
became a great friend, despite being forty-seven years older than I
was. I regarded him with affection rather than awe; he made me feel
that I was a colleague rather than a pupil. Vaughan Williams was to
become quite an influence in my life because I was privileged later
to record almost all of his large choral works with professional
orchestra. He was very encouraging to me on all those occasions, as
was his wife, Ursula Wood, a poet and friend, whom he married on
the death of his first wife, Adeline. Meredith Davies and I stayed
during that week in Gloucester in a house party with Ralph
Vaughan Williams and Ursula Wood (they weren't married then, of
course) and Gerald Finzi and his wife Joy and their two children,
and one or two other friends of the Festival. It was a nice little
gathering under the shadow of the Cathedral. We used to meet to
have drinks in the evening and to chat about the events of the day.

O.   How did you feel about Vaughan Williams at this time?

W.   He was so kind and he always treated one as an equal. Later in life
I asked him when I was conducting one of his works whether
I was interpreting it as he would wish. He would reply: 'I wrote
the music; it's up to you to interpret it. I'm not one to dictate to

others how they should perform my music. I've often heard performances, particularly from John Barbirolli, which made the music more beautiful than I ever conceived it in my head.' I thought how modest he was to pay such a tribute to a conductor of his works. But he recognized that composers are not necessarily the best interpreters of their own music. He would say, 'Just think of Bach, how many different ways there are of performing his music. I've seen enormous changes in my lifetime in the way in which people have performed Bach. Who is to say exactly how a piece of music should be performed?' Vaughan Williams was one of those who was against attempting to recreate original performance conditions. The question that he would ask when performing Bach's music was not, 'What did Bach do?' but 'What would Bach do if he were alive and with us today? Would he use modern instruments? Would he sometimes perform in a concert hall instead of in a church? Would he use women and girls instead of boys?' He would always pose those questions. He would rarely give his own answers; but you knew perfectly well what he thought, because he had asked the questions. Whether or not one agreed with Vaughan Williams's approach to Bach there was no doubting his sincerity or intellectual honesty.

O.   So Vaughan Williams gave you little performance advice?

W.   He would say, 'I want people to feel my music living within them.' Well, during the next seven years I conducted most of his big works in front of him: *Hodie, Job*, and *Sancta Civitas*, and *A Sea Symphony* in Birmingham. He was always very kind, and said they were fine. He said, 'Do what *you* think is right because the chances are that you know just as much as the composer does about the performance of his own works. Sometimes the composer is thinking in an abstract way, or of a different acoustic and different circumstances.' I always remembered that, because on another occasion I asked Benjamin Britten the same question. He said, 'I've put in my score exactly what I want—every metronome mark, every *legato*, every *staccato*, every shape of phrase. If you do that, I shall be happy. If you do anything else I shall be very unhappy. Many people put their own interpretation into my music, and I don't like it! I want to be remembered by what I wrote, not by what I ought to have written. Does that satisfy?' I said, 'It certainly does.' He was a very commanding sort of person. He and Vaughan Williams were two very different people.

O.   Tell me about Gerald Finzi.

W.   He was a very nice chap, rather shy, who died relatively young. I'd heard his songs a bit and played one or two accompaniments. He obviously steeped himself in Wordsworth's poetry and loved it. I loved his *Intimations of Immortality,* which I heard in 1950 when it was performed for the first time at the Gloucester Festival. Finzi always tried to get to the heart of the matter. He was a slow composer, spending a lot of time just getting one little chorus right, whereas with Britten you felt he picked up his pen and worked right through without stopping. Finzi's Clarinet Concerto is beautiful. He wasn't a particularly good conductor, a bit angular. He formed his own little string orchestra near his home near Newbury, where his wife, who was a good artist, used to paint. They were a very happy family and their two sons were both musical.

O.   Did you work with Finzi very much?

W.   He was present when I performed his works. He was always very kind. He never altered anything, but said it was lovely, 'just the way I wanted'. I did his *Intimations* in Birmingham, and I also took it to America.

O.   Tell me a bit about the Festival's history.

W.   It has a great history. It is not known for certain when the music meetings of the Three Choirs were first held; it seems that they began at least as early as 1715. But it was in 1724 that it became a charitable institution. In that year the Chancellor of Hereford suggested at Gloucester that the meetings be made the means of raising funds for the relief of widows and orphans of the clergy of the three Dioceses. That proposal was unanimously approved, and to this day remains the main object of the Festival: to raise money for the poor, and particularly the families of poor clergy. Since those early days, the Festival has grown in stature, and many famous musicians have been attracted to it, some having conducted their own works for the first time. Elgar was a major figure, having been born in a little village near Worcester called Broadheath. When he died in 1934, his mantle was inherited by Vaughan Williams, who had been closely associated with the Festival since 1910, when his *Fantasia on a Theme of Thomas Tallis* was first performed. He conducted the first performance of *Hodie* at the Worcester Festival of 1954 at the age of eighty-two.

O.   I believe you commissioned *Hodie*?

W.   I wanted 'Uncle Ralph', as we referred to him, to write a special work for me for my 1954 Festival at Worcester. I thought he probably did not have much longer to live because his deafness was increasing and also he was losing control of his hands. He said he would love to and could he show me something in a few months' time. He wrote occasionally to say how he was getting on, and then in early 1954 asked if I could go to London to hear the new piece. When I met him in his studio he had his professional accompanist, Eric Gritton, there. I noticed immediately the work was based on Bach's format of having an Evangelist, but instead of having a man singing the story, he had all the boys telling the tale. It was the story of the birth of Christ interspersed with big choruses. I was very excited by the modernity of it. The first chorus is 'Hodie Christus natus est' and is quite syncopated rhythmically. He said, 'That's thrilling. I'm glad you like that.' He played one of the slower movements and some of the music for the boys. He asked, 'Will all the boys sing it or just some?' I said, 'Probably all of them, they're used to singing together.' He said, 'I'll send you a score, probably by April or May, for you to have a look at.' The Festival was coming up in September, and I thought it was getting a bit late. He came down and conducted it himself. I well remember the final rehearsal of that work in the Cathedral. Vaughan Williams by then was getting very deaf, his eyesight was poor, and he was conducting from his own illegible handwritten full score. The chorus, including the Worcester Cathedral boy choristers, the soloists, and the orchestra were apprehensive but eager to give of their best as the first performance was to be broadcast live to Britain and overseas. In the first movement Vaughan Williams either lost his place or failed to cope with awkward changing rhythmic patterns. Everything came apart. Everybody wondered what Ralph Vaughan Williams would say—would he blame the chorus or the orchestra? Not a bit of it! He banged the conducting desk and in feigned anger said, 'I have told you all a hundred times, *don't* watch me . . . then things will go right!' We all followed his advice! And the performance in the evening was very successful. I was playing the piano right beside him because he asked for a piano accompaniment for the boys. I was able to nod to the chorus when they were due to come in. He was really very pleased with it all. Vaughan Williams, as usual, had won our respect and affection by his candour and modesty.

O. What is the supposed debt to Herbert Howells in *Hodie*?

W. A year after the first performance he asked if I'd noticed any likeness to anything by any other composer. I said I hadn't, but he said, 'I reckon I owed something to Herbert Howells. You must look and see if you can discover what that is.' I said I would, but he died before I had the chance to put my answer to him. I think it was that he made use of certain scales. He used one where you leave out a particular note—it's a special scale which is a mixture of some of the old modes, which he was very interested in. I'm certain that's the answer.

O. Was it difficult planning your first program for the 1951 Festival?

W. I built on some suggestions of Ivor Atkins, although I obviously wanted to include works which I particularly liked and felt that we could do reasonably well. I had to bear in mind the shortage of time for rehearsals, but I thought that Herbert Howells' *Hymnus Paradisi*, which had been first performed in 1950 at Gloucester, was such an outstanding work that we ought to give it a second performance. Many works never get a second performance because people seemingly only want to hear an established work or the premiere of a new one. The other piece which I borrowed from the 1950 Festival was Finzi's *Intimations of Immortality*. Howells himself conducted *Hymnus Paradisi* as he had at the first performance in Gloucester, but Gerald Finzi was very modest and didn't want to conduct his own work. Everybody was delighted because both works had been very popular when they were first performed in 1950. The first performance of *Hymnus Paradisi* had gone very well, even though the last pages did not come until a week before the first performance, but I felt much more comfortable a year later when we had plenty of rehearsal. I think both composers felt their works went better in 1951 than they did in 1950, but that is not to run down Herbert Sumsion, who made every effort to ensure the success of both works. I actually sat with him during *Hymnus Paradisi* while he played the organ just behind the choir. In Gloucester Cathedral the organ is right in the middle of the building, so the back row of the choir went right up to the organ loft; he could really support the choir from that position.

O.   What else did you include in the 1951 Festival?

W.   In that Festival I wanted to recognize composers who had worked in Worcester or been born in Worcestershire. Accordingly, I included, for the first time at a Three Choirs Festival, the Mass in C by Julius Harrison, who was a Worcestershire composer. It is a full-length work with four soloists. He was present at the performance, which went well. Herbert Howells conducted his song cycle for soprano and orchestra *In Green Ways*. Other major works included the Piano Concerto for the Left Hand by Ravel. You can guess whom I employed to perform as soloist! It was with great pride that I was able to offer that opportunity to my beloved teacher, Douglas Fox.

O.   Did you conduct?

W.   Yes, I did. It was lovely to have Fox there. He was, as always, desperately nervous, but he played supremely well and everybody marvelled again at his dexterity. I don't know how many more performances he gave after that, because he was already more than sixty years of age. I conducted *The Dream of Gerontius* again, and for the first time Elgar's Second Symphony, which I very much enjoyed. I entrusted to John Sumsion the Elgar Violin Concerto. He had, of course, heard Elgar conduct it on more than one occasion. Sumsion also conducted Elgar's *The Kingdom*. Vaughan Williams conducted his *Wasps* overture, and Sumsion conducted RVW's Fifth Symphony, which he had dedicated 'without permission' to Sibelius. Other works performed during the week included Bach's Mass in B minor, *Messiah,* Mozart's Symphony No. 40, and Cherubini's Overture in D. It was quite a busy week, for in addition to the concerts given by the three choral societies, there were the daily evensongs sung by the three Cathedral choirs (boys and men). Each day from Tuesday to Friday there was a morning concert, an afternoon concert, evensong, and an evening concert. The Festival traditionally begins with an opening service on the Sunday afternoon, featuring the choirs and full orchestra. This was attended by the Lord Lieutenant of the county (representing the monarch), the Deputy Lieutenants, the mayors of the three cities, and the senior clergy. This was followed by our one day of final joint choral and orchestral rehearsals for the performances on the next four days.

O.   Were all the concerts held in the Cathedral?

W.   Yes. I was surprised when I arrived at Worcester to find that at concerts in the nave the audience were still sitting facing each other, at right angles to the performers, because the choirs were placed on tiered seating at the west end looking east. The Dean and Chapter thought that it was unseemly and irreverent for the members of the audience to be seated with their backs to the altar.

O.   So they used English choir seating?

W.   Yes, it was necessary for members of the audience to crane their necks to the right or the left, as the case may be, to look at the performers, which was very unsatisfactory. I could not understand why there was anything wrong in people sitting with their backs to the altar. Even the bishop has his back to the altar in some cathedrals when he is sitting in his throne. I tackled the Dean on this matter, explaining that I was perturbed about this and asked if we might turn the chairs around. Many audience members had told me that they found it embarrassing to sit a few feet from people looking at them for two or three hours. I remember, as a boy at the 1936 and 1937 Festivals, I sat opposite George Bernard Shaw. It was interesting for five minutes but not for two hours. More than once I pleaded with the Dean, 'May we turn the chairs around?' He said, 'We haven't got the staff to do it because for evensong we cannot have the chairs facing west.' I said, 'I shall be happy to move the chairs myself, Mr Dean, and if I can't, I shall find volunteers to help me. There will be no cost to the Cathedral. Immediately after evensong we shall reposition the chairs for the evening performance.' I said that if necessary we would move the chairs twice each day. I pointed out that I could find nothing in scripture that forbade people sitting with their backs to the altar. I said, 'After all, when we leave the choir stalls in procession after a service, we are walking with our backs to the altar.' The Dean eventually gave in, and from that day in 1954 onwards the problem was solved.

O.   You later also had problems with the Dean and Chapter about performing Walton's *Belshazzar's Feast* in the Cathedral, didn't you?

Figure 5.1. Worcester Festival, 1951; David conducting the Festival chorus and orchestra in the Cathedral, with the audience facing each other

W.   That was a work I always felt ought to have been performed at the
          Three Choirs Festival. It was written in 1931 and yet twenty years
          later it still hadn't been performed at a Festival. I couldn't see any-
          thing wrong in performing it. I persuaded the Dean and Chapter of
          Worcester that there should be no objection to performing the
          work in Worcester Cathedral. It is a marvellous setting of the text. I
          think the objections from some cathedrals had been that Walton had
          placed too much emphasis on the actual orgy of the feast, the drink-
          ing, and the blasphemy in it. But I said, 'If you can read it as a lesson,
          why can't you sing it?' It is a very exciting and dramatic work and it
          made quite an impact on the audience when I performed it for the
          first time at the Three Choirs in 1957. It's not all that easy for a choir.
          In fact in 1931, when it was first performed at the Leeds Festival, the
          choir found it extremely difficult, because they'd been used to
          singing works like Mendelssohn's *Elijah* and Haydn's *Creation*. Today
          people accept it as being just part of the repertoire. I believe before
          the first performance of *Belshazzar's Feast*, Sir Malcolm Sargent or-
          ganized extra rehearsals, playing the piano himself. He felt it was the
          only way he could get them to learn it in time.

O.   When did you begin your work in Birmingham with the City
          Choir?

W.   I began conducting the choir in 1950 when I moved to Worcester.
          I succeeded George Cunningham (conductor from 1926 to 1948)
          who had been the City Organist of Birmingham and widely rec-
          ognized as one of the leading organ recitalists of the day. He was
          always known as GD, after the initials of his first names, and was
          greatly loved by the choir members, who enjoyed his quiet
          humour. The choir had been founded in 1921 by Joseph Lewis,
          who had established a tradition of performing new works with the
          City of Birmingham Symphony Orchestra. When I took over,
          singing members numbered about two hundred, all of whom were
          auditioned regularly. As they were all good sight-readers, we were
          able to continue performing enterprising repertoire, much of
          which was broadcast by the BBC, which had a department in
          Birmingham. The Town Hall had excellent acoustics, which the
          recording engineers understood well. Among those works which I
          performed in the Town Hall with the CBSO was the Duruflé
          Requiem, soon after he had written it. Our two performances in

1952 were the first to be given in Britain. The work has since become very popular worldwide. I loved it from the moment I saw it
and was delighted when Duruflé came to Birmingham and agreed
to play the organ part. His wife also came. I didn't realize at that
stage that she was a brilliant organist as well, and later used to play
joint recitals with him. It was a little difficult at rehearsal because he
didn't speak a word of English; he couldn't even say 'Thank you'. I
wasn't very fluent in French, but between us we got through somehow and he was very complimentary. He said, 'How can I thank
you for those marvellous performances?' I said, 'You can give me
this full score, autographed.' My wish was cheerfully granted and he
wrote very nice things in French. I treasure the score to this day.
About a month later I got a letter from his publishers, 'I gather that
you've bought the full score of the Duruflé Requiem. I should be
grateful if you would settle the account as soon as possible.' I fear
that I lost that letter and have not yet had a reminder!

O.   You said his English wasn't very good. Was he involved in the
      rehearsal preparations?

W.   No, he just sat at the organ, and played his part impeccably. I
      remember wishing that he could have advised me about balance
      from the auditorium. I tried to communicate with him in my
      limited French, as best I could. He seemed to be happy with the
      rehearsal. I was glad to be able to invite him in later years to give
      one or two organ recitals in King's College, Cambridge. I always
      consider that as a composer Duruflé was a supreme craftsman
      because nobody would wish to remove or add a single note in his
      pieces. The Requiem is economical and scholarly in the sense that
      he makes use of the traditional plainsong in a very subtle way. It
      has the melodic lines of Fauré but with more advanced harmony,
      reminding the listener of the harmonies of Debussy and Ravel. It
      is beautifully constructed and I still enjoy conducting that work.

O.   How often did you go to Birmingham?

W.   I went every Tuesday to rehearse the choir. It seems strange that in
      those days I just left my car outside the Town Hall or our rehearsal
      room. Now it is impossible to park anywhere in the city centre.

O.   How many performances were there a year?

W.   There were a minimum of four, to which were added extra con-
      certs if there was to be a broadcast of a particular work. Several of

the works that we performed were most unusual. I've never heard some of them since. One was by Granville Bantock, a setting of 'Omar Khayyam', which required an enormous orchestra with extra brass. The choir certainly enjoyed the challenge.

O.   Who was this composer?

W.   Sir Granville Bantock had been the first President of the City of Birmingham Choir and a respected figure in Birmingham music. Speaking of Bantock, on a different occasion we performed his extended arrangement of the British national anthem, 'God save the King'. On the opening drum roll the whole audience stood up, including the Lord Mayor. There followed a long instrumental passage building up to the first choir entry. At first there seemed to be no thematic reference to the national anthem, so after a minute or two the Lord Mayor and audience sat down.

O.   Oh, dear.

W.   Eventually the writing became fugal and the subject bore resemblance to the first six notes of 'God save our gracious King'. Rather sheepishly the audience had to stand up again.

O.   What other repertoire did you perform with them?

W.   We presented a wide range of works which the choir had not performed before. They had performed much of the standard repertoire many times, but works like the Tallis forty-part motet *Spem in Alium*, Tippett's *A Child of our Time*, Britten's *Spring Symphony*, Bloch's *Sacred Service*, and Thalben-Ball's *Sursum Corda* had never been tackled.

O.   Did you work with Tippett on the performance of *A Child of our Time*?

W.   Yes. He came to hear the performance and was pleased that the choir obviously enjoyed the work, having initially found some of the movements very difficult. I went to consult him at his home in Wadhurst, in Sussex, not so much about the music, as about the meaning of the text, some of which he himself had written. I found some of the words by no means clear. For example, I wasn't quite sure what the very opening meant: 'The world turns on its dark side'. My guess was that it referred to the alternation of light and darkness, or good and evil. We talked for about two hours and Tippett explained the deeper thoughts behind the words, though when I came away I realized I was little further on in my understanding of the text. But he was a man of great charm, gentle and generous with his time.

O.   What other new works did you introduce?

W.   In 1952 we performed Howells' *Hymnus Paradisi* which had so impressed me at the Three Choirs Festivals of 1950 and 1951; also Kodály's *Psalmus Hungaricus*, Maurice Jacobson's *The Hound of Heaven*, and Britten's *Spring Symphony*. I think that the choir relished the new repertoire; for my part, I was glad to have the City of Birmingham Symphony Orchestra playing for these concerts. When I moved to Cambridge in 1957 I was succeeded by Meredith Davies, my friend from Hereford. He in turn was succeeded by Christopher Robinson, who was by then Organist of Worcester.

O.   Did you have time for any other musical activities at Worcester?

W.   I continued adjudicating. In some years I judged as many as ten festivals, most of which would last for two or three days. I tried not to be away from Worcester too much. I felt that having accepted the post I ought to *be* there. I also taught the organ. One of my pupils was

Figure 5.2. Hereford Festival, 1952; the three Festival conductors, left to right Meredith Davies, John Sumsion, and David, with Herbert Howells, seated right (W. H. Bustin & Son, Hereford)

Figure 5.3. Hereford Festival, 1952; left to right: Douglas Guest, Melville Cook, John Sumsion, David, Percy Hull, Harold Darke, and Douglas Fox

Roy Massey, who was then a schoolboy at King Edward's School, Birmingham. He was very talented, and when he was seventeen I appointed him as accompanist to the City of Birmingham Choir. He later became Organist at Hereford Cathedral, among other places. Rather as Ernest Bullock felt pride when I went to these various positions and ended up at the Royal College of Music, so I am proud to see Roy Massey having done so well.

O.   Where in Worcester did you end up living?

W.   In the end they solved the problem of what to do with the Organist and his wife by dividing up the Headmaster's house. I believe they never told the Headmaster and his wife that they were going to do this. They just found themselves one day with builders coming to convert the house into two!

O.   They were living in it?

W.   Yes. They were nice people, very understanding. Obviously we had

Figure 5.4. David playing the organ at Worcester Cathedral, July 1957

to be near the Cathedral, and the Dean and Chapter had no other property that was vacant at that time. All the canons lived in College Green or in College Yard. The Dean and Headmaster lived in the close and the school occupied several buildings in the close. Sir Ivor Atkins had his own house right by the north door of the Cathedral, so of course he preferred to live there. There was no Organist's house as such. It wasn't wholly satisfactory for us, particularly during the later years at Worcester when we had four children. The house was not suitable for children, because it was on different levels with a lot of stairs and beneath the house was the River Severn with a walkway—you had always to be vigilant, lest the children should walk down there and step off.

O.   How many years were you the Director of the Worcester Three Choirs Festival—three?

W.   Yes, 1951, 1954, and 1957. I was lucky in that respect because some
        people served eight years and were Director only twice. It just
        depends how the years fall. I was delighted that when I left Worcester
        they offered the position, on my recommendation, to Douglas
        Guest, who had succeeded me at Salisbury. I had succeeded him as
        Organ Scholar of King's many years before. I think I was able to hand
        over to him nice choirs at Salisbury and Worcester. After Worcester
        our paths diverged, as I went to King's College, Cambridge and he
        went to Westminster Abbey, but we remained friends.

O.   Did you do any teaching?

W.   When I was at Worcester I went to two girls' schools in Malvern,
        St James's and Lawnside, to conduct their girls' choirs. Malvern is
        in a lovely part of Worcestershire; the Malvern Hills have marvel-
        lous views of both Worcestershire and Herefordshire. The girls par-
        ticipated in one or two concerts given by the Worcester Festival
        Choral Society in the Cathedral. The headmistress of Lawnside,
        Winifred Burrows, was a great friend and admirer of Elgar and
        George Bernard Shaw—they had a Shaw Festival there for many
        years.

O.   Did the Festival Choir sing during the entire year or just for the
        Festival?

W.   It was called the Worcester Festival Choral Society, and it was
        like an ordinary community choir, based in Worcester. We had
        several singers who came in from Malvern, and even a few from
        Birmingham. Mostly we rehearsed once a week. Before a festival in
        the summer months we had two rehearsals a week. We needed
        every second of those rehearsals to cope with all the repertoire. The
        cathedral choirs took part in some of the performances, but not all
        of them; for instance, in a work like *The Dream of Gerontius* I might
        use the boys from the Cathedral Choir for the semi-chorus, and
        some men might also volunteer to sing. The Cathedral Choir was
        separate from the Festival Chorus, and had plenty to do that week
        just singing for the cathedral services.

O.   The music schedule at the Cathedral was rather like Salisbury, I
        would think?

W.   Yes, very much so. We sang matins, I think, three days a week, and
        on Friday morning, instead of matins, it was the litany. I always
        enjoyed, just once a week, singing the litany. That has ceased now

at most cathedrals. It can be difficult, if singers are employed in a full-time job, to get the mornings free.

O.   What about your organ playing?

W.   I did everything, normally. I had an assistant, but he would never be there when I was. The assistant's duties were to take the choir and to play the organ when I wasn't present.

O.   Who was your assistant?

W.   Throughout my time at Worcester the Assistant Organist and accompanist of the Worcester Festival Choral Society was Edgar Day, who had also held the post under Sir Ivor since 1912. One of his duties was to play the six-thirty service on Sunday evenings. We played golf from time to time on Wednesdays, a day when there were no sung services. He was a kind and gentle man who kept house for his mentally handicapped brother. He knew Elgar well.

O.   So you did all the hymn playing, and accompanying the psalms and anthems?

W.   That was the general practice in cathedrals.

O.   So the choir really sang on its own?

W.   Yes. You learned exactly where they were going to breathe and where they needed time. Perhaps on rare occasions, if it was a broadcast, you might get the assistant to play so you could conduct to keep things dead together. The ensemble isn't always much better when there's a conductor, because still the organ has to be with the choir. At Worcester and at Salisbury we did not have the same problem as we have at King's, where the organ has to be definitely ahead of the choir for it to sound together. At Worcester the organ is within ten feet of the men on one side and at Salisbury it is up only about fifteen feet above the choir, so it was very easy to be together.

O.   You told me that the Cathedral would frequently be nearly empty for matins except for some of the clergy and choir.

W.   That's quite true. I think we had matins at Worcester at eight-thirty in the morning. Nobody was there other than the Precentor or a Minor Canon, and the Canon-in-Residence. I always felt that we must be just as conscientious over the singing as if the Cathedral were full of people. I remember being told that Dr Harold Darke, on one occasion when he was rehearsing the choir at King's just before a service, said to them, 'I want you to sing particularly well today, because Dr Herbert Howells is going to be in the congregation, and

I want you to do really well.' One of the choral scholars put his hand up and said, 'Dr Darke, I expect God will be listening too, won't he?'

O.   Darke had a little nickname that came from his Service in F, I think, didn't he?

W.   Yes, he was known as the 'Ineffable Darke', which I think pleased people.

O.   What is the organ at Worcester?

W.   A Harrison, but originally it had been a Hope-Jones, with diaphones and that sort of thing. One of the difficulties was that a substantial part of the organ was down in the nave. You couldn't comfortably use the nave organ with the choir organ. I used to use the nave organ for accompanying when there was a nave congregation. When there was a full Cathedral, then one could use both together. It didn't really work ordinarily to couple the two together.

O.   You also conducted the Bradford Festival Choral Society from 1956 to 1974?

W.   Yes, that's right. Bradford Festival Choral Society was one of many northern choirs which had a great reputation for singing, particularly during the last years of the nineteenth century and right through the first half of the twentieth century. Before the days of television and radio, people in those industrial towns took part in choral singing much more than they do today. Some of these choirs couldn't read music—they sang from tonic sol-fa, but they were very well trained by a number of excellent chorus-masters who were good vocalists. Sir Malcolm Sargent used to conduct several northern choirs, including Liverpool, Leeds, Huddersfield, and Bradford. When Sir Malcolm Sargent retired from Bradford in 1956, I think he recommended that I take over from him. I went up about four times a year. I'd go up the night before the concert and conduct a chorus rehearsal. There would be a *tutti* rehearsal on the afternoon of the concert and the concert in the evening. We performed much the same sort of repertoire as I did in Birmingham.

The chorus-master had to 'note bash', but they were very well prepared when I arrived. Once they had sung a piece they would know it for all time. As is so often the case when people aren't good sight-readers, they have a very good memory. We generally had the Royal Liverpool Philharmonic Orchestra to perform with us. I enjoyed the challenge of performing some of the pieces I'd never done before, just in one rehearsal. I found that was useful to me in later life.

O.   Well, it makes you know the spots that need the work.

W.   Exactly. You know what you are going to do if you've got ten, twenty, or thirty minutes, and what the order of priorities is. Sometimes it can seem quite strange. People might say, 'He only looked at that little easy bit with the women', when in fact it is a very difficult bit. Also it meant that you really did have to study your scores. I never play the piano when preparing a score. I like to do it in a train or plane where I can actually hear it. It's not the same when I play it on the piano, because I then hear it as a piano piece—I don't hear an orchestra. You must learn, as I did from Malcolm Sargent, what is necessary to mark in your scores clearly to remind you of metre changes. You have to hear the work really clearly in your head. If you can't hear it clearly you ought not to be in the job. I'd go as far as that. When people ask what I believe is the most important aspect of being a conductor, I think it is to have a clear conception of the work and then balance what you actually hear at rehearsal against that. Obviously you have to correct mistakes first, but after that you try and get the overall conception.

O.   Did you guest conduct at this time?

W.   When I was at Worcester, Malcolm Sargent was occasionally away from the Royal Choral Society in London. If he was away for more than two or three weeks he would ask me if I would take a concert. In those days there were three leading choirs in London: the Royal Choral Society, The Bach Choir, and the newly formed Philharmonia Chorus. There were other choruses like the London Choral Society, but the Royal Choral Society under Sargent had great prestige; the word 'Royal' helped a bit, and of course he was probably the most distinguished choral conductor of his generation. I got experience there of taking a strange choir for rehearsals in works which they may or may not have started to prepare. They were always subconsciously comparing what I did with what he did. I didn't always know what he had or had not done, so I had to try and deduce what would be right. Once, I took perhaps three rehearsals running and a concert in the Royal Albert Hall, which was good experience for me. He seemed very pleased. I got to

know him quite well. He was a very conceited man, really, and I
was able to tease him occasionally. One day he wrote to me when
I was at Worcester, 'Dear Willcocks, I'd like to commend to you a
small boy I heard the other day, aged only eight, who has perfect
pitch. He is very bright with a good sense of rhythm and I'd like
you to hear him to see if he would be suitable to sing in your choir
at Worcester. He could easily go on to end up at least as a cathedral
organist.' I thought, 'How rude!' After I had heard the little boy, I
replied, 'Dear Sir Malcolm, Thank you very much for bringing to
my attention this gifted young boy. I heard him sing. I agree with
you that he is very musical, very intelligent, and has got a good
voice. I think he might easily end up as a conductor at the very
least. I don't think he'd *quite* make the grade of cathedral organist,
though.' He wrote back saying, 'You win.' I just couldn't resist it.
There was a sort of a hierarchy in his mind, with conductor right
at the top and cathedral organist well down.

Interlude 5

Reflections on Worcester

Lady Willcocks was interviewed at her home in Cambridge on 18 June 2003.

RW. We went up to Worcester for David to have a look-see. We wondered if we wanted to move, because Salisbury is a very beautiful place, though Worcester College Green (which is like a close) is also lovely. In those days there was no motorway and great lorries thundered through just outside the cathedral precinct, and on the other side you had the River Severn. We asked about a house to live in, and the Dean took us to one of the houses which had been a canonry and said, 'This is a very big house. We propose to cut it in half. We will make you a new front door, you've got three bedrooms and three rooms on the ground floor and a basement and the garden.' That all seemed very satisfactory. Only when we arrived in Worcester did we discover that the occupants of the house had not been told that we had been shown around their home. We found that this sort of rather eccentric behaviour of Deans and Chapters happens quite often. However, our neighbours, the Kittermasters, were charming and didn't blame us at all for taking half their home. When we first arrived the house wasn't ready, so they popped us into a large, empty rectory, a couple of hundred yards up the hill. I was pregnant and feeling very happy about it. When lunch was ready, we had to run the length of the building to eat it—the kitchen wasn't the sort you could eat in. One day there was a smell of gas so we called the gas board and the man said, 'Are you staying here?' And we said, 'No, we are only here for another two weeks.' 'Well, I should just pour a bit of vinegar down and mask the smell,' he said. That was most alarming, but we soon moved into College Green. Instead of using the number 12A for our newly divided house, we chose 13, not being superstitious. Our four children were all born there in the next seven years. I was told by Lady Atkins that my children were the first to be born in the Green for a hundred years. I didn't have much time for anything else, but I did sing madrigals and sing in the Festival Choir and the Worcester Choral Society concerts.

O.   Tell me about the children.

RW.   Sarah, our eldest, was born in 1951 and then Jonathan two years later; Anne two years after that and a year after that our youngest, James. He was six months old when we left Worcester. So really my time in Worcester was taken up with the children and the Three Choirs, which I took part in when it was in Worcester—I didn't try to take my tribe over to Hereford or Gloucester. In our first year, before I had any children, I spent the week at the Gloucester Three Choirs Festival.

O.   Was that when you went to the house party with Ursula Wood and Ralph Vaughan Williams?

RW.   Yes, that's right. Alice Sumsion, who was the wife of the Organist at Gloucester, fixed up this house party. My memories of it are: first thing in the morning, Ralph Vaughan Williams, talking hard at breakfast; last thing at night, Ralph Vaughan Williams, wearing his dinner jacket with his stiff shirt popping out, telling funny stories— he was always the last to go to bed at night.

O.   Was David conducting?

RW.   Yes, as the newcomer he was invited to. The resident organist is responsible for the Festival, but he would ask various people to conduct different things because he couldn't do the whole thing himself. So we usually had five, sometimes more, conductors in the week. This was very interesting for me when I was able to sing in the Festival Chorus. I think over my sixteen years as a chorus member I had about sixteen different conductors, and by far the best was David! Some of the others, particularly some of the composers, were not used to conducting amateur choirs. Being amateur singers, we found this difficult.

O.   Did you sing under Vaughan Williams?

RW.   Yes, at Worcester. It was hard, because he didn't give us any help, but it was a great experience.

O.   What about the three years that David had the Three Choirs Festival in Worcester? That must have been a lot of extra work for him, and, I'm sure, for you.

RW.   That's right. You spend two years planning. David was extremely clever at balancing the books of the Festival, because he was able to have new works without running into enormous debt. As you know, music is always dependent on money. Initially, my mother, with a girl to help her, took the children down to Cornwall during the Festival, but later I had a very good friend and helper, Mrs Saunders, to look after the children in Worcester. People would say, 'Where are your children?' And I would reply, 'They're in the cellar!' We had a playroom in the cellar, and their routine would go on there as usual.

Roy Massey was a student of Sir David and served as his accompanist for the City of Birmingham Choir. He was interviewed on 31 October 2006 in Tewkesbury.

RM.   The music master at my school was a man called Stanley Adams, who was also rehearsal accompanist to the City of Birmingham Choir. They had just had a new conductor appointed, David Willcocks, and Stanley suggested that it might be a good thing if I met him, so a meeting was arranged where I would go and play to him. I suppose I must have been fifteen or sixteen. I went along and I played my piece, which I remember was the 'little' G minor Fugue by Bach. David listened and then started to test my general musicianship. He made me extemporize, transpose and harmonize, and then modulate. He also gave me some absolutely fiendish ear tests, which I couldn't do. He turned me inside out to find out what I was really capable of. At the end he said, 'Oh well, I'll give you some lessons. Let's meet up in September', which we did. I had a weekly organ lesson. Sometimes it was very short, but I'm sure I learned more from David in ten minutes than I might have learned from lots of other people in a couple of hours. We never talked about money, so one day I asked him how much I owed him. He said, 'Let's not bother about that. When I'm on the parish in my old age you can support me.' He never charged me a penny for a lesson. It was absolutely fantastic that he should do that and I owe him a great debt of gratitude. One day Stanley Adams was unwell, and a message came through 'Could you come and play for the City Choir tonight? It is the B minor Mass.' I was so inexperienced that I may even have had to ask, 'Who wrote that?' So I went along and I sight-read the Bach B minor Mass. On another occasion, I was called in as the choir was learning *Hymnus Paradisi* by Herbert Howells. In those days the music of Howells seemed very modern and I had no experience of it whatsoever. I made an absolute mess of that rehearsal. At the end David said, 'Are you being paid for this?' and I said, 'No,' and he said, 'Well, if you are, you're not worth it. Take it home and learn it, because you're playing next week as well.' Fortunately it was a school holiday, so I took it home, and I really did learn it. When I went back the next week, David, with a slight glint in his eye, put up the lid of the piano and said 'Now, I want plenty of piano tonight'. Afterwards he said, 'Yes, yes, you now play it better than the regular accompanist.' So that was a little pat on the back. Eventually, the accompanist's job with the choir became vacant. David said, 'I would like you to have it, but you have to apply for it.' So I applied and was appointed. Here I was, at the age of seventeen or thereabouts, sitting every Tuesday watching one of the very best choir trainers in the country at work. It was a fantastic experience, and if I know anything about training a chorus, I learned most of it from watching David. From the *Hymnus Paradisi* experience I learned that you *never, ever* went unprepared to a rehearsal. David was always well prepared and expected you to be the same. He was a great technician in terms of intonation, vocal colour, words, blend, balance, and style. When he moved to Cambridge, he left behind him a splendid choral society as good as anything in the country.

O.   Did you hear David's choir at Worcester?

RM.   There was in Worcester a set of rather old-style lay clerks—tenors and basses with rather heavy voices and rather hooty altos. Stylistically, cathedral choirs have altered past all recognition in the last half-century, and it was people like David who helped to accomplish this transformation. In the 1950s David produced a wonderful set of boys and made the men blend as best they could in the lower parts. He was brilliant with his boys, and I well remember a performance we did in Birmingham Town Hall of *Hodie* by Vaughan Williams. There is a special narrative part for boys' voices, and a group of Worcester choristers sang it. They were absolutely brilliant in every way, and one felt that they would have lain down and died for their choirmaster, so devoted were they to him. He had a wonderful way with them. His total commitment to the job in hand became *their* total commitment, and this resulted in superb singing. David helped me to focus on what real musical standards were. It suddenly became that you tried to play every note absolutely correctly. If you were conducting a choir you made them sing absolutely in tune. Nothing less was good enough. You never achieved his sort of perfection, but at least you tried.

O.   Do you see much of David now?

RM.   We met at the Three Choirs Festival in Worcester in 2005 when my wife and I had the pleasure of staying with the same hosts as David and Rachel, and where we had a very enjoyable time together. On the day after the festival there was a 'do it yourself' *Messiah* which David directed. There was an orchestra, and I played organ continuo. I said to him, 'Do you realize the first *Messiah* I ever played was in this building under your baton, and this might be the last one I shall ever play, but at least we've come together again!' From the moment he picked up his baton everyone performed absolutely brilliantly.

Henry Sandon was a bass lay clerk at Worcester Cathedral from 1953, and sang for four years during Sir David's tenure there. He was interviewed on 14 June 2007 in the Music Library at Worcester Cathedral, which had been the sitting room in the Willcocks' former home.

HS.   I saw a position advertised at Worcester Cathedral and applied for it. At the audition I was met by David Willcocks at the station—he said he'd hurried through matins to get to the station in time to meet me! It was 1953—Coronation year—and we had lunch and he took me for a drive round to the old hills. Then I had the audition, which was to sing some Bach in the Cathedral with him on the organ, and then met the Dean and was offered the lay clerk post. The choir had been reduced from eight lay clerks to six to save money, and to raise the stipend of those that were still there. The number of services was very large: Monday morning matins—but Cyril Stevenson (who had sung for David at Salisbury*) got that stopped because he claimed that wherever you worked first on a Monday morning, that place had to pay your health stamps.† So we started with Monday evensong at quarter past five, then Tuesday morning practice and Tuesday evensong. Wednesday was plain, Thursday morning matins, Thursday evensong was boys only, Friday morning was litany and then evensong. Saturday was matins, then practice, then evensong. Sunday was three services: matins, communion, then evensong. So it was a tough routine.

O.   You sang the litany every week?

HS.   Yes, there was no organ. It was *accompanied* by David Willcocks going around the Cathedral in the nave kicking chairs whenever he heard something wrong—a wrong note, or wrong tuning or something—which happened quite often because the choir was a bit ancient.

O.   Did the boys sing the litany as well?

HS.   Yes. It was tough on the boys at half-past eight in the morning, without breakfast. One or two of them used to faint every now and then, or be sick. There were special services occasionally, and of course the Three Choirs Festival for which we got twelve pounds per annum. This involved twelve sectional rehearsals, three re-hearsals with the full choirs, and then the whole week of the Festival—all for twelve quid! All three Cathedral choirs sang, except that not all the boys went to the away Festivals. The full choristers of the home Festival sang with four each from the other Cathedrals, but all the men sang. It was invigorating but mentally and physically quite exhausting, especially the Festival week itself, beginning with Black Monday. Black Monday was three long rehearsals: no concert, but a rehearsal with the full choirs and orchestra in the morning, a rehearsal with the cathedral choirs in the afternoon, and a full rehearsal again with everybody in the

* See p. 82.
† At that time each employee had a card recording the mandatory National Insurance contribu-tions. These were paid in the form of stamps that had to be affixed to the card by the employer each week.

evening. Everything was rehearsed on that one day, and at the end you were sung out. All three cathedral organists were at you to sing louder and better, so by the Tuesday you'd got hardly any voice left, which was a bit stupid, but that's how it was. It was a tough, tough week, but we did some marvellous music.

O.   What sort of repertoire were you singing in the Cathedral when you came here?

HS.   We took over a lot of the Elizabethan music which Sir Ivor Atkins had introduced. Willcocks brought in a few modern pieces but it was mainly Elizabethan and Victorian. Sir Ivor preferred earlier music. He was a strange man. After my audition Willcocks invited me to sit in the organ loft during evensong, which was wonderful. At the end of the service there were a dozen people crammed into this organ loft and he said, 'Who's the youngest here?' A little girl put up her hand rather shyly and he said, 'You can choose the voluntary, what's it to be?' 'Ooh,' she said and stuttered out a certain Bach toccata and fugue, so Willcocks played it, on the spot, without the music and it was going fine, when all of a sudden into the loft came this wizened old fellow who, of course, was Sir Ivor Atkins. The atmosphere fell about twenty degrees! At the end of his playing, Willcocks looked up in fear and trembling and Ivor said to him, 'Can't you span a tenth, Willcocks?' 'No, Sir Ivor'; David's got very small hands. 'I can', said Sir Ivor and thumped it down on the organ. That was my first introduction to him. I've heard from some of the boys that the treatment he gave them was pretty tough and they used to call him 'saliva'. He was a martinet, but a great musician, everyone admitted that, though not a great conductor, apparently. I met a number of singers who sang under him and they all spoke equally badly about his conducting. Of course David was a brilliant conductor and the Three Choirs began to be great fun with him.

O.   What about the clergy at the cathedral?

HS.   I remember Canon Brayley—a funny old boy, always drunk—and we used to say in the Lord's Prayer 'Give us this day our *Brayley dead*!' His daughter got married in the Cathedral. We sang the usual wedding stuff, and were invited back to College Hall afterwards to participate in the wedding feast, which got very alcoholic. Everybody got plastered and come five o'clock old Nicholls, who was Senior Lay Clerk, realized we should be going up to sing evensong. We all trooped there very much the worse for wear. I don't think anyone remembers very much about that service although people who attended it said it was the most memorable one ever. A tenor—Llechid Williams—was next to me and on the far side of Llechid was Kirkby, who was a retired captain from the navy. He'd never been to sea but he'd run the stores at Portsmouth. About half-way through the service, it might have been during the first lesson, he turned to Llechid and said in a very high-pitched alto voice, 'What's next?' Llechid said something back quietly and Kirkby said, 'Christ! I've already sung that.'

O. Can you talk a little bit about David's work with the Cathedral choir?

HS. He was mad keen on the psalms, which I was too—I loved the psalms. Now cathedrals have abridged the psalms, which is an appalling business. David was wonderful at the psalms and we spent a long time rehearsing them. He had a different stop for everything: he used to make the birds twitter, and the plagues in Egypt would have different stops for the bugs and the snakes. When we got to verses such as 'my foot had slipped' he would slide his foot down the pedals, beaming like a sunbeam. He used to play the service with the curtain by the organ console pulled back, so we could see him. Sir Ivor Atkins would have the curtain closed and would watch the choir through a periscope, peeping over the top.

O. What about David and the Festival Choir?

HS. Willcocks was at his absolute best rehearsing a massed choral society and they loved it. The ladies used to get to sit in the front row and he had his great fan clubs there and they revelled in the jokes—he had some incredible stories. He was brilliant with amateur choirs, but could be tough on the professionals.

O. Did you see much of Rachel?

HS. She would come to the Three Choirs and would put on little teas for us and things like that, which was enjoyable. And we saw his children, of course. He once told me that he'd been offered the post at Eton College—not a great post, but they told him that all his children could be educated at Eton with no fee! But he decided not to and was happier, I'm sure, at King's College.

O. Was there any resistance from any of the lay clerks to some of the music that David introduced?

HS. No, I didn't feel that. I think some of them found it difficult to do modern music because they'd been brought up with eighteenth- and nineteenth-century music, which is pretty easy to sing. Something like Benjamin Britten was thought to be really, really difficult, but there were no objections to it even though it meant more rehearsal and practice.

O. Here in Worcester, we must talk about David and Elgar.

HS. He was a great lover of Elgar and I learned a lot about Elgar from him. He did all the great oratorios, which were marvellous—they never sounded better to me. David was good with Vaughan Williams, but his Elgarian skills were tremendous. His style was truly Elgarian.

6

Director of Music, King's College

1957–1974

O.   How did your move to King's come about?

W.   The circumstances were somewhat unusual. Boris Ord had been
       my mentor when I first went to Cambridge in 1939 and then
       again in 1945 when I returned after World War II. He was the
       person to whom I looked for advice, counsel, and help. I was told
       by the Provost of King's in 1955 and 1956 that Boris Ord's health
       was failing rapidly. He had a degenerative disease which meant he
       was gradually losing control of his hands and then his feet. He
       could barely conduct and could not stand for very long. The
       Provost said, 'I don't know how long he can last doing this, but we
       obviously want him to carry on as long as he feels he can. Could
       we beg you to come back to King's? We can't actually appoint you
       Organist because we don't want to deprive him of that title, but
       we would like you to help him. When he can no longer continue,
       we would love it if you were to succeed him.' I thought it was
       rather peculiar for a Cathedral Organist suddenly to become an
       Organ Scholar again, but I was so fond of Boris Ord, and I loved
       the whole atmosphere of King's. There was another advantage in
       that Rachel's mother lived in Cambridge, and it would be nice for
       Rachel and the children to be near her. We still had many friends
       in Cambridge, so I determined that we would go back. When I
       arrived in September 1957 I found Boris Ord still very cheerful,
       and he didn't seem to realize that he was going to get much worse
       fairly quickly. I think with that particular disease you have a sort of
       euphoria—you are very happy.

O.   Do you think it was something like Parkinson's?

W.   He didn't actually shake but he just lost control. I think disseminated sclerosis is the correct term.* First of all he started dropping things, then he would trip over the carpet. He would blame the carpet if he tripped, when in fact he had lost control of his feet when walking. He was still mentally perfectly all right although his speech began to get a little bit slurred. I found him much more relaxed in some ways than when he was younger. He lost all that burning ambition and just wanted to enjoy life. When I returned, it was really like going back to 1939 to be his Organ Scholar again! He took the rehearsals, and I played the organ. In the end, the College decided the best thing to do was for me to be appointed Organist, and invent a new title for Boris Ord . . . Director of Music. There had never been a Director of Music at King's; there had always been just an Organist, as in the statutes of King Henry VI: 'There shall be an Organist and sixteen boy choristers of sound condition and honest conversation.' I was awarded a fellowship of King's and a university lectureship, and also made University Organist, a post which Boris Ord had held but obviously couldn't continue. I became associated with the Cambridge University Musical Society (CUMS), a university chorus numbering about two hundred and fifty singers, and also the University Orchestra. And I took over the conductorship of the Cambridge Inter-village Choral Society, a group of village choirs from the Cambridge area, which combined to give performances of oratorios.

O.   When did you actually take over from Boris Ord?

W.   When I returned Boris continued to direct the choir very well, and a lot of singers felt very loyal to him. He conducted the Christmas Eve carol service in 1957 and I played the organ, just as I had in 1939 as Organ Scholar. Then in January 1958 I took over. He continued to listen to the services. At first, he could get into the Chapel with help and listen from the antechapel to what was happening. When that was no longer possible, one of the choral scholars rigged up a means so that he could listen to the services in his bed. Three or four times a week I would go up to his rooms in college after evensong and chat with him and have a glass of sherry. He was very supportive. He never said, 'Stanford in G was too fast' or 'Stanford in A was too slow'. I don't think he would

* Now known as multiple sclerosis.

have minded if I changed things, but I didn't want to. I didn't consciously think to myself, 'I don't like the sound the boys make, I'm going to alter it.' The tone, phrasing, and sound of the choir do perhaps alter slightly with a change of director, and very gradually the sound may have changed. I think if you heard a recording of the King's College Choir under Boris Ord or me—or under Philip Ledger or Stephen Cleobury—it sounds almost the same. Of course the Chapel is a unifying factor. I think each Director of Music should encourage the sort of sound he likes, and each Director may have his own vocal exercises which produce a different sort of tone. I would hate it if one felt that it was necessary to carry on exactly as one's predecessor did.

O.   Can you describe the difference in Boris Ord's sound and your own?

W.   It is very difficult to describe. I think we were both aiming at the same sort of freedom. Some people found King's too effeminate and they wanted a more robust sound. I aimed at what I call a 'pure' sound. I don't often like vibrato in boy's voices, especially singing Elizabethan music, where to me the line and tuning are so important. There is only *one* place where a major third can be, and it can't vibrate. However, when there is a solo line, I do like a little bit of warmth or very slight vibrato here and there in a phrase. But I can't bear an uncontrolled wobble. Boris Ord never had it, and neither has Philip Ledger or Stephen Cleobury.

O.   What were your duties with your university lectureship?

W.   I taught harmony and counterpoint and some music history and music appreciation. That was only twice a week, so it was a fairly light load and most of my day was directed towards the King's College Choir. I taught undergraduates and a few postgraduates in the university; most were reading for a music degree.

O.   Were they large classes?

W.   They would be about four to eight. One got to know most of the Organ Scholars from the other colleges, because they were generally studying music.

O.   What did the post of University Organist entail?

W.   I played in Great St Mary's Church, with its famous Father Smith organ. I just had to play a voluntary before and after the University Sermon, which was on a Sunday afternoon. There was no choir.

Figure 6.1. King's College Choir, 1958–9; Boris Ord, seated, second from left; David, seated, third from left; Simon Preston, back row, second from left; Robert Tear, back row, third from left (photograph, Edward Leigh)

Figure 6.2. David conducting King's College Choir in the Chapel

Occasionally there were special services, as when the judge came for the Assizes.

O.   You had a really illustrious roster of Organ Scholars during your time at King's.

W.   My first Organ Scholar was Simon Preston, who came in January 1958. I had been all on my own from September until Christmas 1957 but impressed on the College that I just *must* have an Organ Scholar. I just couldn't do it all on my own, with Boris Ord ill. Simon was a very talented boy from Canford School in Dorset. He had been at the Royal Academy of Music, studying under C. H. Trevor. He tried for a choristership at Salisbury when I was there, but didn't get in because I felt at the age of eleven he was too old. I thought I'd much rather have a boy of eight or nine and bring him up, rather than take a boy of eleven even though he was obviously very musical. I'm not sure Simon Preston has ever forgiven me for that! When he came in for the Organ Scholarship he was up against a man named Graham Mayo. Mayo had been at Clifton College, as a Scholar. He and the school knew perfectly well that both Boris Ord and I had come to King's from Clifton. Everybody at Clifton was assuming that he would become Organ Scholar, and I think Boris Ord had been asked, once Mayo had completed his FRCO, what he would like him to do before coming up to Cambridge. Against him was this young chap called Simon Preston who had only got an ARCO [a lower examination than the Fellowship].* Well, they played! Mayo played very well indeed. It was good, as was his sight-reading, transposition, and extemporization, and I thought 'That's it'. In came Simon Preston and played after him. I thought, 'Bless me, he's playing even better.' I think he might have played a movement of the Reubke *Sonata*. His transposition was also good, as was his sight-reading, score-reading, and extemporization. It all came down to the boys' rehearsal. Graham Mayo took them first, and he said, 'You are singing very well, boys, it's lovely. I like the sound, you're phrasing beautifully.' I thought what a nice chap he is. In walked Simon Preston. He said, 'Stand up when I enter the room!' After they sang, he said, 'When I was a chorister here, we sang much better than that. I want you to do it again. Now sing it properly!' The difference was electrifying and I thought, 'This is the man we must have.' I felt sorry and still feel sorry for Graham Mayo, because on any other day he would have got it. There was nothing wrong with him at all. He got a scholarship to Corpus Christi the same day. Simon Preston . . . I just couldn't refuse. I never regretted it.

O.   He is one of a kind.

W.   Yes, one of a kind. He led me on a dance at times. I had regularly to be on the q.v. . . .

O.   'On the q.v.' . . .?

W.   'On the *qui vive*'. It's an old military expression meaning 'on the alert'. '*Qui vive?*' was the challenge that French sentries made to strangers who approached. Simon was followed in 1961 by John Langdon, who was also excellent. He had been a former chorister of mine at Worcester and I started him on the organ. He had perfect pitch and I was really delighted that such a musical boy was able to come to King's. Then in 1963 along came a boy who was undecided whether to study music or classics. He was immensely

* See p. 32.

gifted. I don't think either of his parents was musical. I hadn't heard anything about him; nobody had lobbied me for him beforehand. His name was Andrew Davis. They were all wonderful Organ Scholars. Simon Preston was probably the most conscientious. When he was practising he would write in fingerings, and would be in the Chapel even practising chants and fairly easy services which he could play perfectly well, but he wanted to be absolutely certain he never made a mistake. I don't think I ever did hear him make a mistake. Andrew Davis you could throw in at the last moment, and he'd just go sailing through. He was naturally extremely gifted. At that stage one didn't know he was going on to become a great conductor. Simon Preston, of course, has gone on to become a great organist.

O. Who followed?

W. Then came John Wells in 1966, who has done extremely well in New Zealand as an organist and conductor. Ian Hare followed in 1968, and he has been responsible for music-making in the Lancaster area. Then in 1971 I had James Lancelot, who is now the distinguished Organist at Durham Cathedral. Finally, I appointed Francis Grier in 1973. He is a very gifted organist and has become a well-known composer.

O. So your first carol service as Director was in 1958?

W. That's it, yes. Now for that service, I thought how dull it is always to have the hymns just sung in unison. I thought I would like to add one or two new descants and arrangements. We had had descants at the Advent carol service—I think Charles Wood had written a book of them. I don't know why King's hadn't had them at Christmas, except for one for 'While shepherds watched their flocks by night' by Alan Gray. There were no descants that I knew of for 'O come, all ye faithful' or 'Hark! the herald-angels sing'. I thought, particularly at the very end of the service, it would be nice to have descants for those two hymns. I also thought we must have something simple for children listening at home, so I also inserted a very simple little setting of 'Away in a manger'. We thought of the audience at home putting up the holly. The carol service was broadcast as usual, and a lot of people afterwards wrote to say how much they had enjoyed the descants. Well, somebody from Oxford University Press heard these and asked if they could have the three carols. I had never had anything published before, but I thought, 'Let them have it'. They sold very well, so they then asked me if I would do a book of fifty carols. I said that I couldn't do fifty on my own, but they wanted fifty, so I said that I would do it if somebody else did twenty-five. They suggested Reginald Jacques, who was the conductor of The Bach Choir. Oxford felt that he could arrange some that were suitable for big choirs, and I could do some for small choirs. I met him and liked him very much. At that stage I never dreamt I was going to succeed him as Musical Director of The Bach Choir. We selected fifty of the best-known carols and decided who should arrange which ones. The editor at that time was Alan Frank, who delegated most of the detailed consideration of manuscripts to Christopher Morris, a fine musician whom I got to know very well indeed. He worked with me, seeing all these arrangements through the press. The book was eventually called *Carols for Choirs*. We never thought it would be particularly success-ful, but it was extremely well received throughout England and abroad. People liked having one volume of carols, which were basically not too difficult, and didn't involve a lot of *divisi* work. It was well within the range of the average parish church choir and wasn't designed for professional choirs. It was so successful that ten years later Oxford University Press said that they would like another fifty. By that time Reginald Jacques had died. I again said that I couldn't do more than twenty-five. They asked me, 'Who should we have for the other twenty-five?' I said, 'I know an under-graduate here at Cambridge who is the most gifted composer that I've seen pass through the university. He is not only very able but quick, neat, and you won't find any mistakes at all in his manu-scripts.' They said, 'We don't know him at all.' I said, 'Believe me, you *will* know him because he is very, very gifted. I've conducted one of his pieces called *The Falcon* and it is really lovely, imaginative and beautifully scored. He has already written a number of carols as well.' So they said, 'OK, we'll see him.' I don't know whether he went to be interviewed or not, but they readily agreed. That was the beginning of a friendship with John Rutter that I have enjoyed for very many years. I am a great admirer of his works, because I think that they are highly original and approachable. There is not one of his pieces that I don't like. He manages to appeal to people of all ages. Children love his music because there is always melodic interest and subtle rhythmic vitality. These qualities endear him to the general public who aren't professional musicians.

O.   As Americans say, 'You go away whistling the tune.'

W.   Exactly. The tunes seem so obvious that you think, 'Why has nobody else thought of that one first?' I often wish that I could have thought of some of John's melodies. His scoring, once he started to write for instruments as well, is so imaginative. Like Vaughan Williams, he adapted his works so that if you do not have all the instruments available, you could perform them with less. That makes his music agreeable to choral societies that might not be able to provide a full orchestra.

O.   So he was your co-editor for the second collection?

W.   Yes. Of course we had to re-name the first book *Carols for Choirs 1*. John Rutter took the really interesting new ones or new arrangements, while I tended to take the old hymns. I had the easier task! Well that was successful, and then ten years later came *Carols for Choirs 3*, and later still *Carols for Choirs 4* for high voices (soprano and alto). In 1987 Oxford University Press published *100 Carols for Choirs*, which was our last joint effort. About seventy were drawn from books 1–3 and, for the rest, thirty new arrangements and pieces were brought in. That's done very well.

O.   The first volume became wildly popular in the United States and Canada, and I think that helped spread the name of King's and David Willcocks to every English-speaking church. Many people bought it for your 'Adeste fideles' descant.

W.   It's nice to think that people are able to share some of the music which we actually sang in King's, because by that stage the King's College Choir had become known more internationally. It was famous, of course, within the British Isles, because radio had aired the Christmas Eve service ever since 1928, apart from one year when Dr Mann died. Many people in the United Kingdom listen to the service, and it has increasingly been heard in different parts of the world. People could buy the book, and sing the same arrangements that they heard at the King's service.

O.   Do you remember much about writing the 'Adeste fideles' descant? That's known in America as the 'only' descant, and when someone does a different one it is considered heresy by some.

Figure 6.3. John Rutter and David celebrating the publication of *100 Carols for Choirs* in 1987, on the roof of the University Church, Cambridge, with King's College Chapel behind

W.   I feel each generation should provide its own. I am quite relaxed about the fact that Philip Ledger, after me, wrote a quite different one, and Stephen Cleobury has written a quite different one again. Probably Stephen's successor, when he's appointed, will write yet another one. Philip Ledger and I have often joked that it's going to get more and more difficult because if you have a chord of G major and I've chosen to have B at a particular point, Philip has chosen D, and Stephen Cleobury has chosen G, what's the next person going to do? There is a limit to the number of variations you can have in a descant. I think already I have heard a number of versions which are sailing very near to mine or Philip's or Stephen's.

O.   We talked a little bit about radio and television beginning to spread the reputation of the choir—that really came about during your tenure at King's. Obviously the Christmas service was broadcast on radio but you were broadcast on a much more regular basis, not only on radio but increasingly on television.

W   Yes. I think the first television broadcast was in the 1960s and then they came every year. They didn't televise the actual service on Christmas Eve. People thought they were seeing the actual service, but it was always filmed beforehand. King's is just the wrong shape for television. The Chapel is very high and rectangular and not the shape of a television screen. King's is a wonderful place, but once the cameras have been up and down the windows and you've shown the Rubens painting there is very little else to show. We found it was much better filming in a place like Ely Cathedral. We went to Lincoln Cathedral to film Berlioz's *The Childhood of Christ* (*L'enfance du Christ*) and to Ely for *Messiah*.

O.   Did Boris Ord ever have a televised service?

W.   Yes, he did. There is a DVD of the carol service in 1954 that shows him directing the choir. Again, not live television—it was filmed. That is very interesting, because it shows the economy with which he conducted and the response of the choir. In fairness to me, and in fairness to Philip Ledger and Stephen Cleobury, the music which we included in our services was much more difficult than the music which is on that DVD. Boris Ord used just a tiny little bit of movement with an index finger, but I think the choir would have been able to manage without that. I was always influenced by Boris Ord. He said, 'Never do any gesture which is unnecessary,

because if people are watching they will see just the slightest movement of your finger. If they are not watching, they won't see you if
you're flinging your arms around.' I have always agreed with that.

O. Were the radio broadcasts live?

W. Yes. The carol services have always been live on radio. I think
it would be a great disappointment if the service ceased to be
broadcast.

O. What about recordings? The choir started recording much more
during your tenure.

W. Yes, I was fortunate to be there during the 1960s, a decade when
gramophone records were really coming out in large numbers.
Moving from the old 78s to the long-playing record was a real im-
provement.[*] There was a keen demand for these records, particularly
outside England. They became quite popular in the United States,
Canada, Australia, and New Zealand. Many people became aware
of Tudor music, for example, through the King's recordings. There
had been other choirs singing this music, but somehow they didn't
get the same publicity. Boris Ord made a number of recordings of
Orlando Gibbons and also a recording of Easter matins and an
evensong. There wasn't the same demand for recordings before the
war and in the immediate years afterwards. I found it stimulating
doing these recordings because some of the music we performed
probably hadn't been heard for four hundred years. We had great
scholars like Thurston Dart and others editing the music. We were
also able to work with orchestras such as Neville Marriner's
Academy of St Martin in the Fields. That was rather nice because
his son, Andrew, was in the choir. We also worked with the London
Philharmonic Orchestra, the London Symphony Orchestra, and
the English Chamber Orchestra. It was a wonderful, stimulating experience for the choir to be doing those things. Of course the BBC
came to record programmes as well. Knowing that these recordings
were going to be available for a long time made us much more
careful to get things absolutely right. I know that one should be just
as careful whether there are the microphones present or not. I used
to say to the choir, 'Sing just as well whether there are two people,

---

[*] Twelve-inch long-playing (LP) 33 rpm records superseded the earlier 78 rpm records in the
1950s. They had a much greater playing time and less surface noise.

two hundred, or two million listening. You've got to get it right for yourself.' I think that one should instil in people the burning desire to make sure it is done to the very best of their ability.

O.   Who determined what the recordings were going to be? Did you make those decisions or was the recording company involved?

W.   Normally you would look around to see what hadn't been recorded. It was much easier in the 1960s because there wasn't the same number of recordings already available. If we took any anthem it was quite likely that nobody else would have recorded it at that time. Today, if you decide to record 'Blessed be the God and Father', or 'If ye love me', the record company probably already has many good recordings available.

O.   And of course that's also true of a larger piece like the Fauré Requiem.

W.   I think when we recorded the Fauré Requiem there might have been one or two others in the catalogue, perhaps one very authentic French one. Now there are lots. With many of the pieces we were recording, we weren't competing against anybody else. In those days many people also liked hearing boys' voices, and preferred the sound of an all-male choir to a mixed choir. Now there are so many good mixed choirs. In England we've got some of these professional choirs where they've got the former choral scholars from Oxford and Cambridge with a new lot of women on top who sing without vibrato and to a very high standard. So we've got competition now on that front. The choice of repertoire depended really on what had been recorded already, except for something like *Messiah* where even though there might have been many in the catalogue, they felt they would like one from King's, especially, because it would be popular. In general we tried to record things that hadn't been done.

O.   What about some interesting recording stories?

W.   Well, I did some of the carol arrangements because the record companies never liked paying large copyright fees. Many of the carol arrangements in volumes 1 and 2 of *Carols for Choirs* were done specifically in order to avoid paying copyright on them. Sometimes for those sessions I was very late getting the music ready, and I would be scribbling out a new arrangement or a descant on the floor of the Chapel. Then the choir would sing it, and while the

Organ Scholar listened to see whether anything was wrong, I'd be writing out the next one. I think some of the descants that are being used widely now were written at the very last moment in that way. We didn't have photocopies in those days, but we had those dreadful things called Banda copies. The ink got wet and smudged. Luckily the boys were very good sight-readers, and the men got used to reading my writing.

O.   What about the Allegri *Miserere*?

W.   When we recorded that, Roy Goodman seemed to me to be the obvious person to sing the solo, so I told him there was going to be a session at half past four that afternoon. I didn't realize that he was playing in a rugby match at the school. He was captain and so all that afternoon he was shouting and cheering people on. I think they ran into overtime as well. He had to run all the way down from the school to the Chapel and arrived red in the face, with bloody knees and apologizing for being late. I said, 'You are recording the Allegri *Miserere* now.' I made him sit down for about five minutes, then I placed him in the quartet at the far end of the Chapel, and he sang absolutely beautifully, and on one take.

O.   Extraordinary.

W.   I thought we had better have some spare ones but we actually used the original take. There is one minute little 'fluff', where it just wobbles for a moment, and I said, 'We'll keep that' because that is what it actually was. It has been one of the most popular records that King's has ever made. That recording has been heard around the world. It is often chosen by people for funerals, or by people on programmes where a favourite record is chosen. I've never asked Roy Goodman what he got paid. My guess is, he got a pound.

O.   He's doing a little better now I think.

W.   Yes, he's a very fine musician. He was an excellent violinist when he was a boy at the school, then he played violin professionally, and now he conducts full-time around the world. He founded his own orchestra and is Principal Guest Conductor of the English Chamber Orchestra. He always says how much he owes to King's, as indeed we all owe him for having been in the choir. I know what I owe to Westminster Abbey, and I think my son, Jonathan, recognizes what he owes to King's as well. There's comradeship—it's like being a member of a soccer team, you are all contributing something to it, and you rely on each other. You're supportive if you are not given a solo, and if somebody else gets one you accept it. You learn so much about languages, because your repertoire ranges widely. We sang frequently in German and French, and now the choir sings much more music from other countries in their native languages.

O.   Well, it has been a glorious tradition. One of the things I love about King's, and any of the university choirs or college choirs, is the fact that there is a new group of choral scholars and a new set of boys every year, so there is always this very fresh young sound.

W.   Yes. People forget, really, that the choir changes—a quarter of the boys change every year on average, and a third of the men change every year, so a complete change takes place every four years. Yet there is an unbroken tradition going right through, and the change in the sound is almost imperceptible. You think that the choir is never going to be the same again in three years' time when all these lovely people have gone. Somehow those little boys who were doing very little in the last year will be doing a bit more the next year, and then they will be leading the choir three years later. That's what's so lovely—the continuous progression. Each generation feels that it is responsible for maintaining a tradition, and, if possible, enhancing it.

O.   Is it possible to name two or three favourite recordings that really stand out?

W.   There are so many. . . . I love the early music like *The Western Wind* Masses of Tye and Taverner—the music is timeless. Then there's the Tallis forty-part motet, Fauré Requiem and Allegri *Miserere*, Palestrina *Stabat Mater*, and the *Coronation Anthems*—the music is all wonderful. I remember as a small boy singing 'Zadok' looking at the statue of Handel in the south transept in the Abbey. All those things go around in my mind when I listen to this music. I don't only think of one performance, I think of countless other performances.

O.   And Bach?

W.   Bach, of course, has always been a great favourite of mine. I loved performing and recording Bach cantatas with Gustav Leonhardt in Holland and the *St Matthew Passion* with Nikolaus Harnoncourt in Austria. Those were great occasions for the choir, working abroad in that way. The tours with the choir were very interesting and it was stimulating going to different countries. The choir now tours more each year than they did in my day, because I think in those days the Headmaster and the parents didn't want the boys to be away for more than perhaps two weeks in a year. Two weeks was probably enough, with perhaps some little tours across the channel to the festival in Bruges or to concerts in Holland. Recently the choir has gone much further afield to Australia, New Zealand, Hong Kong, Japan, Canada, and the USA. It means, of course, the choir is singing less in King's. Some people are very disappointed to come to King's College Chapel and find the choir's not there, so you can't win!

O.   What was your most memorable tour?

W.   Probably when we went to Africa. We went to Ghana, Nigeria, and Sierra Leone, which was very interesting, because I'd never been to that part of Africa before. It was wonderful singing to people of a quite different culture. We met the King of the Ashanti tribe, and his staff gave us presents. We gave the King a present; I forget what it was. I told our Senior Chorister, 'The King would like it much better if you make the presentation speech. What you should say is, "Your Majesty, I hope that you will be graciously pleased to receive this gift from us all as a thank you".' He got it nearly right by saying, 'I hope you will be gracious enough to receive this gift.' My heart sank, but I don't think any harm was done. On another occasion, we were invited to take the boys to sing carols to the Royal Family at Windsor, and at the end refreshments were provided. Again, I said I thought it would be appropriate if the Senior Chorister thanked the Queen for her hospitality. At that time the newspapers had been saying that the Royal Family had been ex-travagant over this and that, and that they'd been spending too much money. This little boy had obviously read the papers and he made his speech, saying 'Your Majesty, I'd like on behalf of the King's College Choir to thank you very much for your marvellous hospitality.' I looked around at all the sausage rolls they had con-sumed and the lemonade. The chorister said, 'I realize it's even more kind of you, because we've read in the papers that the Royal Family is very hard up and short of money at the moment.' There was momentary silence, after which the Duke of Edinburgh roared with laughter and said, 'Quite right, my boy, we're very hard up!' The Queen said, 'We like to splash out at Christmas!'

O.   Any other stories about the choristers?

W.   Auditioning and interviewing new boys often provided happy moments for me. When young Andrew Marriner came for his test, I asked him, 'How old are you, my boy?' He replied quickly, 'I'm eight, sir . . . How old are you?'

O.   Tell me about the Cambridge University Musical Society (CUMS).

W.   This was a big society of about two hundred and fifty singers and a full orchestra, which I conducted. I felt that every person going through the university who wanted to join this choir ought to experience some of the major classics like the Mass in B minor, *The Dream of Gerontius*, and the Verdi Requiem. I never performed *Messiah*, because I knew they'd meet that in their colleges and elsewhere. I preferred full orchestra works rather than ones that employed just part of the orchestra. We would try and perform new music as well. Benjamin Britten was writing a lot of new music at that time, and I was able to get him to conduct his own works when they'd only had perhaps one or two performances.

O.   Was Britten in Aldeburgh then?

W.   Yes. Cambridge of course is near to Aldeburgh, where Benjamin Britten founded the famous Aldeburgh Festival in which many of his works were performed. He became very attached to the CUMS and thought that they sang and played well. We performed several of his works with him conducting: the *War Requiem*, the *Spring Symphony*, *Voices for Today*, *Saint Nicolas* (with text by Eric Crozier), *Cantata Misericordium* (with words by Patrick Wilkinson, Vice-Provost of King's College, Cambridge), and the piece he wrote when he got a degree from the University of Basle in Switzerland, *Cantata Academica*. He also invited CUMS to sing at the Aldeburgh Festival in the lovely Maltings hall with its beautiful acoustic. We sang in the old hall and were due to give a concert on the very day that fire destroyed the Maltings. We were all in our buses in Cambridge early in the morning ready to drive off, when somebody listening to the radio heard that the Maltings had burnt down during the night. We thought it must be somebody making a joke, but it wasn't. We rang up Aldeburgh, and found that what was said on the radio was quite true, so we didn't go that day. But Benjamin Britten said, 'Well, we'll invite you again. We're going to rebuild the hall. We've made the decision already, you must come for the opening.' He honoured his promise and we went back to give a concert in the newly built hall exactly a year later.

O.   Did he work with the King's College Choir as well?

W.   Yes, he was quite attached to the King's College Choir. He wrote for boys' voices in a number of works, including the *War Requiem* and the *Spring Symphony*. He came to Cambridge from Aldeburgh to rehearse with them himself. He used to come to breakfast and he would chat about the boys. He didn't waste time in rehearsals— he just got down to working straightaway and was always encouraging. We recorded his *Ceremony of Carols* and *Voices for Today* and he was quite pleased. Britten invited the King's College Choir to provide the semi-chorus in Elgar's *The Dream of Gerontius* in the recording which he made with Peter Pears and the London Symphony Orchestra Chorus. It was a work I hadn't associated with Peter Pears at all, but he was a very dramatic interpreter of the role of Gerontius, and the King's College Choir provided the sort of ethereal background that Britten wanted. In that recording, if you listen carefully, you will hear the organ part which I played on the King's College organ. I sat all on my own in the organ loft at King's wearing earphones. They had recorded it without the organ part, and I played the organ and they 'fed that in' afterwards. It was a funny experience not having anybody conducting, just listening over the earphones and playing. Of course I had the

Figure 6.4. David and Benjamin Britten in June 1966 after recording *Voices for Today*

famous little chord on its own toward the end which I played with just the two notes: 'Spare us, Lord'.

O.   The other thing I think is so important is the way you performed the psalms at King's, which was unique and quite beautiful. I know psalmody has always been a great love of yours. Tell me about that.

W.   Ever since I was a small boy, I've always loved the words of the psalms. Of course, we sang them every day in Westminster Abbey, either the morning or the evening ones. I think I can still recite many of the psalms to this day, because when you learn something at the age of eight, nine, or ten you remember it for the rest of your life. I felt that if a choir could sing psalms well, it could sing anything well, because it's like chamber music—you must work together as a small team. I used to tinker with the pointing of the psalms (the word or syllable on which you change the chord) and try to make the rhythm as near as possible to good speech. I also studied the structure of the psalms. In some, the sense goes right through the whole verse; in others the sense changes at the colon in the middle, and you get what is called the 'answering' effect. A good example is the opening of Psalm 114: 'When Israel came out of Egypt: and the house of Jacob from among the strange people, Judah was his sanctuary: and Israel his dominion.' In these cases it is nonsense for one side of the choir to sing the whole verse; the two sides of the choir should answer each other. But where the sense goes right through it is bad to divide the choir. Therefore, I think it is right to vary the way in which each psalm is approached. You also have to consider, 'Where does the main stress come?' In a verse like 'God is our hope and strength: a very present help in trouble' [Psalm 46: 1] is the stress on 'very', 'present', 'help', or 'in trouble'? You have to work in rehearsal to make sure that the entire choir feels the words in the same way, at the same speed, and with the same emphasis, in order to make the psalms vital to the listener. You also have to plan your dynamics very carefully, and sometimes the organ can be a good adjunct. I like some psalms sung *a cappella*, others using the organ. When you have got a verse like 'Tremble thou earth' [Psalm 114: 7], it is very exciting to hear the organ in the background, reinforcing the meaning of the words. There are some verses in which it is extremely difficult to know what stops to use. There's one verse that says, 'Like as it were a moth fretting a garment' [Psalm 39: 12]—I don't know which stops you use for that! Another example is 'For I am become like a bottle in the smoke' [Psalm 119: 83]. I was always conscious of the need to prepare the psalms as much as possible. If there was only one hour's rehearsal, I would often spend as much as forty minutes on the psalms and perhaps ten minutes on the anthem and ten minutes on the canticles. We were constantly changing our minds concerning the pointing, and I'd make everybody bring pencils so that they were prepared to make the necessary alterations. I very often used to take a vote.

O.   You were the first person to make an entire record of Anglican psalms, weren't you?

W.   I think so. Now that occurred by accident. We were going to record some hymn arrangements and the record company set up all the equipment, but I'm afraid the arrangements were not complete and we had to cancel that session. I said, 'Don't just pack up your gear. Surely we can do something.' The producer, Christopher Bishop, said, 'What about some psalms?' The man at EMI headquarters thought no one would want to hear those. 'It's just the same tune going on and on.' But I said, 'People often comment after a service that they enjoyed the psalms very much. It's worth trying and we wouldn't need to rehearse because we sing them every day.' So they agreed and we recorded seven or eight psalms in one session. They were so pleased we completed a whole record's worth, and to our astonishment, and even more to theirs, the record sold extremely well. The company came back and said, 'Could we have another volume?' I think Philip Ledger did a third volume and I'm sure Stephen has recorded some. Again, you'll find, if you listen to each of them, that there's a difference in the speed of the psalms. Each person has his own idea and I don't think I would necessarily sing the same psalm the same way two days running. It's how you react to the words on a particular day. I'm very fond of those records, because I love the psalms. They cater to every mood, and speak of joy, sadness, sorrow, love, hate, redemption, and reconciliation—every mood experienced by man is to be found in the words of the psalms.

O.   Would you talk a little bit about what many people call the glorious King's tradition? It's gone on for so many centuries and is probably one of the oldest continually singing choirs in the world, isn't it?

W.   Oh, no. Worcester and Salisbury are older. Westminster Abbey is older still. King's College wasn't founded until 1441, and the Chapel took nearly a hundred years to complete. In English cathedral terms, it's just a little baby, only been going five hundred and fifty years or so. The tradition as we know it today probably only dates back to Boris Ord's predecessor, Dr Arthur Mann, who was Organist for fifty-three years. It is to him that we owe many of the traditions associated with King's. Even the dress of the little boys, walking to the Chapel in their top hats and their flowing gowns, isn't a very old tradition. The first carol service, as we know it, was during Mann's time in 1919, and it was first broadcast by the BBC in 1928. It was devised by Mann and the Very Reverend Dr Eric Milner-White, then Dean of King's. Much of the King's tradition comes from these annual broadcasts. Few people actually come to services in King's; the tourists are there, but the regular worshippers are relatively few. In some places like Westminster Abbey there is a sense of a long tradition, and it's possible to name many of the Organists throughout that history, but in King's that's less true. Few people could name anybody who sang or played there between the time of Christopher Tye (a chorister in the sixteenth century) or Orlando Gibbons (who died in 1625) and that of Dr Mann. So the King's tradition is relatively new, and I think we owe a great deal to 'Daddy' Mann and Boris Ord.

O.   When did the choral scholarships begin? Am I correct in thinking there were originally lay clerks at King's as in cathedrals?

W.   Yes. I have been told that the boys, until the beginning of the twentieth century, served in Hall as little waiters and received free education. The choral scholars gradually came in the 1920s, and replaced the full-time professional men. I wish we had a recording of the choir in those days—it would be most interesting to hear what it was like. Of course, the sound of the choral scholars, whether at King's or any other college at Oxford or Cambridge, is quite different from the sound of the average cathedral lay clerks, where you have men with mature voices aged from twenty to sixty-five or even seventy. There may be better soloists in some cathedrals, but the blend is normally better in university colleges, because they're all young. Against that they may lack maturity: it is rare to get some really good deep second basses, but from time to time we even managed to get those. Many of the choral scholars later become professional singers. Some of them sing as soloists; others in groups such as the King's Singers.

Figure 6.5. Choristers of King's College in front of the Chapel, including Jonathan Willcocks, sixth from right, facing to the left (photograph, Edward Leigh)

O.   Were you involved in the founding of the King's Singers?

W.   Yes and no! We had a very good bunch of solo singers in the men of the choir around the mid-1960s, and two of them, Simon Carrington and Alastair Hume, were very good double-bass players. They both applied to join the BBC Northern Symphony Orchestra and got good jobs. I was surprised when, along with Brian Kay, they came to see me two years later and told me they'd made a decision to sing and not play. They had loved their time in the King's College Choir and found playing tonic and dominant in the BBC Northern Orchestra for a long time pretty boring. They wanted to form a new male-voice choir and earn their living by singing. So I said, 'What sort of forces will you have?' They said, 'We'll have two altos, two tenors, and two basses.' I said, 'Well, that seems a strange group—how much music can you think of for that?' They said, 'There are various pieces we could sing. We've sung a lot at college feasts in May Week, and we've gone around to sing after some dances and been very well received.' I said, 'Well, it's one thing to sing two or three pieces of music, but to earn your living you have to do much better than that.' They responded, 'We'll find some way of doing it. We'll commission music!' I said, 'Commission! Well, someone's going to have to *pay* for that. Are *you* going to pay for that?' They said, 'If necessary, we will. Some people may want to do it for us.' So I said, 'Well, don't come crying to me in ten years' time if you are out of a job with no money.' They said, 'We won't.' They were most engaging people, and I rather believed them immediately, because they were all determined to make a success of it. So they set off, and the first thing I knew they'd done was to ask John Rutter to write a piece for them. About a year later I heard that they were doing very well, singing in Oxford and Cambridge colleges and also at one or two dates in London. They seemed quite happy. Then to my surprise they started touring abroad, and they ended up in New York City, where they did some broadcasts and were very well received. I asked, 'Are you still singing with two altos, two tenors, and two basses?' and they said, 'Yes, that's all we need.' I said, 'If you had two sopranos, you could do a lot of double-choir and eight-part music.' One said, 'We don't want to do that.' So I left them to it, and to my great surprise they did extremely well during the next ten years, singing all over the world and recording. I think Simon and Al stayed with the group from its foundation to around 1993. The others were choral scholars who joined them for different lengths of time, all good singers and beautifully trained. Bob Chilcott, who is now a well-known composer, was one. They were brilliant presenters: each of them in turn could come out and say the words to the next number and make jokes about it.

O.   And they never said, 'I told you so.'

W.   No.

Interlude 6

Cambridge Voices

Lady Willcocks was interviewed on 18 June 2003 at her home in Cambridge.

RW.   The move from Worcester came much sooner than one would have liked really, because Boris Ord became very ill. I rang up my mother and said, 'Quite soon I *may* want you to look for a house within ten minutes of the King's Choir School with a garden and a garage and three bedrooms.' To my surprise, only three days later she rang back and said, 'I heard in the butcher's that Lady Barcroft is moving. Her house isn't on the market, but I think you had better come and look at it.' David was away in Hull giving a recital and so I tucked the current baby under my arm and came over incognito to look at the house. I made an offer subject to contract and then I rang up David and said, 'I've found a house with a minstrel's gallery, I think it will do.'

O.   This was the house in Grange Road, where you've lived ever since?

RW.   Yes. It was much bigger than anything we had lived in before, but it's proved to be very satisfactory. It had space to have live-in help for the children, and we had a string of au pairs until the children decided they didn't want people looking after them any more.

O.   How did it feel, coming back to live in Cambridge?

RW.   All my Cambridge world had gone really; it was all quite new to me. I had spent the war years down in Cornwall, because my mother thought it safer than Cambridge. We were there on holiday when war broke out and we stayed there. Back at Cambridge women who weren't academic were very much pushed aside by the university. I remember David went to a feast in King's and the wives were invited to come down later to hear the speeches. So you ate your boiled egg at home, cycled to college, and then sat up in the gallery, where you were given sherry and listened to the speeches while the cigar smoke came up from below, where they drank their fifth wine. It was a few years later that women academics were invited to dine, and now of course colleges are co-educational and have women dons.

O. What was it like raising children in Cambridge?

RW. Well, I think it is a lovely place to have children. Ours went to the local primary school, and then the girls went on to the Perse School for Girls, and the boys went where David very much wanted them to go, to Clifton College. Jonny went there on a music scholarship, having been a chorister at King's, and James followed him. I found myself bringing up the children really on my own. David was out at eight o'clock in the morning, then again at half past three, and usually he didn't come back until half past ten. He always had holidays with us, three times a year, but he didn't see the children much in-between times.

O. What about David with the boys at King's?

RW. I think he most enjoyed working with the choristers and had a great rapport with them. He would struggle along at ten past eight in the morning and be greeted by these bright little faces; their enthusiasm really got him going. He had various little tricks to keep their attention and one of them was that the boys were allowed one yawn, but after a second yawn they were taken out-side into the yard and their heads put under the cold tap. This kept everyone amused. If things were getting slow, David would do a couple of yawns himself and the boys would leap to action, 'Sir, sir, under the tap, sir!', and drag him off for a soaking. It all added to the general spirit of things.

O. You said when they were laughing the pitch was better?

RW. Yes. I forget what the technical thing is, but you're less likely to sing flat if you are laughing and relaxed. I don't think he necessar-ily had that trouble with the boys, but with adult sopranos getting a bit tired at the end of the day, he'd find something to make them laugh to stop them going flat. He has various ploys to keep a choir's attention. He never lets anybody sit about. If the tenors are having to work on a special thing, the sopranos would be asked to do it too, to see if they could do it better.

O.   You went on some of the choir tours, I think, didn't you?

RW.   Yes, I did. I was asked if I would like to go as second matron while my son Jonny was a chorister, but when I asked him what he thought, he said 'Daddy organist, yes; Mummy matron, no!', so I waited until he had left the school. I was only in charge once, for just two days in Holland. The regular matron didn't come for some reason. The other times I was in charge of shirts and surplices, which was much more my line, though I must say in West Africa it was difficult to get them dry in that very humid climate.

O.   What about the choral scholars, did you see much of them?

RW.   Not really, though we had a tradition of entertaining them here at the house at Christmas, as well as having a party for the choristers. We used to give them tea after the carol service in one of the rooms in King's, which we used to do ourselves. I was a great one for 'do it yourself'—I'm a peasant at heart, you know!—instead of having a caterer. The children and I would listen to the carol service on the radio while we got things ready. My whole first year of marriage I thought, 'If I can save money, David won't have to work so hard.' Little did I realize, that wasn't what was driving him.

Anne Willcocks is Sir David's younger daughter. She was interviewed on 25 June 2003 at the Athenaeum Club in London.

AW.   Dad was much stricter as a conductor than he ever was as a father. He would say, 'Rachel, are they allowed to roll the tomatoes along the table?' He would never ever discipline us, that was entirely Mum's province. When he was at home he was very focused on us, playing cards, ball games, anagrams, and all sorts of things. When we got older we would go to France in the summer. We went to different places which Dad had searched out with the map. What he really wanted was somewhere exactly like Cornwall but without the crowds. So he'd work out from maps somewhere that was west-facing, with good surf, high cliffs, and long sandy beaches. Surfing was not really known in Brittany at that time; we were thought to be extraordinary with our old wooden boards. Mum's mother was one of the first people to surf on a board. We were inveterate surfers with these old wooden curved boards, and in fact Mum and Dad still surf.

We'd try to catch the same wave and come in together. Dad would also do these fantastic mazes on the beach, carving them in the sand with a spade. At home, he'd sometimes tell us these rather exciting stories at bedtime, then Mum would have to tell us a nice, quiet, soporific story to calm us down afterwards. Mum made sure we got our prep done and did our practice and got to school on time and had the right clothes. When Dad was recording, we'd usually go away for a week because it was so intense. We'd go off on a narrow boat on a canal, and Mum would leave little instructions: 'Tuesday lunch', 'Tuesday supper', all neatly in a row in the fridge. I don't think many of them were eaten—he'd be quite hungry by the time we got back!

O.   What about grandchildren? How have they reacted to him?

AW.   Well, they absolutely adore him. Whatever he does he really focuses on it. Even if he's playing 'Grandmother's footsteps', he plays to win. Mum would always let us win if it was late in the evening, but Dad didn't make any concessions, so if you actually beat him you know you've beaten him fair and square. Sometimes he gets the grandchildren to play a tune. They play a few notes and then he improvises around those notes—they love that.

O.   That spirit helped with choristers too, I'm sure.

AW.   I remember one time during a choristers' party some carol singers came to the door. He got the boys to hide up the stairs, then invited the carol singers into the house. They plodded through a couple of carols, and then Dad asked them to sing 'O come, all ye faithful'. When they came to 'Sing, choirs of angels', this almighty descant broke out from high up the house! Those poor carol singers must have left wondering what on earth was happening. We did give them some mulled wine, but we never had carol singers at the door again.

The Very Reverend Michael Till was Chaplain and later Dean of King's College, Cambridge from 1967 to 1981. He was interviewed on 14 June 2003 in the Deanery at Winchester Cathedral.

MT.   I first met David when I was one of the candidates for the chaplaincy at King's. The Chaplain had to sing the service, so an important part of the session was to go across and be heard by David.

David, I think, found me the least musical of the candidates, and my secret hunch is that the college appointed me out of a sense of malice for the Organist. But he set about turning a pig's ear into a pigskin purse by getting me singing lessons. We were very good friends, and it was good working with him. Later, when the Dean left, I was asked to stay on and be Dean and Director of Studies and a fellow and so on.

O.   David tells a wonderful story about your appointment to the Deanship. He changed a certain hymn for evensong?

MT.   There was no hymn for evensong—he included one. I thought evensong was over, but then the head choral scholar got up and announced the hymn; it was 'Now thank we all our God'! It was the first I knew that *they* knew I'd been appointed, because I'd only been told on my way over to evensong that I'd been elected at the Congregation in the College.

O.   Do you remember your first carol service?

MT   Yes. The choreography of these things had to be worked out very carefully with the choir behind closed doors. The Chaplain had to say, 'Look, forget about the music for a moment, just make sure we all get from A to B'. They were never entirely tolerant of that. I remember on a choir tour with David, in Canada, one of the boys said to me, 'Why do we always have to rehearse getting on and off the platform?' And I said, 'Because if we don't, you'll end up in a broom cupboard.' We arrived in Prince Edward Island and there was no time to rehearse because in fact the plane was late, and at the interval they went off into a broom cupboard!

O.   What about tours?

MT.   The one to West Africa was tremendous. David was asked to give a masterclass in the Cultural Centre in Kumasi. The local choirs had chosen to sing 'Crimond'* and the 'Hallelujah Chorus'. We left David to it and soon he had this *huge* crowd of people from different choirs singing 'Crimond' wonderfully, and he was getting them to show the King's College Choir just how to sing the 'Hallelujah Chorus'. We combined in a concert outside that night. He was great with a crowd of people he'd never met before and getting them

* 'Crimond' is the name of the popular melody by Jessie Seymour Irvine (1836–87) written in 1872 for 'The Lord's my Shepherd' (Psalm 23).

to sing. I found the first time I really began to understand who David was, was when I got around in *front* of him when he was conducting—that's when you really saw the quality and the character of him.

O. You were Dean at that very difficult time at the end of the 1960s and the early 1970s, when 'traditional Church' was . . .

MT. A rude word! David had a strong sense of tradition in a college which was trying to be as radical as it could be and which found the traditional side of the Chapel's existence a deep embarrassment to its forward-looking, liberal, atheistic self. At a distance, that's quite funny, but there were days when it wasn't. We had to work very hard to make sure we inhabited that world happily and successfully. At the same time, the number of people who were there at that time that have been ordained since is really quite remarkable. I think Chapel and the choir and music had a lot to do with it, because you could find it accessible without having to sign up to anything. You could be there on your own terms.

O. What about the big choral concerts? You often allowed CUMS to use the Chapel for big events.

MT. One of the things about that Chapel is that it is one of the five-star buildings of Europe. It and its music tradition are part of a national, certainly, cultural heritage. Therefore you have an obligation to be sharing this with people, while still allowing it to function as a college chapel. I liked to make these things happen.

O. Your Deanship overlapped both David's and Philip Ledger's time at King's.

MT. One day in Cambridge I was with David and Philip Ledger when one asked the awkward question, 'What do you think is the difference between us in the way we conduct the choir?' So I said, 'I think David has this strong sense of the chord and the pitch, and Philip seems to have this strong sense for the shape of the phrase.' Luckily they agreed—I might have been murdered by both of them!

O. Do you have a favourite David story or anecdote that lingers in your mind?

MT. Whenever I meet anyone who was one of his choral scholars or his choristers, they immediately start imitating him, for example by the way he strokes the side of his face or his 'hmmm'—no matter whether he ever does these things any longer, he does them in the popular memory. But some of the happiest memories of David are of him as a fine player of ball games, or polishing off the crossword puzzle pretty fast in the morning, or spotting hilarious misprints in documents. We were rolling around with laughter at some of David's discoveries!

O.   Is there one performance of David's that really lives in your memory?

MT.   I think the one that lingers is a *Dream of Gerontius* which they did with Benjamin Britten conducting and Peter Pears singing Gerontius. David was utterly part of that. I'd forgotten to get any tickets, so I sat in the organ loft. It came to that point where there's that shimmering line which says, 'here every instrument shall play as loudly as it can' before the main 'Take me away'— that wonderful, wonderful moment. At that point David breathed in to support his way into that huge chord he was about to play, and as he did so, all the music fell off the organ, all over the floor. It was so old, his score, that every sheet was severed from every other, and there was no retrieving any of it. But he didn't notice, by then he was on another planet, and he was straight in—it was tremendous! Those three musicians were making music as best they could and at the top of their game—it was a wonderful occasion.

Sir Philip Ledger was a student at King's College, Cambridge when Sir David returned in 1957, and succeeded him as Director of Music in 1974. He was interviewed on 21 June 2003 at his home in Gloucestershire.

PL.   I first met David in 1957, when he became my supervisor and I later played as the accompanist for the CUMS chorus, which he conducted.

O.   I think he played for your wedding?

PL.   It was in 1963 when I was Organist at Chelmsford Cathedral. David had asked me what I would like him to play before the service and I'd said, 'The Prelude and Fugue in A Major by Bach.' He said, 'Oh I know, you'll be sitting there listening to see if I make a pedal mistake!' Of course he didn't make any pedal mistakes; he was a very accurate player. I remember Boris saying, 'You listen to David. Most people hurry when they get to a difficult bit, even good musicians, but David just slightly steadies himself.' That, perhaps, is how he approaches a lot of things. When it gets difficult, he just slightly steadies himself.

O. You must have a good Willcocks story from those days.

PL. Well, there are some oft-repeated stories. One that I remember was after the broadcast of one of the carol services. The Director of Music received a huge number of letters after these, most of them extremely complimentary. David replied to all these letters punctiliously. He loved corresponding. This letter said that the only thing which marred the service was that the choral scholars' hair was too long and unkempt. David replied graciously and in a post-script added that he had it on good authority that Our Lord himself wore his hair long. I thought that this was a marvellous way of answering that letter! On another occasion one of the choral scholars saw David driving his car along Grange Road at great speed but leaving it in first gear. He asked David later why he'd done this, and he said, 'I was in such a hurry that I didn't have time to change gear!'

O. Then, of course, you followed David as Organist and Director of Music at King's in 1974?

PL. That's right, yes. I succeeded him as Conductor of CUMS in October 1973 and took over as Director of Music at King's in January 1974. In some ways, it was the most difficult task that I've had in my career. The problem was that David was doing everything marvellously, so it was a case of trying to maintain something which was running at peak. David was very encouraging. The dominant thing about the Chapel is the acoustic, which is very resonant. It doesn't let you sing *fortissimo*. It loves you singing *pianissimo*, provided it's beautifully in tune. You have to be careful that you enunciate the consonants very clearly. So there's a kind of tradition of singing in King's which works, and David taught me how to use it.

O. What about the difference in working with King's and with large amateur choruses?

PL. Well, all the choristers and choral scholars were excellent musicians, so one could expect the highest possible standards, but choral societies are a bit different and tend to be made up from a wide range of people. This would certainly have been true in David's case when he conducted The Bach Choir, and it was true of CUMS. The conductor is doing a major job of 'encouraging', and that is where David is so skilful. He can stand in front of any group of singers in any part of the world, and they respond because he encourages them, he makes them laugh, and they want to give of their best.

O.   So was he one of your principal teachers and mentors?

PL.   I regard two people as having had the most influence on me as a musician. The first was David because he taught me everything about music-making, the professional music scene, how to conduct myself, and how to get the best out of people. The other person was Benjamin Britten, with whom I worked very closely. He was a completely different character who taught me about chamber music and orchestral conducting.

O.   Any other memories?

PL.   I remember coming back to Cambridge on the train from a Bach Choir rehearsal in London. David had been conducting and I'd been playing. He was writing the descant to 'O come, all ye faithful' for the verse 'Sing, choirs of angels', later published in *Carols for Choirs 1*. He said, 'I thought to myself, "What would angels be singing in heaven? They'd be singing *Gloria, hosanna in excelsis*" ', and, in his descant, he quotes the music for these words from the first two bars of the refrain for 'Ding dong! merrily on high'—the 'Gloria' sequence. I have always thought this was brilliant!

Sir Neville Marriner and the Academy of St Martin in the Fields performed and recorded frequently with Sir David. His son, Andrew, was a chorister at King's College, Cambridge during Sir David's time. He was interviewed on 18 January 2005 at his home in London.

NM.   David and I started working together in the 1960s when he invited us to work with him in recording choral repertoire. The Academy was immensely indebted to David for putting them on record, because our reputation was fairly local whereas his reputation at King's was international. David has this extraordinary, quiet authority, which orchestras admire. It's the authority of someone who knows exactly what he's doing and what he wants from the music. The discipline within the choir itself was extraordinarily high and so we behaved ourselves while we were there! But once the work was over David was a very good host, and I remember we had splendid evenings at King's. Most recordings were in the summer because in the winter the temperature dropped to sub-zero and recording companies are not over-enthusiastic about working in those conditions.

O.   Did David do all the conducting and you were the leader?

NM.   Absolutely. It was a good combination, because David did not wish to get involved with the purely technical aspects of orchestral playing like up and down bows, but he knew interpretatively what he wanted, and because he knew the acoustic of the Chapel so well, he always got a good sound from the orchestra. One of his great virtues was that he was able to encapsulate a choral piece as a whole unit and get the relationship between the various sections and the tempos to work so well. He was undoubtedly the boss in these recordings, always.

O.   What about his move to London?

NM.   He was a breath of fresh air at the Royal College of Music, because he brought his experience of working with young people. His flair and conducting experience made a difference to the quality of the orchestras at the College and the choral work suddenly assumed a new standard. The students were very fortunate to have David as their head. He was good at the administrative burden—or perhaps he surrounded himself with very able administrators—but certainly the building ran very smoothly.

O.   How did the orchestral players respond to David?

NM.   Usually with choral conductors, orchestras are immensely dismissive. I don't know whether it's a natural instinct, or they don't like the gestures, or they don't like the technical efforts that the choral conductors make, because certainly some of them do have to make rather looser gestures to the chorus to get the sounds they want. David didn't suffer from these sorts of frailties. Technically he could always get the orchestra to produce the same ensemble as he could with the chorus.

Roy Goodman was a chorister at King's College, Cambridge from 1959 to 1964 and was the treble soloist in Sir David's famous recording of the Allegri *Miserere*. He was interviewed on 16 September 2003 at his home in Bishop's Stortford, Hertfordshire.

RG.   I suppose my claim to fame was the recording of the Allegri *Miserere* which David had transcribed. It wasn't a very famous piece at that time. I'd been playing rugby that afternoon and rushed rather breathless into the Chapel. David went down the line listening to one boy after another, and then it was my turn and I had just about got my breath back. He said something very simple like 'that's the one'. We recorded, I suppose, a couple of complete takes and I had to sing like a bird and hope all the top Cs worked out.

O.   Did David choose his soloists like that on the day?

RG.   You never knew very far in advance that you were going to sing a solo. It was always really who was the best on the day, and you just hoped that you were going to be on form. That would happen for the Nine Lessons and Carols, for example. We would be waiting outside the vestry, very quietly, and there would be maybe two or three boys whom David had heard singing that morning, and he may have made his mind up already, but you were not told until just literally a few minutes before.

O.   I am sure singing with David at King's was a huge part of your early life.

RG.   I loved him; he was wonderful with the choir. David came out with magic somehow: reasons for us to give of our best.

David Briggs was Headmaster of King's College School from 1959 to 1977. He was interviewed on 19 June 2003 in Cambridge.

DB.   The relationship between the Headmaster of a choir school and the Organist has certain problems in that both officials, in their different capacities, are concentrating on a particular aspect of the boys' work, but we managed to get on together very well. We had a curious ritual attached to the school's outdoor swimming pool. One of the things I remember most about David was that he loved dressing up in all sorts of extraordinary garbs. Every year in May, when our pool was opened, the boys put a couple of long poles across the pool and he and I dressed up in various things and approached each other with a pillow from opposite sides. We then had a sort of pillow fight over the pool to see who was knocked over first. This was sometimes preceded by a trumpet flourish from one of the boys. Silly things like this helped us to work happily together. The thing I connect him with particularly is carols. I remember when David was given a doctorate somewhere or other a little boy asked, 'Is he a Doctor of Carols?'

O.   Tell me a little about David in his role with the boys.

DB.   A choirmaster has the same difficulties as a schoolmaster. You have to steer a course between being strict and being indulgent, but mostly it's a matter of leading by example. David's energy was infectious. Obviously there were occasions when people would displease him, but on the whole, considering the rigorous timetable that the choristers had, I think it really all worked remarkably well. I remember him as a very lively and generous person.

Christopher Morris was head of music publishing at Oxford University Press from 1975 to 1986. He was interviewed on 11 June 2004 at his home in London.

CM.   Alan Frank, who was my predecessor as Music Editor of OUP, and I discussed who should replace Ernest Bullock and Harold Darke, who had been joint editors of OUP's church music leaflets. We both thought of David, and so he became general editor. We got to know each other quite well because, being a very meticulous person, David read all the submitted manuscripts and proofs. I looked after the church music. I am an organist, and Alan Frank was not, so he left the church music and carols to me. I had decided that the *Oxford Book of Carols* was miles out of date, because it was strictly a carol book. This meant that certain popular carols like 'Hark! the herald-angels sing' and 'O come, all ye faithful', which everyone thinks of as Christmas carols, were excluded by the editors because they were considered to be hymns or songs. However, I discovered that the contract with the three editors of the *Oxford Book of Carols*—Vaughan Williams, Martin Shaw, and Percy Dearmer—stated that the contents of the book could not be changed without their permission. Fair enough, but they were all dead, and their widows would not agree to any changes. So I did a new edition, adding original texts for the carols, which made it a more interesting book, but wasn't what I really wanted. I then approached David, who said it would be very nice if we could find a book, for instance, for choral societies' annual carol concerts, that had everything included, so that the singers, instead of having fifteen sheets of paper under their seats, could merely turn to page seventeen for the next carol! So we worked on the idea of having a book which would provide music for a whole concert. In fact we originally thought of calling it *Carols for Concerts*, but we soon changed it to *Carols for Choirs*, because we realized that it was suitable for church choirs as well. The first book was edited by Reginald Jacques and David. After Jacques died, David very cleverly brought John Rutter on board, and they edited the next three books, which are still best-sellers. They finished with *100 Carols for Choirs* in 1987, which contained what they saw as the best from their other books, plus some new ones. It's a fine book. I have a dedication in my copy: 'For Christopher, the father of *Carols for Choirs*', and it is signed 'David and John, 1987'.

O. Now, when you were compiling the carols did you make the lists, or did David?

CM. It was marvellous fun. We used to meet at Reginald Jacques's house, because it was down the road from me, here in Kensington. We all brought our little lists of what we thought should go in —it was definitely a joint effort. We always managed to get a unanimous agreement on a carol. They had to decide who was going to do the arranging of each carol, and David used to say, 'I bags that one'. Jacques didn't really mind very much who did it.

Christopher Bishop was a recording producer and then chief producer for EMI from 1964 to 1979, and was responsible for many of the much-loved recordings of the King's College Choir under Sir David and Sir Philip. He was interviewed on 1 November 2006 in Aldeburgh.

CB. I went to EMI as a 'cub' producer in 1964, and one of the first things I managed to do was to persuade them to get the King's College Choir under contract. It wasn't a very difficult thing to do because my boss was very keen on the idea. I thought the one thing I could bring to a huge company like EMI was my knowledge of the choral world. It worked very well. We went on making records with David until he left in 1973. What EMI wanted above anything else, not surprisingly, were carols, because the carols from King's are a huge seller. Where would David be without Christmas? Or Christmas without David? He was not inclined to give us that straightaway. We started recording in August 1964 with *Byrd and his Contemporaries*, which is a fairly esoteric record, but a very beautiful one. We made another record called *Christmas to Candlemas,* which has anthems for both those feasts but no carols. Then in January 1965 we made *Family Carols.* This was David's sop to us. We did a very enjoyable record, but it was with The Bach Choir and the Jacques Orchestra, not with the King's Choir. Then we did *Hodie* by Vaughan Williams and *Dixit Dominus* and then *Sing Praises.* The first carol record proper we got was in July 1969—that's five years he strung us along without any carols from the choir! But the next year we made another record called *Once in Royal David's City.* David managed to persuade us that we weren't there just to make carols. Part of the game was that he recorded for Argo, then an independent record company, and they made some smashing records. Argo had recorded Boris Ord doing carols, among other things, and we were always slightly afraid that they would take over, but they didn't. One of my very favourite records with David was the *Paukenmesse* of Haydn, which with *Dixit Dominus* were his early records with orchestra for EMI. He hadn't done a great deal with orchestra for Argo, but we could offer him that chance. We did a lot of Vaughan Williams and the Bach motets. We did these unaccompanied,

except for *Lobet den Herren*—you have to have the organ bass or
you get second inversions, as David pointed out.

O. What about the Fauré Requiem and Bob Chilcott's lovely solo?

CB. EMI liked the idea of doing the Fauré Requiem with the King's
Choir, but they wanted Victoria de Los Angeles to sing 'Pie Jesu' and
Dietrich Fischer-Dieskau to sing the baritone solo, and I said, 'No,
no, no, if we're going to do it, we must do it as Fauré did it originally,
with a boy treble as soloist, and why don't we use John Carol Case,
who had been a choral scholar and made the King's sound, as the
baritone.' That again was a success. Chilcott sang beautifully.

O. Tell me the story about the famous and much-loved recording of
psalms.

CB. EMI wanted a record of hymns with descants, that David does so
well. In due course he did produce that as *Hymns for all Seasons*, but
the first time we went to record these I arrived up there with all
the equipment, and David hadn't finished the hymn arrangements.
I think he was just too busy. I asked what we could record instead.
David suggested a Tye mass, but even a mass by Byrd wouldn't have
sold close to what we were aiming for. We looked at the music lists
and thought, 'How about the psalms?' The choir wouldn't need to
practise as they sang them every day. I rang up EMI and spoke
with my boss, Kinloch Anderson, a Scot, who was the chief producer at the time. He said, 'What a terrible idea, how dreadful', but
he thought we meant Scottish metrical psalms, which are really
very dreary. I said, 'Anglican psalms are wonderful.' Anyway, I got
permission to do it, having really put my head on the block. But
of course, it sold very well. David was wonderful at psalms. I have
those records in my car, and whenever I feel stressed I play them.
I find them most wonderful: the words, the fabulous choir, the
fabulous singing, and David's word rhythm—absolutely perfect.

O. What about the practical issues of recording in King's?

CB. We used to get quite a lot of traffic noise. You could filter it out to
some extent. Nowadays you couldn't, but in those days the fre-
quency response at the bottom end wasn't that good. We did have
trouble with birds. We'd sometimes record quite late in the evening
in the summer, and they would sit up on the west window chirp-
ing. We had space mikes at the back, and they picked up all these
blasted birds. It was like Messiaen! So I wrote a note for the record

of the quadraphonic version of *Anthems from King's*, issued in 1974: 'This quadraphonic recording was made with some microphones at the west end of the Chapel, in order to give a spatial effect. Listeners with good ears (and equipment) will notice the sound of birds outside the west window, singing their own evensong.' This did the trick and we had no complaints. King's College Chapel is a difficult place to record in.

O.   Did you keep the choir in their normal divided position in the stalls for regular choral works and have separate microphones on decani and cantoris?

CB.   If we were doing something antiphonal, like psalms or a double-choir piece such as 'Faire is the Heaven', we certainly would have done that, but if it had been something in four parts, we would normally put them all on the same side. We would have had one central mike, very high, which got the acoustics, and probably three microphones down each side, so you could really control the sound. The problem is you have to have high ones to get the men, because the boys are at one level and the men are at a higher level. We didn't always record in the choir stalls; sometimes, for example for *The Creation*, we set up in front of the organ screen, facing the west end. There's no room for an orchestra in the choir stalls. But straight choir music we usually recorded in the choir stalls. It doesn't sound like King's if you don't.

O.   What about working with boys?

CB.   The King's boys were so professional and so used to recording and performing all the time. They wouldn't do more than one session a day, normally. The sessions lasted three hours with a break in the middle. Sometimes we'd do two sessions a day. I don't remember there ever being a problem with tiredness, unless we did some-thing very, very difficult. They were so well trained.

O.   Did David spend much time listening to takes, or did he pretty much trust you?

CB.   He didn't spend a great deal of time. To start with he used to want to come and hear it all afterwards, but then he gave that up after a time. If a producer gets the trust of the conductor, it's marvellous because you don't then have to waste time listening on sessions. But sometimes you want a conductor to listen, so you can show him what's wrong. It's best if the conductor gets the balance right in the studio. It shouldn't be done by the engineer. You should record the performance that's going on. I'm very much opposed to the system where you have endless microphones and lots of tracks, and you fiddle about with the sound afterwards. The balance has got to be natural. It's not that difficult to get a choir properly balanced, but much harder when you have an orchestra as well.

O.   Were you aware of any great changes in the sound of the King's College Choir before and after David?

CB.   The choir's conductors that I've known have been Boris, David, and Philip. I think there was a much greater change between Boris and David than there was between David and Philip. Boris was so relaxed and could be immensely emotional, doing things like the Collegium Regale service of Howells. There's much more precision with David, all the lines were much clearer, but you have to be careful comparing because recording techniques have developed dramatically. When Boris made his records they were only in mono. I don't think recorded sound has improved much since about 1970. There may be more bass, and there's certainly no 'crackle-and-pop' on CDs, but I don't think many of them are a great deal better.

O.   You have worked with some of the greatest conductors in the world in your career. How was working with David from a practical standpoint?

CB.   David was a marvellous person to work with. He was wonderfully easy at taking ideas and was full of ideas himself. He didn't get overexcited about things. He'd come back after a marvellous take, and I might say, 'David, that was absolutely superb', and he'd say, 'Oh, yes, good'. He was sort of restrained, *English*, you know, in that sort of way, and yet in his performances that's not the case, you can hear the drama. In that respect, I think *The Creation* is marvellous.

Bob Chilcott was a chorister and choral scholar at King's College, Cambridge with Sir David, and also a student at the Royal College of Music during Sir David's tenure.

BC.   I enjoyed the choristership audition. I remember it was all rather marvellous and slightly misty. Of course David had that glint in his eye which he still has now. He was extremely kind, and made it very easy to do the audition. At that time we all came from different backgrounds. I don't think that's quite the same now because there aren't the number of boys' choirs singing in churches from which the boys can be gathered, so they tend now to come from a much more particular type of background. I went up in 1964. David's impact with the choristers was immediate. We learned by example—that is purely how we did it. The younger boys would sit next to the older boys, and they would have to beat time with their fingers, and you would just learn from what they did.

O.   Do you remember much about David's rehearsals?

BC.   Yes, we all adored him. He had a tremendous gift with boys. He was very tough, actually. He wouldn't let you get away with anything, but he did it in a way that never discouraged. He could get furious, but always in a way that made you want to do better. David was a man with a passion for doing it right. He could be so marvellously silly and open. We rehearsed in a classroom you would have the piano facing out into a horseshoe of tables, three sides of a square, and on either side of David was a junior boy, and then a senior boy behind, one each side. The junior boy in front would have to turn the pages, and if he got it wrong David would cajole or scold him, but in an encouraging way. It was a very good way of monitoring what was going on; he let the older boys lead, so he gave them their wings. On the rare occasions he was late, we were absolutely thrilled. We'd be playing football out on the front field, waiting for him. He would come on his bike and he'd put the bike down and join in. That was a spontaneous thing that made us realize he was always on our side. It was marvellous, but the trouble was, as you know, he was a fine sportsman: he could outrun you, he could outskill you, everything. One would never get away with this now, but when we had a Christmas party, the big thrill was all sixteen of us getting into David's station wagon, his estate car which was an Austin Princess, with the back open, and he'd drive through Cambridge with everyone in the back— boys with their legs dangling out the back. David set everything in motion really for all of us. We were massively influenced. There was no going back, because he'd shown us a glimpse of something which was new and so exciting. It was a level to which most of us never even aspired or knew existed. We were shown the beauty of what we could do. I was lucky—I sang the 'Once in royal David's city' for three years running.

O.   That must be a record.

BC.   Yes. At that time there wasn't the thing they have now of saying, 'You're going to sing it today.' David prepared me. I can remember standing with him in the antechapel of King's in front of the organ screen, and he said, 'Imagine there are hundreds of people sitting there, and they are all cabbages.' He was marvellous, and it did prepare me. The ultimate for me was to sing the 'Pie Jesu' on the Fauré Requiem recording in 1967 and that was a marvellous thrill. My voice was nearing its end then, and I remember struggling a bit with the solo and struggling with nerves and that sort of thing, but it worked out quite well. David was very encouraging. The release of that recording in 1968 coincided with the death of my father, which was quite a dramatic time in my life. I was only twelve years old, and I'd been away from home for four of those years. David was incredibly sympathetic. He said, 'Chilcott'—because they always called you by your surname—'I'm very, very sorry to hear about your father.' He said it a few times and graciously, and it was beautifully expressed. He said no more than he had to, and then he said, 'Now run along.' That was a fine, kind of 'Now get on with the job' comment.

O.   Probably what you needed to hear.

BC.   Absolutely right. One of the last times my parents met David was when we went up to London to sing in a performance of *The Hymn of Jesus* by Gustav Holst at the Royal Festival Hall in April 1968. David conducted. The recording engineer, Christopher Bishop, had a pre-release version of the Fauré there, and he gave it to my parents. They were so proud. My father died the month after.

O.   So your father got to hear it.

BC.   Exactly. It was a very special thing in my life, and my family's life. A few years later, I went to hear the choir perform the *Five Mystical Songs* of Vaughan Williams, and I was totally overwhelmed by how good the choir was. I remember the experience of going to King's College Chapel and seeing the magnetism of that choir. It was a magnetism David had instilled. I thought, 'I've got to get back in that choir,' which I did as a Choral Scholar. I just had a term with David, and then Philip came. That was an exciting time, too. After King's, I went to the Royal College of Music for two years, so I came across David again as Director and with the chorus in the College. This was very important for me when I took over the chorus at the College in 1997—it was the first real conducting that I'd done. The very first thing I did with the College chorus was the Brahms Requiem, and David was going to conduct it. I was very determined to prepare that choir as I knew David would want. We worked very hard, and it was a fantastic choir, I have to say. I think David was rather thrilled, and he was lovely. He made a fantastic impact on that choir and gave a great energy. He was seventy-nine at that time. The nineteen-year-old sopranos would come up and say, 'Bob, how old did you say he was?' I said, 'He's seventy-nine.' They said, 'Oh, but he's gorgeous.' I told David that, and he was sort of very coy and said nothing, but he was obviously very pleased. The following year he came back again and we did the Fauré Requiem. He got the head of the Student's Union to get stereo equipment on the stage for the final rehearsal. He said, 'I'll give five pounds to anyone here who can tell me who this is.' He played the 'Pie Jesu' from the Fauré Requiem I had sung, and someone put a hand up and said, 'It's Mr Chilcott.' David said, 'Yes, good,' and handed over his five pound note. I find now in my conducting work it's David who is always there in the back of my mind. There are lots of other influences as well, but David is the kind of starting point really, because that's where it all started for me.

O.   How was David as an administrator at the Royal College?

BC.   He was very clever in that role. He was fantastic at it, actually. He left that place in fantastic shape. Behind it there must be a tremendous iron will. Because he commanded a lot of respect, he could get the right people to help him achieve what he thought was right for the place.

O.   Is there a particular genre of music that you associate with him or a particular composer?

BC.   One of the things that had the biggest influence on me was psalm singing: the way he dealt with text and stress and shape. He had a very special way with psalms. We used to rehearse them sometimes to the point where you would want to shoot yourself! I think in terms of composers, Howells and Vaughan Williams always stick in my mind. That was a massive influence. I do remember, too, the Haydn masses which we recorded. He also had a huge flair for those Handelian pieces—the style, actually. I heard his last performance of the *St Matthew Passion* with The Bach Choir in Symphony Hall in Birmingham. I hadn't heard The Bach Choir for years and they sang that piece with such delicacy and style . . . to hear a big choir sing like that was incredibly impressive.

John Rutter CBE was a student at Clare College, Cambridge during Sir David's tenure at King's, and was co-editor with Sir David of volumes 2–4 of *Carols for Choirs*, and *100 Carols for Choirs*. He was interviewed on 24 June 2003 in Duxford, near Cambridge.

JR. I first met David through his music and his music-making, and I think the year must have been 1961, which was just after the first volume of the *Carols for Choirs* series had been published. I remember the scene vividly. I was in a Presbyterian church in Kensington, where my school friend John Tavener was the organist. He rushed in one evening—I occasionally sang in the choir to help them out—and he had a green book in his hand. He said, 'Just listen to this', and he played the Willcocks descant to 'O come, all ye faithful'. Then I felt, as I still feel today, that it lights up the sky, just like the best descants should do and, of course, not so many descants really do. I thought this was just an extraordinary piece of writing that transformed a classic hymn into something more splendid and more inspiring than I could have imagined.

O. How did you eventually meet David?

JR. Word reached David that there was this chap called Rutter at Clare College, next door, and that he had been writing some carols. He evidently felt that his curiosity was roused and by that time he knew me from the harmony and counterpoint classes, and he sent me a little note saying, 'Can you come and bring these to me in my rooms in King's?' So, in fear and trembling, I did, and was just amazed when he said, 'Would you be interested in these being published?' Of course I knew that he was a part-time editor for

Oxford University Press, and he was able to take these manuscripts down to London and recommend them for publication, which he did. The next thing I knew I got an offer from OUP, which has remained my principal publisher ever since, so that's a relationship which I entirely owe to David Willcocks. He didn't make a bad recommendation. I've been, by and large, very happy with OUP for what's now a period of thirty-five years or more.

O. When did your work on *Carols for Choirs* begin?

JR. The year must have been 1969—my second postgraduate year, by which time I'd embarked on a PhD—when he invited me to be his co-editor for the second volume of the *Carols for Choirs* series. That was when we really got to know one another. Our work together on the 'orange book' was a very happy collaboration. By then I was in print, so I had a little more confidence, I think, and we were able to look at each other's work, and I had the courage sometimes to say, 'David, did you really mean *mezzo forte* there, or should that be *mezzo piano*?'—things like that—and he was equally, in a tactful way, able to say to me, 'Do you think that verse is a bit too grandiose? You might possibly recast that.' By and large he didn't, so when he did, I listened. I remember that working with him taught me quite a lot, not only about publication and proof-reading and the whole business of being an anthologist, but also something about leadership. He would grab me at the end of the Friday evening rehearsal of the CUMS Chorus, and say, 'Come back to Grange Road, we need to do some proof-reading.' It would be maybe eleven o'clock at night as we started, and he would make some coffee, and we'd pass proofs back and forth across the table. Midnight would come and go, one o'clock, two o'clock, maybe we'd get another cup of coffee. I would be flagging, for all that I didn't have any pressing engagement the next morning, and I would start to be a little bleary as I read the proofs on the table. David's energy only seemed to increase! Three a.m. would come and somehow the world would seem very quiet and still outside, but he was absolutely full of energy and would say, 'Oh come on, let's finish this off.' I remembered that he had to be up and bright-eyed for the chorister rehearsal at eight o'clock the next morning. I didn't have to be up at any particular time and I was the one who was flagging, and at the same time was considerably younger than he was. What I learned from that was that he never asked people to do things he wasn't prepared to do himself. There's no point in showing fatigue and weakness if you're trying to inspire somebody else. Anyway, the second volume came out and did very well.

O. So you saw David on a regular basis from this time?

JR. From time to time I was a visitor to his office in King's, which was always a hive of activity. There was invariably a large pile of papers and letters and scores and documents needing to be dealt with, and a succession of helpful and usually slightly harassed secretaries—I remember a dear lady called Mrs Radmore who sometimes found what was going on just slightly too much for her! With good reason, because people were contacting David from all over the world and not only writing, but turning up on the doorstep in person, with all manner of requests from 'Can I observe King's College Choir?' to 'Will you write a carol for my choir out in Idaho?'— whatever it may be, or 'Can you explain your twenty most important choir-training points, and will you write them down for me?'—this sort of thing. The demands on him came in from all sides.

Robert Tear was a choral scholar at King's College, Cambridge when Sir David returned to King's in 1957, and continued to sing with Sir David professionally. He was interviewed on 19 June 2003 in Cambridge.

RT. I was only eighteen when David arrived. It must have been difficult for him because Boris was the *grand seigneur* of church music, but he soon settled in. I was with him for three years, and he was fundamental to my subsequent career as a concert singer and an opera singer. David injected a new look into the choir. He was an absolute stickler about tuning. He felt that in the Chapel the major third should be very high, which has lasted with me forever. They almost got to fourths, but not quite. He had these wonderful eyebrows which he would sort of make go up into the heavens, and he would say, 'Flat, flat!' He put a lot of faith in me right from the start. He also beat me at squash regularly, which I found fairly galling. When you are a young man, you think you can beat this old guy, but you can't, you see.

O.   I think you have a very interesting relationship with David, because you went on to become a major international soloist and continued to work with him through the years.

RT.   Absolutely right! David was fundamental in actually starting my career. When I was about eighteen David conducted *The Damnation of Faust* by Berlioz in the Guildhall in Cambridge, and I sang Faust. It was an immense role which I should never have attempted, but he had that trust in what I could do. When I left—apart from, of course, supporting me when I went to St Paul's Cathedral doing a very similar job—he gave me my very first paid job, which was to sing *Messiah* in Great St Mary's. One of the soloists happened to be Dame Gwyneth Jones who was an alto at the time, and we both got paid five pounds.

O.   What do you think about David's work with the men and boys at King's versus the large mixed chorus of The Bach Choir?

RT.   He's got fantastic charisma with all choirs. He once said to all the women in The Bach Choir, 'How many of you think I am looking at you individually?' and about two hundred people put their hands up! King's was a much more sort of tight professional outfit. If we made a mistake in the rehearsal before service, we would have to raise our hands, and if we made a mistake in the service we would have to queue up under the organ screen to say, 'Sorry' personally, even though he may not have heard it. It was a military exercise! But without David my career, should I have had one, would have been totally and utterly different. I learned how to be a musician with him. He was the absolutely seminal influence in my life.

Richard Cooke was a Choral Scholar at King's College, Cambridge during Sir David's tenure. He was interviewed on 15 June 2006 at the Athenaeum Club in London.

RC.   David's flexibility and sense of timing with Christmas carols was better than anybody's I've ever worked with before or since. It wasn't only Christmas carols—his pacing of even basic things like hymns was also very impressive. I still do his tempos, because they strike me as having such dignity and depth.

O.   As a tenor, you should probably talk about David's bright thirds and tuning.

RC.   He was very keen on that sort of thing. We used to have a joke scale we would sing in the pub after evensong, where the major third was slightly higher than the fourth and the major seventh slightly higher than the octave. It was very hard for him, incidentally, when we went to Vienna—the first time he'd worked with original instruments. The idea of anything down a semitone was agony to him, because his perfect pitch was being pulled to shreds. That and the fact that these fundamentalists, as we call them these days, the original instrument people, liked flat major thirds. There is a very funny story when we were recording the *St Matthew Passion* with Nikolaus Harnoncourt and the Vienna Concentus Musicus. We'd arrived in Vienna and were absolutely exhausted from yet another tour of Holland. We had had to learn a lot of new repertoire. It was the summer holiday and we settled into this unclean university hostel. The floors were dirty, the loos were dirty, the whole place was pretty scrubby, and I was staying in a room with two other choral scholars. David flew in and in the afternoon he managed to find his way into our room—I suppose it wasn't locked. I found him rubbing these brand new Breitkopf copies of the *St Matthew Passion* on the floor. I went in and said, 'David, what in God's name are you doing?' He said, 'I think it's got to look as though we've done some rehearsal!' The copies had to look used.

O.   You are famous for your David stories—what are some others?

RC.   David was often in a bit of a panic before a concert. He could be very tetchy just as we were about to emerge in front of an audience. He'd be trying to get us to calm down and line up. We sort of knew what was going to happen. One time, he said, 'Yes, boys, line up in pairs in single file!' We would then create more chaos while we would work out how we could create 'single file' pairs.

O.   Any others?

RC.   There was an organist called Margaret Phillips; I'd got to know her when I was a student at King's. I went and heard an organ recital played by her, and it was so good that I thought I could recommend her to David to come do an organ recital in King's. She did that and it was very good indeed. It was just at the time when King's had announced it was going to have female students as well as male, one of the first three colleges in Cambridge to take women. Afterwards I met David downstairs, and he said, 'She's absolutely marvellous, isn't she! She's absolutely first class.' I said, 'Yes, David, she's fantastic.' David said, 'I can't understand how she reaches the pedals, but she was absolutely splendid, don't you think?' So I said, 'Yes, David, very good indeed.' He said, 'The time must come surely where we might have to think about having a female Organ Scholar in the College, don't you think?' So I said, 'Yes, David.' He said, 'I think if we have forty people applying for the post of Organ Scholarship, thirty-nine of them are men and one of them is a woman, and the woman is better than all of the men, then we'd have to take her, don't you think?' So I said, 'Well, yes, David.' He added, 'Well, yes, especially if she's sung all the music as a boy.'

Tim Brown was a Choral Scholar at King's College, Cambridge during Sir David's tenure. He was interviewed on 17 September 2003 at Clare College, Cambridge.

TB.   I came up in 1965, and joined the choir, and, as I always tell my choir here at Clare College, I was aware of the standard that was demanded by Sir David right from day one. Without him saying anything, he instilled such respect and discipline within the ranks of both the undergraduate men and the boys, that you knew that you just had to do your level best to get it right. And that was what it was like for three years. If you got it wrong, if you sang something wrong in a rehearsal, he was merciless. Because, and I think this is perhaps the thing I most remember about David, there was the sense in which you ceased to be an individual person, a personality. When you were in the choir, you were a cog in a wheel. In those days, in the mid-1960s, there was a kind of disciplined atmosphere, which I, coming from an independent boys' public school, was quite used to. It meant that you prepared and knew what you had to do. He was very clear and explicit in his instructions. Nobody had any doubt about what his standards were, and you wanted to give your best. I suppose if I had to sum up David in one single sentence it would be that 'he was an inspiration'. He was absolutely obsessive about tuning, ensemble, and, of course, correct notes. It took me a long time to come out of that extra-ordinary atmosphere that was David. Even now when he came in May 2003 to conduct my choir in evensong at the age of eighty-three, there was still that sense, when he walked into the room and started conducting my choir, youngsters he didn't know, that he has immense control. Not in a freakish way, but people just realize that here is somebody who has ears like nobody else's, and is able to spot immediately what's going wrong, what he can improve, what can tighten the ensemble, what can bring this into a unit. It's this kind of extraordinary sense of unity that he created when I was a student, which he does now, all these years later, which I just think is inspirational. David is one of the great organist conductors who learned their trade really in the organ loft, and not in the concert hall. Some people would criticize him for that. But I think the kind of discipline that was part and parcel of life in a cathedral choir and organ loft was something he brought to his work at King's, and he's taken it all over the world. He took it to the Royal College and to The Bach Choir. That's lost, I think, at one's peril. It's all very well having performances which are flamboyant and authentic and so on, but if they lack that kind of inherent sense of real musical discipline, I think one's lost something. His ability to create a *pianissimo* was astonishing. Likewise, his ability to create the grand sound was also wonderful, for instance in Parry's 'I was glad'. He had an instinctive feel for tempo, for pacing something, all those things of course are essential. I learned all those at his feet. He never made a big show about it, but that's just how he was, very disciplined. He worked himself harder than he worked any of us. That's the sign of a truly great person. He never stood back and let other people do the job. He was there working completely, intently, and that's what he expected of us.

O. Are there any special works you particularly associate with David?

TB. I suppose if there's one type of music above all, it's psalms. He had a wonderful sense of psalms. If anybody sang something wrong, if anybody got the pointing wrong in psalms, he would say, 'Oh, that probably means there's a mistake in the pointing.' He was terribly

aware of how we responded, and if somebody found it difficult to
sing the pointing, we'd very often change the pointing to accommodate that. He was constantly trying to get a way of singing
psalms that really communicated the text.

Brian Kay was a Choral Scholar at King's College, Cambridge during
Sir David's tenure and was a founding member of the King's Singers.
He was interviewed on 19 June 2006 at his home in Oxfordshire.

BK.   I will never forget the day that basically changed my life. I was shown
into this rather darkened room where all these strange-looking men
sat. I walked in there feeling very alone, very young, and desperately
inexperienced. There I was, coming from a Methodist school, with
a Methodist chapel upbringing, walking into this great seat of
Anglican worship and music. Mr Willcocks said, 'Mr Kay, would you
kindly sing this little piece of music by Mr Thomas Tomkins?' I'd
been brought up properly to do as I was told, so I did. I've never yet
worked out why I could sight-read, but for some reason I could, and
I sang it through. He said, 'Oh, that's very good, thank you.' Then he
said, 'I've got another little piece here called "The dove descending"
by Igor Stravinsky. Would you sing the bass part of this?' And again,
I sang it through. He gave me a few scales and ear tests, the usual sort
of thing, and then I went to sing in the Chapel of St John's, because
King's was closed at that time, and sang an aria from Bach's *Christmas
Oratorio*, 'Mighty Lord'. I worried around for the rest of the day
while everybody else had a go, and in the evening we all met in the
Senior Combination Room. David Willcocks and Alec Vidler, the
Dean, walked in and said, 'Thank you all for coming. The following
people we've selected: King's it's Kay. . . .' So that was the start of my
entire life in music. One of the many remarkable things about David
is his ability to choose the right voices. You needed to have the kind
of voice that he could obviously mould into his very rounded sound
and that wouldn't stick out in the choir. There is the story of a choral
scholar who became a very distinguished tenor. At one point David
reassuringly came up and said, 'Dear X, how are things going?' The
young man replied, 'Fine, David, I'm just beginning to sing out.'
David said, 'Oh, yes, *don't*.' There was in that word, *don't*, such a 'fear

factor' that the lesson had been learned in that single moment. David did have a remarkable way of making his feelings very clear, sometimes in a single word. You don't mess with the Big Man.

O.   Do you remember much about your first term there?

BK.   The Senior Choral Scholar, Bruce Pullan, took the new chaps under his wing and said, 'This is what we do. We go into the chapel in the morning and we pick up our little pile of music and we take it to our room and we learn it, and we come to the rehearsal at ten past four, knowing it. We rehearse for an hour, we have tea, and then it's evensong. That's the way it is for the rest of your three years.' So I did what I was told. I went and picked up my pile of music, learned it, turned up, and did the business. The first thing we sang was the final response, 'Thanks be to God'. Just those four words to those chords, and when we finished that final chord, and that sound just went on rolling around this building for a number of seconds, I thought I'd died and gone to heaven. David's influence was huge and has remained with me ever since. Forty-five years later I still think of him when I'm doing certain things.

O.   What about founding the King's Singers? David says he was a little bit sceptical in the beginning.

BK.   Oh, he said, 'Give it a go, but it won't work.' He's probably quite right. It's only been going now for thirty-eight years! He was genuinely concerned that we should all do something worthwhile in our lives. He didn't think this was going to be it, and I think he was probably right, but we happened to play the game reasonably successfully, and the thing took off. There was nothing quite like it at the time because we mixed sacred and profane in somewhat equal measure, and then it became slightly more profane and slightly less sacred as audiences demanded it. David advised us, and he is very proud to say, 'I said no, but you were right'. He's very happy to admit that it was worth a try, and he's always been wonderfully supportive. We took out of the college everything that he had to offer: a sense of pitch, rhythm, a sense of purpose, a sense of blend, all those things, straight down the line from King's. We couldn't have done it without him. He had his own reputation to maintain, and he had, even more importantly for him, I'm sure, the reputation of the King's Choir to maintain. If he didn't get what *he* wanted, and if he didn't get what he felt was worthy of the choir, then he made his feelings perfectly clear. I remember in my first term, he let Andrew Davis—now Sir Andrew, then an Organ Scholar—play the service and the two Senior Choral Scholars on each side beat out the time. David looked over the organ screen to see how things were going, and there were a couple of first-year people who weren't watching. He stormed into the choral scholars' vestry afterwards, and gave us hell. He did it in his own very forceful way. He came in and very determinedly said, 'If you do not watch, you are not worth a place in this great choir.' He let that hang for a minute, and then he left the room. My legs were like jelly. That's all he had to say. I think we were all absolutely shaken to the core. He was very good at that, and boy, did we work harder.

O.   What do you think is unique about David as a choral conductor?

BK.   He instils in everyone who sings for him a very specific sense of rhythm. I think what matters to him as much as anything is blend and balance between voices, which is just the basis of good choral singing, full stop. One of his most important attributes is his incredible charm. He can charm the birds off the trees and fantastic singing out of any number of singers. People would give their lives to sing under him. He stands there—as he gets older he gets more venerable—and everybody just worships him. People will watch him because they can't take their eyes off him. But if they don't, he's got all these techniques—the handkerchief on the head, and all those things—that get the results. People often describe it as the old saying 'Iron fist in a kid glove', but it's there. You don't mess about with him.

O.   If you had to choose one genre of music or one specific piece in which you think that David really excelled, what would it be?

BK.   One piece that always sticks out in the memory of choral scholars in my generation is the anthem with which we always ended the last service of the year—William Harris's 'Faire is the Heaven', which is such a masterpiece of unaccompanied double-choir writing. It was one of those little traditions, and it says such a lot about life and death and everything and music. Being so wedded to King's when you were there, your last day was a day of immense emotional upheaval. None of us could ever get through it. We would end up in floods of tears, completely out of it, and left it to the first- and second-year people to see the choir through the anthem. David was himself feeling that emotional tug. We all wanted to leave King's, we all wanted to leave Cambridge, we all wanted to go out into the real world, but our emotional ties were to this place.

Jonathan Willcocks is Sir David's elder son and sang with him as a chorister at King's College, Cambridge. He was interviewed on 20 June 2003 at the Royal Academy of Music in London.

JW.   It may surprise you that at home my father didn't actually play music very often. My earliest musical memories are of my mother playing the piano. She was really rather good before she married my father—I have found pieces of music with her name on that are really quite complicated and sophisticated—but after marrying my father I think she realized that, as far as serious music is concerned, one in the family was quite enough! My father was always completely involved in music. Some of my earliest memories are of childhood holidays down in Cornwall, but when I was playing on the beach, wanting him to do the usual father-like things—building sandcastles and kicking balls—he was often quite tied up sitting there on the beach doing carol arrangements. From the age of seven I became extremely involved in his musical life because I became a chorister at King's. Choristers are chosen by competitive audition— all the boys who wish to be considered come along and sing little prepared pieces or scales, just to assess the potential of their voices. These are boys aged about seven or eight. I think my parents might have had some doubts as to whether it was a good idea for me, as the son of the Director of Music, to be put in there. The first time I entered these contests I was not successful, which didn't worry me particularly at the time. One year on, I entered again and was selected, and from then on I had the very strange circumstance of seeing my father professionally for many hours each day for choir practices, but later seeing him at home as Daddy. I saw him much, much more in the musical guise than I did at home, because he was always very busy and quite often worked very long hours. So from the age of about eight through to twelve or thirteen I got completely used to calling him 'Sir' in the choir and he called me 'Willcocks', because the boy choristers were called by their surnames, and it didn't seem strange to me at all. As soon as we got outside or in the car, then it would be 'Daddy' and 'Jonny' again, completely as a normal parent. I saw much more of him than my brother and two sisters did—they were not involved in music in the same way, and so my involvement with him as a child was of a very different nature from theirs, which is quite interesting.

O.   What was life like for a chorister?

JW.   Remarkable. You're making music at a very high professional level from a very early age, for many hours every day. By the time I was twelve or thirteen I'd acquired a musical instinct purely through being involved in it. I could sight-read almost anything, I had a very good understanding of harmony and counterpoint, I had relative pitch, and an understanding of a very wide range of repertoire, just by immersion in the choir. He was a very firm disciplinarian. He was very clear about what he wanted, and wouldn't put up with any, even light-hearted, misbehaviour from the choristers. Choristers are boys and they like flicking candle wax and passing notes along in hymn books, but he treated them as professional musicians and expected exactly the same standards of concentration and punctuality and attention at rehearsals as he did from adults. The self-discipline that develops from that is very valuable and transferable to any other activity. His greatest skill, just viewing him as a musician, is bringing quite extraordinary things out of large amateur choirs. Whether he's working with one hundred or three hundred singers, or sometimes, as in concerts in the Royal Albert Hall, with four thousand singers, he has a fantastic ability to bring a discipline to them—to bring out a performance and ensemble— which is so far removed from the sum of the individual parts. Each singer will think he's really involved with them personally, and that's a great skill. I think there's a connection with the involvement he had in military service in his early twenties. He has great discipline as a conductor, and nothing gets him more angry than people— whether amateurs or professionals—who are late for rehearsals, who don't come well prepared, or who don't act professionally. He expects singers in an amateur choir to turn up on time and to be equipped with a pencil—if he's asked them to mark something in, it angers him greatly if they haven't. It's because he expects high standards of everybody he works with that he gets such exceptional results. That's very different from the life at King's College, of course, where once choristers were trained they were working at a very high level. In selecting choristers my father looked for a bright intelligence in the boys, because they then have an alertness and a natural inquisitiveness about them, which means that they are able quickly to develop their innate ability to sing. A natural voice is obviously a great help, but more important is their ability to learn fast. Music was always an important part of my life, but I had never really thought it would be my career too. It was only when I realized what being an engineer (and the involvement of studying engineering at university) entailed, that a 'road to Damascus' moment occurred and I decided that it had to be music for me. I think that this came as rather a shock to my parents and I know exactly how they were feeling. I've got a son myself who is a musician and is trying to carve out a career and livelihood for himself in his twenties. I think all professional musicians are delighted if their children show interest, aptitude, and ability, but are horrified if they show any signs of trying to earn a living at it!

O.   So you came to Trinity College, Cambridge to study music. Was there much contact with your father?

JW.   I came across him only peripherally. He made a point of never being involved in teaching me. I was never in any of the classes that he taught at Cambridge. He was on the faculty, and it was a bit of a worry for him. However, I did come across him regularly as a cellist, as I played cello in the CUMS Orchestra, which he conducted. I think he quite enjoyed that because we both took a similar pleasure in spotting mistakes that others made, so quite a lot of eye-contact was made throughout rehearsals, which was quite fun.

7

The Bach Choir

1960 – 1998

O. Let's talk about The Bach Choir and your association with that wonderful chorus.

W. It begins in 1960, when I was adjudicating in Trinidad in the West Indies. I'd been asked to go out to adjudicate at a festival in Port of Spain. It was quite an experience for me, because I had to judge many steel bands, and I didn't know one steel band from another. They played the most extraordinary things with immense precision (sometimes twenty or thirty in a band) and I was terribly impressed. They had arranged things such as the first movement of the 'Moonlight' Sonata, and played old steel oil drums which they had tempered and got beautifully tuned. I think in one class there were probably fifty or sixty competitors, one coming right after another. I thought, 'I just don't know how to judge these people', so I judged them purely on the pleasure they gave me, but I think I got it about right. I heard a lot of singers as well, and I had to judge them, give prizes, and encourage them. I really enjoyed it.

Then a telegraph message came to me, asking if I would conduct The Bach Choir in a concert in June. Reginald Jacques, who had been a friend of mine for several years and with whom I had co-edited the first *Carols for Choirs* volume, had had a heart attack during a performance of the *St Matthew Passion* and had been advised to give up conducting. I hadn't much experience with The Bach Choir, although I had heard them when I was a child at Westminster Abbey. I knew it was a very prestigious choir, so I agreed. It happened to be the Mozart Requiem and Walton's *Belshazzar's Feast*, both works that I knew well and enjoyed. When

Figure 7.1. David in Trinidad with steel drum, 1958 (photo Trinidad Guardian)

I got back to England, I started weekly rehearsals with The Bach Choir. I wasn't appointed Musical Director—I was just asked to do this one concert. We rehearsed through May and June and the concert went well. Immediately afterwards, I got an invitation to become the permanent Musical Director, which I readily accepted. In the space of six or seven weeks of rehearsals I had made many friends, including some with whom I'm still friends to this day.

O.   Tell me a little of the history of the choir.

W.   It was founded in 1875 to give the first complete performance in England of Bach's Mass in B minor. It's astonishing to us today to realize that it was almost a hundred and fifty years before England heard one of the greatest works ever written. It came about because Otto Goldschmidt, who was a pupil of Mendelssohn, came to settle in England, and he brought with him his wife, Jenny Lind, the famous singer. They decided to form a little choir to give the first performance of the B minor Mass in London. I think they started rehearsing in the autumn of 1875 with a view to giving the first performances in April 1876. These performances were very successful and so the choir decided to carry on. Over the years the choir has broadened its repertoire from Bach to include composers from the sixteenth century right up to the present day, and has expanded to a choir numbering between two and three hundred singers. When I joined, they normally had perhaps four or five concerts each year. There would be a concert in November, one carol or Christmas concert in December, another concert in March, followed by the two performances of the *St Matthew Passion* (which had become traditional in English with modern instruments), and then a May concert to end the season. Occasionally, there would be an additional concert some time in the summer months. Gradually during my time (I was there for thirty-eight years) the repertoire of the choir grew and the number of concerts increased as we started being engaged in recordings and in tours. It became a much more busy appointment than when I started. I enjoyed the variety of the concert-making—not only the concerts but the actual rehearsals. In many choirs they have a chorus-master, and they bring in a professional conductor to conduct the concerts, but I always felt that it was important that the person who trained the choir should also conduct the concerts. We did occasionally invite outsiders to perform, particularly if they were composers. I was very anxious that Britten should conduct the choir when we were performing a Britten work because I felt he was the creator of the music, and therefore he should show us how he wanted it performed. We also got people like Pierre Monteux and Horenstein to conduct, but these were rare events.

O.   I think Britten conducted his *War Requiem* with the choir?

W.   Yes. Among the highlights of my time with the choir was when Britten asked us to give the first concert-hall performance of the *War Requiem* in London. It had received a good performance originally, but under difficult conditions. It was written for the re-dedication of Coventry Cathedral, which was rebuilt after World War II and consecrated in 1962. To mark the opening of the new Cathedral there was a festival, the centrepieces of which were the first performances of this new *War Requiem* and *The Beatitudes* by the Master of the Queen's Musick, Sir Arthur Bliss. I felt sorry for Bliss, because the demands of the *War Requiem* were such that all the rehearsals had to be in the Cathedral. Bliss was told, to his great disappointment, that his work would be performed in the local cinema because they couldn't fit in enough rehearsals in the Cathedral to accommodate his work as well. It must have been a slight for the Master of the Queen's Musick to be relegated to a cinema and Benjamin Britten, a younger man by many years, to have the full use of the Cathedral, but it was the right decision, because the *War Requiem* is generally acknowledged to be one of the great works of the twentieth century.

O.   Were you involved in the first performance?

W.   No, I was at King's in those days. I heard it, though, and was very impressed. Britten felt that he hadn't received the sort of performance he really wanted because of the difficulties of performing in the Cathedral, and the fact that it was a locally recruited chorus, drawn from several different choirs with just a little professional support. They naturally couldn't be quite so carefully rehearsed under these conditions, because there were additional works to be performed during that week. Meredith Davies did extraordinarily well to keep the whole thing together; he conducted the major choir and orchestra while Britten directed the chamber orchestra and the tenor and baritone soloists. There is quite a lot of duo work, where one conductor has to follow the other. Normally the person conducting the main orchestra controls things, but Meredith had to keep an eye on Britten and didn't dare argue with him! The tenor soloist was Peter Pears and the baritone Dietrich Fischer-Dieskau. He was going to have a Russian soprano, Galina Vishnevskaya, the wife of Rostropovich, who had a gorgeous voice, but she couldn't get a visa. Instead, Heather Harper took on the role, and did so well on the first reading of it that she got several subsequent performances when Vishnevskaya wasn't available.

O.   So you came on the scene with The Bach Choir for the second performance?

W.   Actually, it was the third, five months after the first performance. The first was in Coventry and the second was in Westminster Abbey, on a night when it was terribly foggy, and anyway the Abbey acoustics are not ideal for a work of that sort. Britten was delighted when The Bach Choir agreed to perform it in the Royal Albert Hall. He directed the chamber orchestra and the two male soloists and I conducted the full orchestra, the main chorus, and the soprano soloist and the boys. Britten was very pleased, and the work was then recorded by the choir under his direction over a period of four or five days; it was very well received all around the world. The sessions went very well and he had lots of recording time (I think he had about three hours for every fifteen minutes of actual recorded music). For the recording he did have Vishnevskaya, although she didn't know it as well as Heather Harper did. One of the boys singing in the boys' choir from Highgate School in London on that occasion was John Rutter, aged seventeen. It has been one of the highlights of his life to have sung under Benjamin Britten at that age. At the recording sessions there were great breaks when the boys were not singing, so they had to just sit and listen and be quiet. Some of the older boys had cigarettes, which of course they were not allowed to have. Someone would have to say, 'Boys, cigarettes out!' As a result of the success of the recording, Britten was asked to conduct the work all around the world. He couldn't accept all these himself, so he suggested that they invite me. The first performance abroad was in Italy, at Perugia, a beautiful city near Assisi. We took, I suppose, a hundred and fifty members from The Bach Choir, plus a number of professional singers from the Ambrosian Singers. Britten was too busy to complete that tour, so he asked me to look after the further two performances in La Scala, Milan, and one in the beautiful theatre, La Fenice, in Venice. Those performances went very well indeed and they were the first of many tours which the The Bach Choir made. Mind you, the performances nearly didn't happen at all. When we unloaded the instruments in Italy—I think they'd come out by plane—for some reason the customs people wouldn't allow us to come in unless we paid a large cash deposit. (We had to find several million lire, which sounded an enormous amount, but of course the lira was several thousand to the pound.) None of us had much money and we didn't know what to do. We all shouted 'Leo!'—Leo being Leopold de Rothschild of the great banking family and a member of The Bach Choir—and hoped that his name would satisfy the customs officers!

O.   What followed?

W.   An invitation came to me from Japan to give the first three performances there of the *War Requiem* in 1965. I didn't know what to expect because I didn't know how much European music the Japanese had done at that stage. It was still only about twenty years after the end of World War II. But when I got there, I was very surprised to see that the repertoire being offered in the concert halls was the usual sort of thing: Beethoven's Fifth Symphony, the Grieg Piano Concerto. You wouldn't have known it wasn't the Festival Hall in London or Carnegie Hall in New York. Instead of a boys' choir they had prepared a large girls' choir of sixty or seventy for me. They sang beautifully, but I think Britten would have been horrified, because he liked the sound of boys' voices and he never really warmed to girls' voices. The main choir consisted of two professional opera choruses that were very good indeed, and we had the Yomiuri Nippon Symphony Orchestra which was also excellent. The concerts were in a beautiful new concert hall in Tokyo. It was possible to alter the acoustics in the hall. You could alter the amount of reverberation from one second to two or three, so you could have one acoustic at the rehearsal and a different one when the audience was present in the evening.

O.   How was your Japanese?

W.   Well, I needed interpreters! We went on tour to Hong Kong, the east coast of the United States, France, Germany, Israel, South Africa, Australia, and New Zealand. We sang the *War Requiem* in Lisbon in 1967 at the invitation of the Gulbenkian Foundation. The only place big enough to accommodate a really large audience was in an out-of-doors circus arena. I remember rehearsing to the smell of the lions who'd been there the day before. We also gave two performances in Holland in 1971, one in Utrecht, where I shared the concert with Paul Hupperts, the conductor of the Utrecht Symphony Orchestra, and one in Amsterdam in the Concertgebouw.

O.   It really became your piece. Could you talk a little about the work itself?

W.   It is a wonderful piece and highly effective. The Agnus Dei with the tenor solo is remarkable, as are the battle scenes, with full brass and drums rattling. There are some wonderful effects in the Sanctus where the choir just speak, 'Pleni sunt caeli et terra gloria tua', while the orchestra is playing its part. I felt that was clever. Britten wanted the effect of the whole world exclaiming, which is so imaginative. Everything in the B minor Mass, or in the works of

Haydn, is musical, but here was something quite innovative. You see people coming out of performances of the *War Requiem* with tears in their eyes, because they find it such a moving experience, particularly those who have lost people in the war, a husband or son who had died. It had a strange effect on people—more than the Bach, because Bach belongs to everybody; this piece belonged particularly to the two World Wars. Most of the text was from the World War I poet Wilfred Owen, and World War II, from which our nation suffered so much, had ended only a few short years before. I think there was more warmth towards Britten after this work. Many people who didn't like his music particularly came around to him afterwards because they felt it was for *them*.

O.   What about your performances of the Bach *Passions*?

W.   A central feature of The Bach Choir was the annual performances of the *St Matthew Passion*—it was an important part of the musical calendar of London as well. People used to come year after year to hear it, even though they knew the work inside out. Equally, we realized that there were young people hearing the work for the first time. Nowadays, it's rather more difficult to put on a work like the *St Matthew Passion* in English, because there's a new generation that wants to hear it only in German, with imitation instruments of Bach's day. They feel that performances in English miss so much of the original. It's true that the notes fit the recitatives much better in the German original, but it's so important to understand what the text is about. Even so, these new performances are not really authentic. Bach used boys, of course, in the choir of St Thomas, Leipzig, but people now are quite happy to have women's voices. Bach would never perform the work out of context—it would always be part of divine service—whereas we perform it in concert halls. Bach would also have had a lengthy sermon in the middle—I don't think our audiences today would want to have a sermon lasting perhaps forty-five minutes between Part I and Part II! So when people say, 'I went to an authentic performance', I say, 'No, you didn't. You had central heating in the hall, and you had no sermon.' One year I had the chance to record the *St Matthew Passion* under completely different conditions. I'd just performed it with The Bach Choir in London singing in English with the English Chamber Orchestra playing modern instruments. Very soon after I was asked to conduct it in

German with the boys of Regensburg Cathedral and the Choral Scholars from King's College, Cambridge with Nikolaus Harnoncourt. Well, I enjoyed them both. They were absolutely different, but I felt that Bach would have approved of both as well.

O.   Tell me a little bit about Vaughan Williams' continuo on the piano. That was all written out, wasn't it?

W.   I think it was, yes. Eric Gritton was the person who actually played the keyboard. He was a very fine player. The continuo was very florid—it was almost the sort of music Mendelssohn would have written. I didn't actually hear one of those performances, but I'm told they were deeply moving. Vaughan Williams loved Bach's music, and felt that Bach would have let him do whatever he felt was right. They were great occasions—people used to come from far and wide to Dorking to hear his performances but the critics were beginning to debunk his approach. They stayed away towards the end, but I don't think he minded. He went right on, and people loved performing with him. I've been conscious in my time that the critics have ceased to review performances in English. I don't mind. I'd rather have no criticism at all than people trying to stop me performing the way I want to.

O.   I believe Peter Pears sang the Evangelist for you many times.

W.   Yes, he became a favourite tenor of ours. He was a wonderful Evangelist in both the *St John Passion* and the *St Matthew Passion*. Of course, when we performed Britten works I always tried to get Peter, because I knew he had the music absolutely inside him. I went on using him possibly longer than I should have (in his late fifties and early sixties he was beginning to give up singing) because I thought so highly of him musically.

O.   Tell me about his interpretation.

W.   Some people felt Peter was too expressive. I remember one *St Matthew* performance where every cadence he sang ended 'and he s—a—i—d.' It was so beautiful, but you wondered what would come next. When Jesus entered it was almost anticlimactic! It is more convincing if the Evangelist just tells the story and Jesus does the expression. However, I could never say, 'Peter, now don't be so expressive'. People just loved to hear him sing it. He always wanted the scourging of Jesus section very *staccato* and sharp, so you could almost feel the lashes. I shall never forget, in the *St John*, the way he sang 'and he wept bitterly' after the cock crowed three times. I always felt I didn't want to go on with the next bit—you just wanted people to sit and enjoy it.

O.   With The Bach Choir, you sang it in both languages or always in English?

W.   The *St Matthew* was always in English, but for some reason we sang the *St John* in German, and more rarely in English. Of course the Magnificat was in Latin and any cantatas and motets we would sing in German. But the *St Matthew* seemed to be rather different, because it was telling a story. People used to come as if it were part of a service. For many, I'm sure it was their Easter experience. You saw many people in the audience at those performances of the *St Matthew Passion* with vocal scores following the text, whereas in an ordinary concert it is very rare to see someone holding a miniature score for a symphony. I should think that at least a quarter of the people would come in carrying scores, some of them marked and obviously falling to pieces.

O.   What about the Christmas concerts?

W.   We used to do a little bit from *Messiah* and a little bit from the *Christmas Oratorio*. I abandoned those because I felt it much better not to take those works out of context. We made them just carol concerts and Christmas hymns which involved the audience at certain points—they would all stand and join in the hymns. I arranged the carols which I had already done with the King's College Choir. I scored them for brass instruments and put in fanfares to make them a little bit more exciting. I think brass in eight parts—four trumpets, three trombones, and a tuba plus timpani and percussion—is a very good background for audience singing, better than just an organ. In the Royal Albert Hall we had two concerts, always, which were sold out. I started to involve the children in a practical way by inviting any children between the ages of eight and ten to come up on to the stage to join the choir in singing certain things. They would sing one or two carols on their own—simple ones like 'Away in a manger'. They would enjoy that and their parents were very proud to see them standing on the stage with the choir. Many have actually joined The Bach Choir afterwards because they had that first experience of singing with a big choir. John Rutter also wrote a number of carols for these Bach Choir concerts, which he scored for brass and percussion. One was 'I saw three ships' dedicated to The Bach Choir, which was a great success. Also, at that time, we had a carol competition for children aged up to eighteen to write a new carol, and several very good ones were produced over the years. Some have entered the repertoire and even been published. (One had to trust that their parents hadn't helped them, but I think mostly they were the unaided work of the children.) Of course, they got a first-class performance out of it.

O.   What about recordings with The Bach Choir?

W.   We were able to do quite a lot of recording of Vaughan Williams' works. Over a period of some years we recorded *Hodie* (involving the Westminster Abbey choristers as well, which pleased me very much), *Sancta Civitas, Five Tudor Portraits*, and the *Five Mystical Songs*. We were greatly encouraged by Ursula Vaughan Williams, who came to some of the sessions. Of course 'Uncle' Ralph had died by then, so I had to remember what he'd said to me about these works, many of which I had conducted at Worcester earlier in my career with him in attendance.

O.   What about other composers?

W.   We sang works by the Welsh composer William Mathias—*This Worldes Joie, Lux Aeterna*, and *Let the People Praise Thee*. He became quite a friend of the choir, and as a result of our recording those works we were invited to sing at the St Asaph Festival in North Wales. We performed there the work that he wrote to celebrate the Silver Jubilee of the Queen, called *A Royal Garland*. In the summer we would go on several short tours, including one to the West Country, where we would sing on three successive days in Exeter, Truro, and Wells Cathedrals. I loved taking people to my favourite coves in Cornwall, and we'd play cricket on the beach. It would be the choir against the orchestra.

I was Director of the Royal College of Music by then, so if we needed an orchestra we'd invite players from the College to come with us on tour. It was cheaper than paying for a professional orchestra to come down from London. They loved the outings as well.

O.   I'm sure they did.

W.   We had many happy events in which The Bach Choir and the Royal College of Music were involved. There were various links there, because many of my friends in The Bach Choir became associated with the Royal College of Music as well. One of these was Leopold de Rothschild, who was Chairman of The Bach Choir and who also became Chairman of the Council of the Royal College of Music. Of course there have been much earlier links—Stanford, for example, taught at the Royal College and was also conductor of The Bach Choir, and of course Parry was also closely involved with both. In later years, Herbert Howells taught at the Royal College of Music and wrote music for the choir. He was present when we recorded his finest work, *Hymnus Paradisi*, with the Philharmonia Orchestra. We enjoyed recording that very much indeed.

O.   You had stellar soloists with The Bach Choir.

W.   We were lucky that so many of them wanted to come and sing with the choir. It's invidious to start naming people, but we had Dame Felicity Lott and Heather Harper, two of our top sopranos, and of course Galina Vishnevskaya from Russia. Also Kiri Te Kanawa from New Zealand, who sang with us in the marriage service of the Prince of Wales to Lady Diana Spencer in St Paul's Cathedral. Among the contraltos Dame Janet Baker was outstanding, as was Catherine Wyn-Rogers, some twenty-five years younger than Dame Janet and a former student at the Royal College. Tenor soloists included Peter Pears, Robert Tear, Neil Jenkins, and Neil Mackie, and in the basses we had John Shirley-Quirk, Stephen Roberts, and Willard White, the great operatic singer who sang the Christus in the *St Matthew Passion* for many years. Bryn Terfel sang *Elijah* for us in Westminster Cathedral. There are just too many to list!

O.   With so many performances over thirty-eight years, do you have a most memorable one?

W.   All the *War Requiem* performances were memorable, in many different ways. Some would be near to Remembrance Day; sometimes a great friend may have died just before the performance, giving a special poignancy. But if there was a single memorable event, it would be the wedding of The Prince of Wales to Lady Diana Spencer in St Paul's Cathedral in July 1981. It was a beautiful day and the sun was shining, but we were all rather terrified, because we'd had terrorist attacks from the IRA just before. But everything was calm on that day—there was no sense of danger and the crowds were enthusiastic. The Prince of Wales and Lady Diana looked radiantly happy. Nobody could have foretold the sort of tragic future that was to come. We just agreed with the Archbishop of Canterbury when he said in his sermon: 'Here is a fairy-tale wedding.'

O.   What were the choral works you sang?

W.   Kiri Te Kanawa sang Handel's 'Let the bright seraphim' and that was followed by The Bach Choir singing 'Let their celestial concerts all unite'. That was just right for the signing of the register, because they needed something like ten minutes while the couple retired behind the high altar to sign the books. That was the big moment for the choir, because they were on their own— the rest of the service was sung by the St Paul's Cathedral Choir, directed by Barry Rose, and the Chapel Royal Choir, directed by Richard Popplewell. The Chapel Royal Choir always takes part in any big state occasion. The organist that day was Christopher Dearnley, a fine player. He played for quite a long time before the service, all English music. The Prince also took a great interest in the fanfares to be played at the Service. He came down to St Paul's Cathedral one morning to have a selection of fanfares played by the State Trumpeters and selected his favourites.

O.   How was William Mathias chosen to write the new anthem?

W.   I was asked to help The Prince of Wales with the choice of music, and I thought it would be good if we had one completely new piece, which would receive its first performance at that service. I told the Prince that I thought he ought to have something 'home grown', and something Welsh seemed appropriate since he is The Prince of Wales. I suggested an anthem about six or seven minutes long, in English, and not too difficult. The Prince was happy with the suggestion of William Mathias, and that he be asked to set verses from Psalm 67: 'God be merciful unto us and bless us . . . Let the people praise thee, O God.' I rang up William Mathias that evening and told him he had four months to do this. He responded eagerly and had the piece written within two or three weeks. It's a very effective anthem with an exciting refrain and a lively organ part, and has become very popular with choirs throughout the English-speaking communion.

O.   How did you manage the logistics of that service?

W.   It was difficult to fit everybody in. We had something like two hundred singers from The Bach Choir, the orchestra of the Royal

Opera House, Covent Garden, leading string players from the English Chamber Orchestra, and brass, including John Wallace, trumpet soloist, from the Philharmonia Orchestra. It was exciting to assemble those forces and to work with them. We timed Lady Diana Spencer's procession so she would arrive at the Prince's side precisely at the end of Clarke's 'Trumpet Voluntary'. Because of her father's frailty, it took longer than originally planned, so I told the orchestra to be prepared to play the whole piece twice.

O.   Can you tell me about some of the other royal occasions where you've been Music Director? I know you did the Jubilee in 2002, but you've done many before that. Which was your first one?

W.   The first of these out-of-door big events was the fortieth anniversary of the Queen's Accession. I was introduced to Sir Michael Parker, a very experienced producer of big events such as the Edinburgh Tattoo and things at the Royal Albert Hall. He devised this pageant called 'QE 40', Queen Elizabeth Forty, which was held at Earl's Court. I seem to remember that I was put on a movable podium and the stages also moved. I had to conduct Parry's 'I was glad' while the podium, which was on wheels, gradually moved backwards because they had to clear the area in front of me for the dramatic entry of the horses.

O.   Was this with The Bach Choir?

W.   Yes, and also with some members of the Royal College of Music, because I could use whom I liked. There was a procession of all the motor cars that had been produced—one of each—during the forty years. There were important people who had done great things including Sir Edmund Hillary, the man who'd first climbed Mount Everest. England had won the World Cup in 1966 and the team entered to loud applause.

O.   What came next?

W.   There was one for the fiftieth anniversary of VE Day—Victory in Europe, the end of World War II in Europe. That was in Hyde Park in 1995. We had the European Youth Orchestra, The Bach Choir, and representatives from the Royal Choral Society and other big London choirs. We had kings and queens and presidents of many nations taking part. It was a wonderful occasion. The music included an arrangement of the last movement of

Beethoven's Choral Symphony (the 'Ode to Joy' is now used as a sort of national anthem for Europe) and other excerpts of mainly English music.

O.   Were there any big problems?

W.   The only disaster that occurred was when Sir Michael Parker devised the Royal Pageant of the Horse which was going to be the biggest display of horses that there has ever been.* But it was cancelled at the last moment because there had been terrific thunderstorms which had made the racecourse at Ascot very dangerous for the horses. Also, the big stands which had been erected for the audience were sinking into the ground. The police decided they couldn't allow the pageant to take place, so alas it was cancelled. We had rehearsed and recorded the music so the horses could rehearse for two months to the actual music.

O.   What were you playing for the horses?

W.   Well, all sorts of things but mainly old folk songs. Many types of music with different speeds, and some that had a gallop.

O.   Any other events?

W.   We celebrated VJ Day, which was the end of World War II, the victory over Japan. That was in two parts. The first part was in Horse Guards Parade, to which the Queen came. There were military manoeuvres—march and counter-march and that sort of thing—and in the evening there was community singing outside Buckingham Palace.

O.   Have you done any since your retirement from The Bach Choir?

W.   The most recent one was in 2002 for the fiftieth anniversary of the Queen's accession to the throne. That wasn't the same as the Coronation because that was a year later. They erected enormous stands outside Buckingham Palace, and The Bach Choir and representatives of other choirs sang while the Queen drove from Buckingham Palace down to St Paul's Cathedral. The music was relayed all the way down the route while she processed and people joined in the singing. Then came the great service in St Paul's Cathedral under the direction of John Scott, then a state luncheon at the Mansion House, and then there was an enormous

* Planned to celebrate the golden wedding anniversary of the Queen and Duke of Edinburgh on 5 July 1997.

parade of children from the Commonwealth during the afternoon. The day ended with the fly-past of Concorde and various other planes, and community singing outside the Palace. All members of the Royal Family were there. These occasions were brilliantly organized, and Sir Michael had to work very closely with the Metropolitan Police, with all the army units involved and the air force, to make sure that it was all coordinated with the fly-pasts. The music was written especially by a man called Barry Hingley. He was actually responsible for RAF bands, but he became the chief musician for all the armed forces, arranging these sorts of things.

O.   Did Sir Michael select most of the music that was to be played and when?

W.   Well he would say, 'We want five minutes of cheerful music. What do we do, Barry?' and Barry would say, 'David, what do we do?' We had conferences and sorted it all out. I think we've had 'Zadok the Priest' in all of them somewhere, even the one with the horses. They had to gallop to that. 'Jerusalem' was another, and of course the national anthem is always used.

O.   And you did 'Land of hope and glory' when the Queen made the balcony appearances. In fact you did it two or three times, I think.

W.   Yes, it was encored.

O.   And you got all sorts of cues as to when to begin?

W.   Yes. I had somebody whose sole job was to sit at my feet. She had earphones and she would cue me when we could start the next piece. One cue meant hurry up a bit if we were getting a bit late, another one meant take more time. There were all sorts of signals, but it was brilliantly controlled. There were film crews from all around the world with their own agenda, talking in their own languages, yet they all had to be briefed as to exactly what was going to happen. Everything had to pass through Sir Michael's hands. I'd say to him, 'What will happen if it rains?', but he'd reply, 'It won't rain!' I don't think there were any plans if there'd been a thunderstorm. There were the players with their instruments: 'Do we keep playing if there's a downpour or does somebody tell us to stop, and if so, who tells us? Can we have umbrellas there, just in case?' And he would reply, 'Oh, it's *not* going to rain.' He was very confident.

O.   I think the choir also did some recording sessions with Marianne Faithfull and Mick Jagger?

Figure 7.2. David with Mick Jagger, *c.* 1969 (photograph, Janet Lewison)

W.   I'd never done anything like that before. We were called for one or two sessions of three hours each. I thought, 'My goodness, this music is going to be difficult!' I asked Mick Jagger if he could send us the music beforehand. He said, 'Oh no, it's quite easy, you'll be able to pick it up all right.' So I took him at his word. When we arrived, he said, 'It's quite easy. Can you get the choir to hum me a chord?' So I sang a triad and asked the choir to hum it. He said, 'Why that's a lovely sound.' He said, 'When you hear my tune—I'll just sing it to you—they can make up their own harmonies. They will have to do it by ear.' I said, 'This is being recorded isn't it?' He said, 'Yes, but we'll just use the best one.' We did it two or three times, with slightly different harmonies each time. I said, 'Let's make the ending a bit more exciting. Sopranos go up at the end. That will make it better.' So we did. He said, 'That's fine, I'm happy with that.' We'd only been recording for about an hour, and I was surprised because everything had gone very easily. Among the people queuing up to get autographs I saw Sir Edmund Compton, then the Auditor General for the government. I asked, 'What are you doing here, Edmund?' He whispered, 'It's not for *me*, it's for my *grandchildren!*'

O.   You made amazing friends through your years with The Bach Choir. It seems like a very collegial, close group socially and personally. Are there any people who sang during your entire tenure with The Bach Choir?

W.   Oh, yes. Several. Among them I particularly think of Leopold de Rothschild. I think he'd been in the choir at least four or five years before I came.

O.   What was your audition and re-audition procedure for The Bach Choir?

W.   With some singers, I'd say, 'That's fine. You can join straight away'. To others I might say, 'You can join and see how you get on, and I'll hear you in a year's time'—because maybe their sight-reading wasn't as good as it should be. I let some people in provisionally, because I wanted to hear them again after one year to see if they had settled down in the choir—many of them became the most valuable members over the years. I would re-audition them every three years, and I was very insistent on good reading when they joined. Instead of giving them sight-reading for the re-audition I would test them on the most difficult passages from works we had actually sung during the previous three years. They never knew what passage it was going to be, but the thought of that coming made them really concentrate. They learned every bit, in case that was the bit they were going to be tested on. I tried to be merciful over re-auditions. If a person had been a member for twenty years I would never turn them out straight away, because I think it's so cruel to somebody who's given so much to the choir and enjoyed it. I would always give them one year's notice. I would say, 'Now, I think you ought to retire in a year's time'—or 'two years' time' sometimes—'and so I suggest that I don't hear you again, but you write to me in about a year's time, offering your resignation, which I'll accept, reluctantly.' In that way nobody knew they'd been failed—I hate the word 'fail'—and they would realize, I think, upon reflection, that it was probably best for them to make way for the next generation. Of course, some people's voices become less good when they're fifty or sixty, others can go on singing until they're seventy. It's very much a matter of individuals, and sometimes people can slow up mentally, as well.

O.   What was your last big performance with the choir?

W.   The last one was the *St Matthew Passion* in Symphony Hall in
         Birmingham. It was a moving occasion and they gave me a
         wonderful farewell. I was presented with a great book which
         everybody had written in, which I treasure.

Interlude 7

Reflections on The Bach Choir

Sarah de Rougemont (née Willcocks) was interviewed on 14 June 2005 at her home in London.

SR.   I enjoyed singing in The Bach Choir because I saw a completely new side of Dad. I'd never sung in a choir conducted by him before, which Jonny had, obviously. I suddenly saw this adored maestro in his element: very witty, which isn't a side he shows at all at home, sparkling, twinkling, with all these fans, women queuing up to talk to him afterwards and then applause. I loved it, actually. It made me feel that I got to know him better. It was a bit poignant, because really it is an odd way to get to know your father, but I did learn a lot about him by singing with him. Everything he said was funny! He was tremendous. It was lovely to see him in his element like that, and I suppose like a lot of very talented people, the family probably isn't his element. He's not really a family person, although I'm sure he adores us all and is very proud of us, in his way. The time my brother James died [June 1990] was quite telling, because Dad didn't cope with it very well. He didn't really have a way of coping with it. My mother was very obviously distraught and unbearably sad for ages, and probably still hasn't completely recovered. She just shut down and grieved for months. But Dad just didn't. He played the organ at James's funeral and although he must have been distraught, he went on that same day to conduct a concert at Birmingham. Nobody mentioned James's death to him because he wasn't open to talking about it at all, and a few weeks later he had an angina attack. A doctor at the hospital said that he thought it was repressed grief. That seemed a very perceptive diagnosis. I couldn't imagine how they'd managed to figure it out when Dad wasn't answering any questions about James at all, but I think it could have been that. I think in some ways he is quite repressed. He doesn't let go very easily except when he's conducting. He doesn't seem to find conducting any more tiring than he used to. He's actually managed to keep music as something that doesn't stress him out at all. He has loosened up, and with more free time now he must occasionally notice that he has a large family who all adore him. But, of course, we don't adore him as much as his fans do! They do the grovelling, obsequious bit, whereas we're more discerning.

Dame Janet Baker was a frequent soloist with Sir David, especially for The Bach Choir's annual performances of the *St Matthew Passion*. She was interviewed on 18 January 2005 at the Athenaeum Club in London.

JB.   The *St Matthew Passion* with David was like an annual punctuation. No matter what else I was doing, there was that one pivotal piece that I never missed. I did it for many years and it became very special, partly because those two performances were like moments of pilgrimage for the audience. The atmosphere was incredible. I suppose everybody who sings the work regularly finds this same feeling of climbing a mountain and being in a different place. What I felt about David in Bach was that his sense of control and rhythm was absolute.

O.   For a singer, I would think that is very comforting.

JB.   Yes, it is; you felt *held* in a particular way. His sense of rhythm and timing were very strong and individual. So one went along with that and it was like being in a big ship: we just started at the beginning and ended at half past four on a Sunday afternoon, and we all felt we had done this journey together, led by David holding it very securely together in the tempo. He listened to what you did. In his directness and stability of rhythm you felt that he was giving you your space to do what you wanted. I think that is what good conducting is—the sense of allowing the person to speak with the individual voice within the bounds of the total concept. I felt that very much and very strongly right from the start.

O.   Would you talk a little about other works you sang with David—perhaps *Gerontius*?

JB.   The Angel was part of my flesh and blood, so to speak. When I talk about being jealous of the role of the Evangelist, the Angel is a role that compares in a sense, and to sing a role like that is quite extraordinary. Again, I sang it so many times I was able to see how I moved to a different place in it. This is so wonderful—if you get the chance to do things over and over again, you see different treasures in them every time you sing them and you realize it's not the music that's changed, it's *you*. It's a question of going back to the score; if we all did exactly what the composer said, there would be no problem. You are the servant and you do what's there as closely as you possibly can. David is a tremendous musician. His priority is always the score. That's what is so good about working with really good conductors: they just bring you back to that, time after time. David always had a clear vision of how the piece should be and we went along with that.

O.   What about Handel? I know you did *Messiah*—did you do any other oratorios with David?

JB.   We recorded *Dixit Dominus* in King's. The rhythm of that—oh my God, I can feel and hear that now!—was wonderful and quite different from Bach. It was amazing how he somehow translated this into his physique and to the clarity of the beat. On the disc you can hear David's remarkable sense of rhythm, completely at the service of the piece.

O.   What other works do you associate with David?

JB.   *Belshazzar's Feast* is one. The big massed forces were a very different path for him. His training and his life were very much bound up with more intimate choirs like King's College, and so to conduct something like The Bach Choir gave him a tremendous opportunity to broaden his work and do the really big pieces. That must have been a real thrill for him. David has always worked at the most tremendous pace. You wonder how on earth he could ever keep all these things in his mind. The energy, which he has had all his life, is possibly an aspect of conducting, which is so physical and seems to rejuvenate people and keep them young and interested. Of course it uses the brain as well. Being a conductor is a good way to grow old and to keep on doing the things which are interesting to you. Conductors are very lucky in that respect. Singers can't do that; we are like ballet dancers and have shortish careers. David was very fortunate to have that breadth and width of repertoire, which he tackled extremely well.

Jane **Watts** was a student at the Royal College of Music during Sir David's tenure as Director, and he appointed her accompanist of The Bach Choir in 1990. She was interviewed on 13 June 2006 at her home in Buckinghamshire.

JW.   I got to know David extremely well over the years. He used to put the fear of God into me sometimes at rehearsal, which is a good thing.

O.   How did he do that?

JW.   You had to be on your toes the whole time, which is such good training. I'm *glad* he was like that. I worked like that the whole time, and then with every other conductor I subsequently worked with. A number of them were amazed at how I was actually 'there'. When they say, 'We'll go from page whatever, to bar 2'—well, I'm *there*, because of David's training. I used to watch him, which way the page would turn, and eventually you got to know the way he was working. Sometimes he'd throw me a googly,* but most times I was able to work out where he was starting.

O.   What about rehearsals with The Bach Choir? Could you talk a little bit about them and how David structured them?

JW   It obviously depended on the programme we were rehearsing. He used to work the choir very hard, and was very particular about pitch and rhythm. He wouldn't let them get away with anything at all, which is why the choir very rarely sang flat or sharp. He would never let anybody get away with not watching. As the accompanist I had to work quite hard to make sure the notes were all under my fingers for the rehearsals, because he would expect it, which was quite right.

---

* A cricketing term: a ball that spins in a direction the batsman is not expecting.

O.   You've played under so many different conductors. I wonder if you could talk a little bit about what you think is unique and special about David?

JW.   What is special about David is that you know exactly where he is and what he is doing. He's got a way, especially with amateur choirs, of being able to make them feel special when he conducts them. I see this particularly with these 'From Scratch' concerts that we do. They are all eating out of his hand, and it's marvellous because there aren't many conductors that can do that. I feel very privileged when I sit there watching this happening, because it's very special to see everybody just doing exactly what he wants.

O.   What pieces do you closely associate with David?

JW.   *Belshazzar* is a good work to quote because it's absolutely in his blood and bones. He doesn't mess around with it. There are lots of conductors that almost wallow in it, but he doesn't. I've done *Belshazzar* I don't know how many times. The first time was at the Royal College; I'd never come across such an absolutely amazing piece. David does a really tight performance of it, which you need. Another piece is something like Parry's *Blest Pair of Sirens*. I've done that a number of times with him, with just organ accompaniment. It's wonderful to do it with him because he just lets the music flow and doesn't mess around with it. It's not that it's a strait-jacketed version, it's not that at all; it's very subtle and just a natural way of doing it. That's what music should be like.

O.   What about his phrasing? I think he has a remarkable ability to get a chorus to shape phrases without making it sound affected.

JW.   This is the whole point, because music is just in him, and therefore he just does it in the most natural way possible, and he gets everybody else to do the same. Because it's not contrived and because it's not affected, it feels easy and natural. I remember, the first time I sang for him in the RCM chorus, I thought, 'Gosh, I've never thought of anything like that before'—he knew exactly where a phrase was going. That's how he influenced me from the very beginning and I still think like that. I very rarely disagree strongly with him, although he does think I'm a very determined person!

Stephen Roberts sang most of the important bass solo work with Sir David for many years. He was interviewed on 17 June 2004 at the Athenaeum Club in London.

SR.   David was always somebody who likes things to be predictable, in a way. He wouldn't be too keen if you were to start stretching things about, so he hoped that all the singers would stay pretty much in tempo. Over the years he had a selection of singers from the various different stylistic Bach camps, and on the whole he coped with them very well. He would try to get some of them to sing perhaps more rhythmically, no names of course, but he knew how far he could push it on that subject. But one thing David required was actually singing in tune.

O.   What about things like cadenzas and interpolations of melodic lines? Did he encourage or discourage that? Did he leave that to you?

SR.   Well, he was of the modern school. He was perfectly happy to have ornamentation in the vocal line as well, as long as it didn't interfere with the pulse and the general shape of the phrase. He wasn't that keen on cadenzas, I remember, but yes, he was happy with ornamentation as long as it didn't get in the way of things.

O.   What about performances of *Gerontius*—you did that with him, didn't you?

SR.   Yes, I did it a couple of times. I don't really think the part of the Priest is totally my role and I always imagine a more bass singer singing it. On the whole, the work is a little bit more operatic than what I would usually sing, but with David it was always a very controlled performance. With Elgar he gave you a little bit more space to expand as a singer, and like all Welsh singers I like to hold on to the odd note every now and again when we feel it's in the voice.

O.   What about David as a conductor? You have worked with a lot of different, fine conductors in your career.

SR.   He liked crisp, rhythmic performances, and especially listening now, as I do occasionally, to the English recording of the *St Matthew Passion* that The Bach Choir did, some of those tempos bear comparison with the modern-day smaller-scale performances. David was always very much up with modern thinking with these kinds of things. I know his performances were normally with a big choir and, on the whole, a reasonably big orchestra as well, but certainly the tempos and the style of playing were very up to date. In fact, look at some of the people who came from his stable at Cambridge—Andrew Davis, for example, a very quick, up-to-date, lively conductor, and Roy Goodman, of course, is a true Baroque performer.

O.   What about his choice of singers?

SR.   I have always been interested in his choice of singers because he used quite a variety of them and surprisingly many of them were Welsh! Beside myself there were Bryn Terfel, Bob Tear, and Catherine Wyn-Rogers, who all have a Welsh background. I think he liked people who sang in a very controlled but musical and emotional way, and I think that is probably what the Welsh delivered.

Roy Goodman was interviewed on 16 September 2003 at his home in Bishop's Stortford, Hertfordshire.

RG.   Quite a few years after I left King's as a chorister, I remember revisiting David at a small private sherry party in his room in Gibbs Building. David was the conductor of the London Bach Choir and they had been approached by Decca Records in 1969. Much to our amazement and amusement, David told us that the choir had been invited to sing on a recording with the Rolling Stones and Mick Jagger! I expect in those days there were quite a lot of bowler-hatted members of The Bach Choir, carrying their rolled-up umbrellas and briefcases and looking very much like city gents, with their wives or ladies in the choir. In the studio they had learned to sing a backing track for 'You can't always get what you want', the song which became the flipside of 'Honky Tonk Woman'. As you can imagine, they sang it very properly and precisely: 'You can't always get what you want, but if you try, sometimes you get what you need'. The music goes very high—right up to a top C rather like the Allegri

Miserere and the sopranos had to hold this high note for a long time, fortunately on a good vowel sound. But the amusing part of all this may seem hard to believe—as David began to embark on an extraordinary impression of Mick Jagger! Obviously Jagger had heard the choir warming up in the studio, singing their opening passage for the backing track, and he was not so impressed by their pronunciation. There was no way he was going to have a posh 'You <u>can't</u> always get what you want'—he wanted something more like 'Yer kannt always git wot yer whannt'. So, there was David clicking his thumb and second finger with both hands and jiving around his room quite like a youngster, giving us his vivid imitation of Mick Jagger! Actually it's quite hard to sing in a rock style the fairly conventional music the choir was given and so they stuck to their guns, creating a deliciously contrasting foil to the band! It was a wonderful moment enjoyed by a roomful of sherry-drinking friends and it certainly showed off a very human side of David.

Jennifer Vernor-Miles sang in The Bach Choir from 1963 and served as concert manager from 1989. She was interviewed on 17 June 2003 in London.

O.   What do you think is special about David's choral style?

JVM.   Enthusiasm. Absolute, straight off. Give him a bunch of people and he'll make music with them. They don't even have to be very good at singing! You know, I've seen him take, frankly, crap choirs, and make wonderful music out of them. I suspect that he prefers making music with amateurs because he just loves their enthusiasm. The fact that everybody's there for the love of making music. He does these 'From Scratch' performances of *Messiah*—four thousand people in the Albert Hall, all singing away—and there he is in the middle, conducting and you can see he loves it! Even if you're up in the 'gods', he'll notice if you're not looking at him! He's one of those conductors that, whether you know the piece or not, you've just got to watch. David's enthusiasm is infectious. I would turn up for choir on Monday nights absolutely exhausted, walk in there with this music, and think, 'Why am I doing this, I'm absolutely knackered.' Five minutes in, you knew exactly why you were there. It was all pepped up and off we went, it was wonderful!

O. Everybody seems to have at least one favourite David Willcocks story and I'm sure you've got one!

JVM. We were singing something like 'Zadok', and we were all semi-quavering away, but David wanted to momentarily pause something —to come in that fraction late that made it extra exciting. David couldn't get us to do this and he put down his baton, turned to all of us and said, 'I think most of you here are old enough to understand what I mean when I say that there are certain pleasures in life which are just that much better if they're slightly delayed!' Collapse of choir!

John Scott was accompanist of The Bach Choir from 1979 to 1992. He was interviewed on 14 September 2003 at St Paul's Cathedral, London.

JS. During the time that I was associated with The Bach Choir I'm sure that we performed the major points of the choral repertory. I remember *The Dream of Gerontius* and *Belshazzar's Feast* being sung two or three times, at least, during that period. What I thought was very refreshing about the programme planning was that alongside the choral classics there were a number of less well-known pieces and indeed some first performances. I thought that was very enterprising and, in a sense, it was taking a bit of a risk, because audiences are notoriously circumspect when it comes to going to things that they don't know, and alas they were not always sell-outs, but I think David felt a great commitment to encouraging some of our younger composers. I certainly found it so instructive just to see how David would take pieces apart and, for the benefit of people singing in the choir for the first time, he would often explain the background to the piece. He did a brilliant exposition on *Gerontius* when we started rehearsing it. He explained all of the musical motifs and how they recur through the piece and what their significance was, and so on. That was always very instructive. It was a privilege to play for pieces such as the

War Requiem which he knew inside out, having been involved in the earliest performances.

The particularly impressive characteristics of The Bach Choir that I admired were their intonation and ensemble. David's reputation for fine tuning in terms of choral sound of course is legendary, and I think one need not dwell on that, but what I thought was so impressive with such a large group of singers was the unanimity which he was able to achieve through ensemble, which was also the result of instilling in the choir an incredible sense of rhythm—this very strongly defined rhythmic awareness. To be able to drill such a large group of singers to sing music of Bach and Handel in a very light and articulated manner I thought was a real challenge in itself, but certainly the ease with which they negotiated things like the final two choruses of *Dixit Dominus*, which are notoriously difficult with all the semiquaver runs at 'Gloria Patri'—was really thrilling, and totally defied all the logic of not having baroque music being sung by more than a hundred and fifty or two hundred singers!

O.   Did you work with him with any other group than The Bach Choir?

JS.   I played the harpsichord on a regular basis for the annual '*Messiah* From Scratch' which he conducted in the Royal Albert Hall. This was an extraordinary, surreal experience because people bought tickets to form part of this monster choir of three or four thousand people! The choir was in various compartments around the hall. The whole of one side of the hall would be sopranos dressed in blue or red or whatever it was, and the altos on the other side, with the tenors and basses in tiered ranks up by the organ. The orchestra, a professional group, was on the floor in the middle of the arena and it was quite a large string group. I played the harpsichord, and it was amplified throughout the hall in such a way that it was just the loudest harpsichord ever! It was relayed through the public address system and I think within each box in the Albert Hall there's a speaker, so when I spread a chord for a continuo recitative there was this horrendous jangling sound coming from all over the hall. But it was essential, I think. David was insistent that it should be there and the volume turned quite high up, because he found it was very helpful to move the choruses along. There was a brief warm-up rehearsal beforehand in which he would give the salient points of each chorus. There wasn't time to sing it through, of course.

O.   I can't imagine the semiquavers with two thousand sopranos.

JS.   No. He made a point of being slightly more cautious than usual with tempi, but even so it was a tremendous achievement to keep people together in the faster choruses. He did it all with a great sense of enjoyment. That's another thing I admire. How many times must he have conducted *Messiah* and yet still make it appear incredibly vibrant and lively? That's always the impression one had. There was never any feeling of being in any sense tired of this music. It always came up fresh, which I think is a remarkable achievement in any individual.

O.   Can you think of anything else about David that you'd like to contribute?

JS.   I once had a rather disarming experience—I remember it was a Bach Choir concert and we were singing in Brentwood Roman Catholic Cathedral just outside London. Part of the programme featured some motets by Mendelssohn, and I remember being concerned that I didn't have a page-turner. I was going to play, as an organ interlude, the Mendelssohn Third Sonata, and I asked David before the concert if I could possibly borrow somebody from the choir to turn over for the Mendelssohn. Without any hesitation he said 'I'll do it!' In panic, I replied 'No, no David, you don't need to do that, I'll find someone from the choir.'

O.   I don't *want* you to do that!

JS   That's what I was trying to say, but he was insistent—'No, no I'd love to do it; I'd absolutely *love* to do it.' It all went well, but the most disconcerting thing was the fugue of Mendelssohn 3 and I knew exactly what would happen, as soon as I got to the first rest, there was an audible sniff on the rest from beside me! Of course he's legendary for the sniff on the rest. It was very funny, and I did point it out afterwards and he was very amused by it. It's a little mannerism of which I think he's quite unconscious. But it's something he would very often get the choir to do in rehearsal if there was a particular passage with a rest and if they weren't quite together. He would have choir 1 sniff loudly on the rest while choir 2 sang, and vice versa—a nice little trick.

Sir Michael Parker organizes important royal and national events. He was interviewed on 11 September 2003 at his office in London.

MP.   When I left the army I started to organize large national events—some military, some civilian—and I tend to do most of the large royal celebrations in this country. David has the misfortune on occasion to have to come and work with me.

O.   I wouldn't say *mis*fortune. . . .

MP.   Well, I think one of the problems with the sorts of events I do, is that (a) they're always on a very large scale and (b) we're always extremely short of time for rehearsals, so it's very important to have someone who doesn't get fazed by the pressure. David is particularly good at not getting fazed. For years, as you know, he has been the principal choral conductor in this country. So whenever I do something big which involves choirs, I always try to find out whether he's available. The first time he and I worked was on the Queen's fortieth anniversary celebrations in 1992, which was a vast and highly complex event. When I look back on it now, I can't think how I had the courage to do it. We built a vast arena in Earl's Court. We built [a replica of] the inside of the Royal Opera House, Covent Garden, and behind it we had a very large stage, enough to get four thousand people on. And we had moving stages, each of which was the size of the Covent Garden stage. We had a full symphony orchestra on one of them that could motor around with the orchestra playing.

O   So you moved the orchestra around—great stuff!

MP   Yes, and at the back we had a thousand-voice choir, which seemed a good round figure, made up from choirs from cathedrals, The Bach Choir, and other major choirs. We basically told the story of the Queen's fortieth anniversary in music, and we had everything from galloping horses (this was in a theatre!) to guns, to the gold state coach used for the Coronation and everything. David was conducting this vast choir. The opening scene was quite something. In the setting the forces all looked extremely small, a very small orchestra, and Ian McKellen, one of our leading actors, did an introduction, and then all the sides of the stage and the proscenium arch moved, motored out, and the roof went up, and the whole of the symphony orchestra then motored back towards the choir, which was about five hundred feet away, playing the while and the choir singing the while. They were singing Parry's Coronation anthem 'I was glad'. Then the King's Troop, which is horses and guns which were fast and loose, galloped through the audience, much to their surprise, and took up their position. The gold state coach came through too, and while all that was going on the choir was singing 'I was glad'. It was hugely complex. David, as always, kept very calm throughout the whole thing. It was just a fantastic success.

O.   What was next?

MP.   The second thing we did together was the fiftieth anniversary of VE Day in Hyde Park. I think it was a choir of a thousand again—we normally do have a choir of a thousand—and this time the orchestra wasn't moving. We built a great big Dome of Peace. David was in charge of all that, and it was very much an orchestral thing. There was quite a lot of choral stuff in it too, and that whole ceremony was done by him. There again we had very little rehearsal. In fact on the day it was so very hot, unusual for this country, that a lot of the children were fainting, so we had to truncate the programme. He was brilliant in coping with the fact that we had to change the whole thing at the last minute. He's unfazed if someone tugs his trousers and says 'Stop the next one early, and jump on to the one after that'. We had an audience in the park of about a hundred and fifty thousand and, of course, many millions saw it on television all around the world. The third event he did with me was for the VJ Day celebrations and again he did it brilliantly. The next thing he did—well he did and he didn't do it—was to be the Royal Pageant of the Horse.

O.   He mentioned this to me—tragic!

MP.   It was tragic. It was to be this great thousand-horse event, which was going to be done originally for the Queen and Prince Philip's golden wedding anniversary. We built a great stadium in Windsor Great Park, but unfortunately we had absolutely deluging rain. We'd completely written the show and recorded all the music—we'd done everything. In fact so much so that I kept thinking we actually *did* the show. We had everything in position, and then literally at the last moment we had to cancel the whole thing because it was just completely unsafe. When we did do it again for the Golden Jubilee celebrations in May 2002, by then it was called 'All the Queen's

Horses', but sadly David wasn't available to conduct it, so we had to use someone else. The final thing we did together was the Golden Jubilee State Procession in June 2002. David was the main conductor for everything. We had an audience of two million live, and that's a police estimate so therefore it's probably more, and he conducted the finale, which again was a nightmare, because although we'd arranged it all, these things never quite happen as you expect. We kept on having to change our plans for the finale because a number of things didn't quite happen as I'd anticipated. I couldn't get the members of the Royal Family to come out when I wanted them on the balcony! We'd arranged it all beforehand, but somehow it went slightly wrong. So we weren't able to play all the beautiful tunes quite where we should, and again we had to be very flexible. But, as always, David was amazing—how he managed to cope—because it's not only a question of getting yourself sorted out, but you've got to get the messages through to the choir as well, so they understand what's changed and that we're not going to do the next three tunes, we're going to do the fifth tune, or whatever it is. Of course, it's very difficult doing all that because most of the microphones are live most of the time, so you can't just shout at them all. That was the last time we worked together. He is a great chap, I must say. He has a most marvellous way with choirs. He's apparently very gentle but very firm underneath it all, and there's definitely a steel hand within that velvet glove. It's marvellous watching him working with choirs because he's obviously enormously respected by everybody. If people know that Sir David Willcocks is going to be the conductor, there's absolutely no problem getting big choirs agreeing to come and take part in massed choir events. One of the problems you have in massed choir events is that there is always the slightly central problem with the conductors of the other choirs wanting to have a part in the proceedings. David is very good and on occasions we agree that they might, but by and large everybody will defer to him, and that's very helpful from my point of view. It makes everything that much easier to do and pulls the thing together much more easily than if you had a lot of different conductors. With these large events, there's no point in losing your temper because you don't actually achieve anything. You have to give the outward appearance of being calm even if you're not quite so calm beneath, and it's lovely having people like him around who have the same sort of approach to life.

O.   Have you been the person who has selected him for these events, or has the Royal Family requested him?

MP.   If anyone was doing anything, he was always the first conductor one would go to and say, 'Would you be prepared to do it?' He has been marvellous. What more nice things can I say about David except he's a very nice chap! I thank him for putting up with me for so long. It's surprising how time flies actually isn't it? He seems to be going on for a hundred years!

8

Director, Royal College of Music

1974 – 1984

O.   How did your move to the Royal College of Music [RCM] in London come about?

W.   I was appointed Director in 1972 and took up my duties in 1974. The RCM is a wonderful institution, founded in 1882 by the then Prince of Wales, later King Edward VII. He was musical and was determined that in England there should be a Royal College of Music which was at least the equal of the Paris Conservatoire in France and the Leipzig Conservatoire in Germany. At that time many of our leading performers took it as a matter of course that they would have to travel abroad for their final training. It seemed wrong that we should be obliged to send our students abroad, so The Prince of Wales summoned the Prime Minister, the Archbishop of Canterbury, the Lord Mayor of London, and many members of the nobility to a meeting at St James's Palace at which he exhorted them to donate towards this new Royal College of Music. It was founded and it flourished. I realized when they invited me to come that the centenary of the founding of the RCM would fall during my directorship. It was something that I thought would be lovely to celebrate, being an important landmark in English musical history. The first Director was Sir George Grove, a distinguished scholar who wrote books on Schubert, Mendelssohn, and Beethoven, and who arranged for the publication of the *Grove's Dictionary of Music and Musicians*, which is known throughout the world. He had a very strong staff in those early days, including Parry, Stanford, and Charles Wood. The second Director was Parry, who, together with Stanford and Elgar, led the renaissance of English music, after at least a century where our music had been dominated by composers from the Continent.

O.   Would you talk a little about leaving King's and coming to the
          RCM?

W.   Well, I was very sad to leave King's in 1974, just as I was very sad to
          leave Salisbury in 1950 and Worcester in 1957. I was always very
          happy where I was. I never applied for any job in my life; I never
          asked to move. It was always an invitation that came, which on
          reflection I felt I just couldn't refuse. The principal factor in this
          case, having been at King's for seventeen years, was that I felt I had
          got the choir to a standard I couldn't actually make better. Somebody
          else might be able to, but I would just be repeating myself each year
          trying to maintain the standard and possibly adding new works. I
          had always looked forward to the next term, but there comes a time
          in every job when you feel, 'What can I do new?' Even with the
          recordings, I felt that we had done much of the music which I
          personally was interested in. I would rather move on to another
          challenge. Even so, it was an absolute surprise when the invitation
          from the Royal College of Music came. After advice from David
          McKenna, Honorary Secretary of the RCM, I agreed to see the
          Chairman and certain senior members of the Council, and they
          offered me the post. Leaving Cambridge, which is such a beautiful
          city, for London was quite a change. We decided to keep our house
          in Cambridge so that we could retreat at weekends, but in fact we
          hardly ever did that because there was always some College activity
          in London. There would be concerts given by present students or
          alumni, and I felt it was my duty and pleasure to go and support
          them. In fact, once I got to the RCM, I found that I had very little
          spare time, although I did continue with The Bach Choir right
          through those years. I hope that the College was glad that their
          Director was seen to be doing things in the mainstream of music.
          Arguably you should be there the whole time, but I think in many
          ways I was fresher, because I was getting this outside experience.
          Also, it was useful for the students for me to be working with the
          leading London orchestras and education establishments, as through
          my various contacts I could then offer advice and help.

O.   How was the faculty when you arrived?

W.   During my early years, there were people on the staff senior to me
          in age and experience, foremost among whom was Herbert
          Howells. It seemed strange, because he had been a boyhood hero

of mine. It was one of those extraordinary experiences where you admire the people under you, and you can't help but hold them in the greatest respect and affection. He was very welcoming to me, and I felt very secure having him as a senior professor on my staff. He should really have retired, I think, at the age of seventy, but nobody wanted to see him go. I was delighted that he agreed to stay with us, and I had many very happy conversations with him. He was full of stories of Parry and Stanford in the early days of the College.

O.   You knew him well from Worcester days and your time at King's?

W.   Yes. He attended every Festival at Worcester and was a regular visitor to Cambridge, being an Honorary Fellow of St John's. A lot of people felt that if he hadn't spent so much time teaching at the Royal College, and for a time at St Paul's (an independent girls' school in London, where Holst also taught), he would have been a more prolific composer. Of course his reputation is really based on his church music and three major works for choir and orchestra— *Hymnus Paradisi*, *Missa Sabrinensis*, and the *Stabat Mater*. The *Stabat Mater* was written especially for The Bach Choir in 1965. Howells was one of those people who would love to have written more. He was a beautiful craftsman and one of the best teachers we ever had at the Royal College of Music. He helped many people with their compositions, rather as Stanford had helped him when he was a boy. He wanted everybody to be able to harmonize a Bach melody in the style of Bach, and take a Mendelssohn piece and be able to complete the lower parts. He wanted his students to be able to understand what was in the composer's mind. He seemed less interested in the *avant garde*. There were one or two advanced composers whose music was very 'squeaky'. One or two of the professors said, 'This is marvellous. This is where music is going.' Herbert Howells said, rather, 'He may be writing very good music. The next generation will tell us.' He was always deferring judgement to a later date. I didn't like that music either. I felt very much in sympathy with him. I feel when you're sixty or seventy or eighty, if you don't like something, you can say so straight away. It's no good pretending you like it, and hoping that somebody in twenty years' time will say it was a brilliant work.

O.   I think you gave the eulogy for Herbert Howells.

W.   Yes, for his memorial service in Westminster Abbey.

O.   When you came to the Royal College, who were the other senior
        professors still teaching?

W.   Angus Morrison and Eddie Kendall Taylor were two. Many stu-
        dents came from abroad, particularly from China and the Far East,
        where Morrison and Kendall Taylor used to go to play. They were
        well known, and people wanted to come to London to study with
        them. I had no intention of turning these senior professors away
        from the College, so I kept them on, despite their age. They were
        the people I was really insistent should stay, but nobody else.
        Everybody else had to go at sixty-five.

O.   How large was the College?

W.   It had about six hundred students across all disciplines, most of
        whom wanted to be solo performers. Of course a conservatoire
        exists primarily for performance, but on the other hand, nowadays
        you have to offer academic studies as well. The College was one of
        those which by Royal Charter could give honorary doctorate or
        other senior degrees, which were conferred sparingly. Prior to my
        coming, the College had awarded two: Queen Mary (1933) and
        Queen Elizabeth the Queen Mother (1973). During my tenure we
        gave Honorary Doctorates of Music to The Prince of Wales
        (1981), Sir Adrian Boult (1982), Herbert Howells (1982), and Sir
        Michael Tippett (1982). I was so honoured in 1998 after my retire-
        ment. We were anxious to preserve the strong representation of
        composers, because so many had attended the College as students.
        I felt my main task was to make sure that we had as strong a
        professorial staff as possible, and also that we attracted the best stu-
        dents, because we were in competition with the Royal Academy of
        Music, which is an older institution founded in 1822. The
        Academy had fallen on difficult times during the nineteenth cen-
        tury, and that had prompted The Prince of Wales to found a new
        Royal College, to replace or exist alongside the Royal Academy.

        The professorial staff numbered about a hundred. Many of those
        would be people who only came for one day a week—they might
        be leading players of London orchestras or people active in the
        profession as soloists. Each student had at least one hour for their
        first study and three-quarters of an hour for a second study. They
        would take part in orchestral playing (if they played an orchestral

instrument) and in chamber music, and in classes of aural training, history, and composition. We offered them a rounded education. Everybody in that building was studying music in one form or another. Most important during my years, I think, was the realization that the College needed an injection of money, firstly to improve and enlarge the main library resources. We had a very valuable reference library, much of it the gift of Queen Victoria, and also an important museum of historical instruments. These were not essential to the main teaching of the College, but were a valuable adjunct and very useful for those who were going to specialize in performance on historical instruments. We also needed to provide better catering resources for the students, so that they could have their meals in better conditions. The most important project of all was the building of a new opera theatre. As Britten had been a member of the Royal College of Music as a student, it was felt right to build a theatre bearing his name—the Britten Opera Theatre. This was a major project, requiring an appeal of several million pounds. Central to the success of the appeal was my own association with The Prince of Wales through music. He was at Cambridge as a student, and he used to come to some of the concerts given by the Cambridge University Musical Society. We persuaded the Prince of Wales to be president of the appeal. Of course that made an enormous difference, because we were then able to approach a wide range of people who were only too delighted to give money to a project which had his personal support. We managed to persuade many leading musicians to give their services for concerts in aid of the appeal. The Prince and his lovely wife were very good at attending those concerts, and they were very kind in offering hospitality on a number of occasions. The Prince asked Leopold de Rothschild, who was by then a member of the Council, to be chairman of the appeal, which he accepted. He devoted the best part of two years of his busy life to the success of this appeal. Quite a number of people came over from America to take part in those celebrations. Among those who gave their services were Sir Georg Solti, Daniel Barenboim, and many others who either played or conducted concerts at the Royal Albert Hall which adjoins the College.

O.   How did you celebrate the actual centenary?

Figure 8.1. Meeting to establish the Royal College of Music, St James's Palace, London, 1882, with The Prince of Wales (standing at lectern), the Archbishop of Canterbury (seated to his right), and William Gladstone, Prime Minister, seated on stage with hat at his feet)

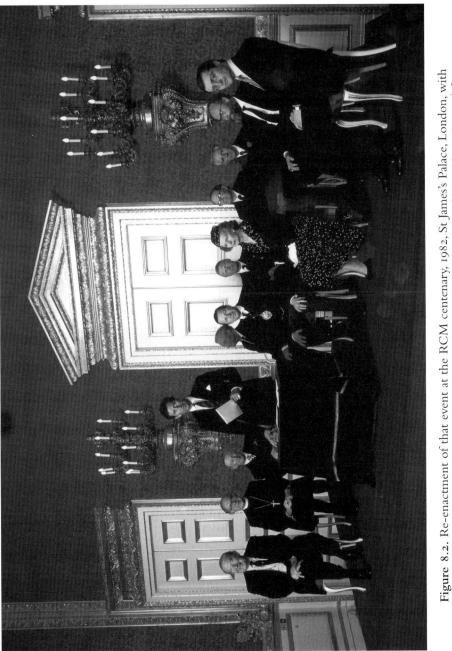

Figure 8.2. Re-enactment of that event at the RCM centenary, 1982, St James's Palace, London, with The Prince of Wales (standing at lectern), Robert Runcie, the Archbishop of Canterbury (second from left), and Margaret Thatcher, Prime Minister (seated fifth from right)

W.   It was a great honour that the actual centenary day, the 28th of
       February 1982, was marked by a broadcast service of thanksgiving
       in Westminster Abbey, in which fine music by many Collegians was
       included. The Chairman of the RCM, Colonel Palmer, and The
       Prince of Wales read the lessons, and the Archbishop of Canterbury
       preached. Afterwards, the 1882 meeting to organize the Royal
       College of Music was 're-enacted' in the same room at St James's
       Palace by the descendants or successors of those present on the
       original occasion. Among those present were the Prince of Wales,
       the Archbishop of Canterbury, the Prime Minister, and the Lord
       Mayor of London, and a photograph was taken of all those assem-
       bled, standing or sitting in the exact location as their predecessors.
       My only frustration was that Prime Minister Thatcher refused to
       place her hat on the floor, as had Prime Minister Gladstone in the
       original 1882 print!

O.   Did you have much contact with students?

W.   I enjoyed my relationships with the students. Most of them were
       very dedicated. I felt sorry for them because some of them didn't
       have very much money and they had to take every opportunity of
       playing in what we call 'gigs' or little engagements to make money
       on the side. But on the other hand, I was always insistent that the
       College had the first demand on their time. They were getting
       government grants, so it was my duty to see that they made the
       best use of every moment of their time. Occasionally, I had reason
       to suspect that some of them were missing a rehearsal or two on
       false excuses. On one occasion I noticed that at a rehearsal we only
       had two out of three trombones. I asked where the third one was,
       and I was told that he was sick, but I thought I saw a smile across
       the faces of some of the people in the orchestra. I was suspicious.
       I thought I would go and call on him that evening. It didn't mean
       my having to spend much time, as I could call on him on my way
       back to Cambridge from London to see how he was. I arrived and
       knocked on the door, and two dear old landladies came to the
       door. I said, 'I've come to see how "Mr Smith" is.' They said, 'He'll
       be so sorry to have missed you. He's out tonight playing in an
       orchestra somewhere.' I said, 'I'm so sorry. I thought he was ill.' 'Oh
       no,' they replied, 'He's very well.' I said, 'Well, do please tell him
       that I called to see how he was.' They said, 'We'll certainly tell him.

Do come in and have a cup of tea. He'll be ever so sorry to have missed you.' I said, 'Tell him when he comes back I would very much like to see him in my office on Monday morning at seven o'clock.' I knew I had to be there anyway, and I thought he might just as well come in to London at seven o'clock to meet me. Well, when he arrived on Monday morning, he looked very sheepish. I asked, 'Do you know why I've asked you to come?' He said, 'Yes, I do, sir.' I said, 'I'm not going to say any more, but never, never, never do what you did again!' He said, 'I won't.' Of course, the news spread around the whole of the College, and the attendance from that day on was very good.

O.   So one of your duties was to conduct the orchestra?

W.   No, not regularly as we had our professional orchestra conductors. I took the choral class every week, because I felt that all students in their first year, whether they could sing or not, ought to join the college chorus. That particularly applied to the pianists and organists because I felt they had lonely lives (they generally have to practise all on their own). It was one way to make sure that the students met people from other disciplines—the trombone players, for example, might otherwise never meet the pianists. I thought also that it was good for pianists to work within a choir, because one day they might have to accompany singers or choirs, and they needed to know that singers need to breathe. I also felt it was useful for aural training, because you had to learn to 'pitch' your notes. For a pianist, this is no problem, you just have to play the next note, whereas if you're a singer you have to think the note ahead. The string players only had to sing for one year, because they needed every single moment to be dedicated to the practice on their instruments. In addition to conducting the college chorus once a week, I conducted each of the orchestras once a year, so that all the students knew me. I felt that was the only way I could really get to know them all. You have to trust their teachers to bring to your attention any real problems they are having. Of course they got expert advice from specialists about their careers, and what they were going to do next.

O.   Did you socialize with the students?

W.   Oh, yes. Every now and again, institutions financially supported by the government are officially inspected. Sometimes they didn't give notice of when they were coming. One day, I was persuaded by the Students' Association to take part in a competition of billiards or pool. We had a table where they had a sort of competition. I said, 'I'm too busy to take part, but I will play the winner.' The table was in the bar. It was twelve noon, and I was there with all the students holding pints of beer in their hands, while I played against the winner of the College pool competition. That was the very day when—unannounced—the inspectors from the government came to see the Royal College of Music. They found the Director in the bar with students cheering! They gave a wonderful report. They said this showed what a wonderful spirit there was in the College! I would have thought that they would have been very angry and report that I had been neglecting my duties.

O.   You mentioned the new Opera Theatre—did you conduct any operas?

W.   No, I didn't, because we had several directors of opera whom I warmly supported in their efforts. I went to their performances. The opera students were all postgraduates, generally in their fourth, fifth, or sixth year of study. It has always been an important part of the College, and one of the showcases, because a lot of the leading critics came to the performances and reviewed them in the London press.

O.   Who was your immediate predecessor?

W.   My immediate predecessor was Sir Keith Falkner, who had been a fine singer. He was one of the soloists in a performance of the *St Matthew Passion* that I heard when I was a boy, aged twelve. I heard him sing the part of Christus in the old Queen's Hall, which was subsequently bombed during World War II. He had a wonderful voice. I remember thinking, 'I wonder if I'll ever see him again?' Years later, when he gave up professional singing, he became the British Council music officer in Italy for a time and then moved to the United States to be a professor at Cornell University, before returning to Britain to be Director of the RCM. He succeeded Sir Ernest Bullock, who had been organist at Westminster Abbey when I was a boy chorister many years ago. It's a small world—these connections.

O.   Now did you enjoy suddenly doing all this administrative work, being a college head, or was that a little bit tedious? You were still performing on a regular basis with The Bach Choir, so you weren't doing administration all the time.

W. I must say I've enjoyed the things I've done in my life. Obviously some things you enjoy more than others, but I found them interesting, if only because of the challenge. The only part I did not like was dealing with the trades unions. The government insisted that if any pay demands came in from the professors they should be through a union. They didn't like people asking for money individually. So they were forced rather against their wishes to join a union in order to get increments in their pay, which was unsatisfactory compared with universities. We had three different unions: the teacher's union, which was called the National Union of Teachers in Further and Higher Education (those would be all the professors); then there was the administrative staff (typists, secretaries), which had a different union called the National Association of Local Government Officers; then there was a third one, the National Union of Public Employees, which would include the porters and the people who moved the pianos and mended the boilers when they broke down. All three of these unions wished to deal primarily with the Director. Of course I tried to delegate as much as I could to the Bursar of the College, but every now and again if there was any dispute I had to be there and available. I liked everybody in the College to feel they had access to the Director, which is a foolish thing to do, really. You ought to be above everything and only intervene, but I like people. If they really had a problem, I wanted them to come and see me. In theory they had the right to go to see the Queen as well, because she was President. Of course, any serious matter would have been referred to the Queen. If a senior professor had a complaint against me, he would take it to the College Council, and if it were not resolved there, it would be referred to the Palace.

O. The Queen actually appointed you, didn't she?

W. No. It was the Queen Mother, because she was the President then and the Queen was Patron. It's a peculiar system, because when the Queen came to the throne, she became the Patron and the Queen Mother became the President, so the Queen Mother was junior to the Queen. The Queen Mother was a wonderful President. She came very frequently to the College, and always to prize-giving once a year. I would sit beside her, and she would chat away, remembering student names from the previous year. I remember once in the middle of a concert, she said, 'Do tell me about that violinist I heard last year. She told me she was going to try to get into the Juilliard for a postgraduate course. I've often wondered whether she actually got there or not.' She had that degree of interest in individuals and remembered their names. She even invited students down to her home in Windsor Great Park to play or sing to her and to her guests. I remember on one occasion, Gerald Finley, now a well-known Canadian singer, was one of those whom the Queen Mother sat at her end of the table when she was pouring out the tea. She sent the staff out of the room to refill the teapot with hot water. She said, 'Promise not to tell the butler, if I give the dog a bit of chocolate cake because he loves chocolate cake!' The Queen Mother cut the cake and gave it to the dog. In came the butler a moment later, and we all sat absolutely still with no smiles on our faces at all. The butler knew perfectly well what had gone on, because the dog was begging beside the Queen Mother with its paws up. People would sometimes ask if the students liked having the Royal Family as their Patron, but I believe they did, because they were such warm friends to the College.

O.   You lunched with her fairly regularly, didn't you?

W.   Yes, and with the Queen. They were very gracious, and it's a great encouragement when people in that position take a personal inter-est, not out of duty, but out of apparent love for the place. The College staff felt they had joined an institution which was proud of its past. I can't see anything wrong in pride, though it is one of the seven deadly sins. Pride, if it means haughtiness and arrogance, can be a sin. On the other hand, it is valuable if it means attention to duty and pride in your institution. A soldier ought to be proud of his regiment, somebody who flies ought to be proud of his squadron, somebody who is in the navy ought to be proud of his ship. I see nothing wrong with that, and I tried to instil a sense of pride in all the students, because the College was a wonderful institution with a great past. I wanted each student to contribute to its reputation.

O.   And you were there for ten years?

W.   For ten and a half years. They were years I enjoyed—to see talent being developed in that way and to see people who arrive at the age

Figure 8.3. Officials of the RCM, *c.* 1976; right to left: David; Queen Elizabeth the Queen Mother, President; Gordon Palmer, Chairman; and (far left) David McKenna, Hon. Secretary

    of eighteen going out at twenty-two ready to enter the profession—it's very exciting. I've been able to maintain friendships with many of them, and they've all without exception wanted to repay the College. They've been very loyal alumni. I think every university in the world has to depend on its alumni because that is where the reputation really ends. To some extent the reputation depends on the academic standing of the staff, but ultimately I think it's on the distinction of its students.

O.   I think, David, you began doing 'From Scratch' concerts at the Royal Albert Hall in London at this time.

W.   When I was at the College, a man named Dr Don Monro came and tapped on my door and asked if I would be prepared to conduct a concert in the Royal Albert Hall with no rehearsal at all, of Handel's *Messiah*. He had done this two or three years before. Don was an amateur musician and a lecturer in chemical engineering at Imperial College. He thought what fun it would be to take his choral society from Imperial College and perform in the Albert

Hall and just invite anybody who wanted to come and join in with them. Well, it was a big risk to take in those days. Booking the Albert Hall is a very costly business: if you only get perhaps a hundred or two hundred people there, you would suffer a thumping loss. But he did so well that he felt inclined to go on with it, and it grew from just a few hundred to three or four thousand. I said I would try it, and I enjoyed it so much that I've been doing it ever since. We perform now not only *Messiah*, but other works like *The Creation, Elijah, The Dream of Gerontius*, Mozart's Requiem, the Verdi Requiem, *Carmina Burana*, and various smaller works. They've always given great pleasure to the singers and audience, and the standard has generally been quite good. People wouldn't pay a lot of money to go and sing if they weren't reasonably good. He charges a lot of money to sing or play, and also a lot of money to come and listen, so he does very well out of it. He has now progressed to employing a good professional orchestra, which is very much better because they manage it well on one rehearsal. At the moment, what happens is that with a work that lasts perhaps an hour—such as the Mozart Requiem—there's time to have a rehearsal as well as the actual concert. The people come, say, at seven o'clock and they rehearse for an hour before performing until ten o'clock. You would think that it would hang by a thread under those conditions, but, in fact, it's generally very acceptable. The audience who come along—generally friends and relatives of the people singing—really seem to enjoy it. They come from all parts of England, Scotland, and Ireland as well as several Scandinavian countries. We've had even one or two from Canada—it's astonishing that they should travel all those miles to take part. I love to see the enjoyment on their faces as they sing. Sometimes we even have parties from schools who take part. What a wonderful introduction for them to sing with other people and with a professional orchestra, especially in a place like the Royal Albert Hall! For soloists, we generally use people who are starting out on their careers. They may have won prizes in national and international competitions, and the chance to perform in the Royal Albert Hall in front of so many people, including a number of critics there to spot talent and others who are promoters of concerts in the regions, is a great experience and very often helpful to them in their careers.

O.   I'm sure it is.

W.   Anne Sofie von Otter was one of the people who sang initially at the Royal Albert Hall, as was Catherine Wyn-Rogers when she was still a student at the Royal College of Music. I've enjoyed this very much, and Dr Monro is a very entertaining man with great vision. We've even taken to going abroad now. We performed a concert of Bach's music with people in Leipzig, and a concert of Handel's music in Halle. We have been also to Barcelona, and to Venice to sing music by Vivaldi, Gabrieli, and Schütz. We went to Paris in 2002 to sing the Fauré Requiem and the Gounod *Messe Solennelle*. In most cases we go for about three to four days, so we get two days of rehearsal before the actual concert. This is ideal because people feel more comfortable when they're performing in a strange country if they've had plenty of rehearsal.

O.   So English people go to Paris, for instance, and then do some Parisians join as well when you tour?

W.   In some instances, yes. In Halle we had quite a large number of singers joining in the performance of *Messiah* there. Of course, it depends on the amount of room there is in the concert hall for singers. In Paris we sang in the beautiful church of St Sulpice, with all its musical associations.

O.   I think you received the wonderful honour of being knighted in 1977, is that correct?

W.   Yes it is. It was the Queen's Silver Jubilee year. In 1971 she made me a Commander of the British Empire (CBE), which is another honour, lower than knighthood. You never know by whom you were proposed, but officially it comes from the Prime Minister's Office. I got the general heading 'For Services to Music', and I'm very grateful that I was so honoured. I felt that I was knighted because of the performances of the King's College Choir, but the choristers and choral scholars earned it; it could, on the other hand, have been a tribute to the Royal College of Music and to all the professors who were teaching there. You can't honour them all. They pick out a person, just as in the army very often after a successful battle a general or a field marshal gets honoured, or in the air force an air marshal gets honoured. He's being honoured not for what he's done, but for what people under him have done.

O.   You represent the group.

W.   Exactly. I was the representative of church music and education. They probably wanted to pay tribute to the institution in the name of the head of it.

O.   And did the Queen dub you?

W.   Yes, the Queen was on duty. On those occasions you are invited to take your wife along with you and any daughters who are unmarried. It's a lovely occasion. You have a little rehearsal and then you're called forward by your name. You kneel on the same stool on which Sir Francis Drake knelt. Then the Queen puts the sword on one of your shoulders and lifts the sword and places it on your other shoulder, dubs you, and she says, 'Arise, Sir David'. You get up and you're knighted!

O.   That's wonderful.

W.   It's nice that these traditions go on, isn't it, over the centuries?

O.   This was in Buckingham Palace?

W.   Yes. There was a little orchestra playing. I think they have quiet music playing, so people aren't embarrassed and so they can't hear what the Queen says to you.

O.   Now what about teaching yourself? You never really did much organ teaching did you, other than working with your Organ Scholars at King's?

W.   I didn't teach them anything—I learned from them! From *all* of them. I think we all go on learning throughout our lives. If I taught anybody, it was that I taught them to be independent and not to take anything without challenging it. I would never say, 'You've got to play it this way.' I might have said to them, 'There are three ways of playing it, you've got to choose which.' I think you learn how to deal with people as well. I've attended some rehearsals where you can see people getting angry with the conductor, and they are not going to be giving of their best if they feel resentment towards the person standing out in front of them. I think if you're directing people you've got to be honest—you've got to say if it's good or if it's bad—but if you encourage you get better results rather than scolding people the whole time. You have got to decide how much you talk, and how much you let people play. I think some conductors talk too much; a lot of mistakes will cure themselves. Many people tell choirs and orchestras what mistakes they are going to make, before they have even played or sung it. I would let them play, and find out for themselves what the mistake is. I've often been to rehearsals where somebody says, 'Sopranos, you're singing B flat incorrectly there.' It's much better to say, 'There was a mistake. Can you tell me what it was?' That way they have to think about it and correct it. These little things you can't teach to people, but they can learn from experience and by watching others. I'd say to any person who wants to be a con-ductor, 'Play in an orchestra, sing in a choir, be at the receiving end, and make up your mind what it is you like about the person up on the rostrum. Is he talking too much? Is he talking too little? Is he encouraging? Is he getting to the really important points, or is he fiddling around with little things that don't really matter?' All those things I think you derive from listening, rather than being taught. I think the best thing you can do is to create opportunities for people to learn for themselves. Now some people disagree with that. They'll say, 'You've got to teach people. You've got to tell them. You've got to show them.'

O.   Good advice!

W.   Well, it depends on the person. Some people have to be bullied because they won't listen or they become lazy. The more you can make people independent, and the younger you make them inde-pendent, the better. Some of the greatest people never studied conducting. I don't suppose Toscanini had a lesson in his life. He was sitting there playing the cello, I think, when he was called out of the orchestra to conduct. I don't suppose he had many lessons, but he just observed what others had done, and then went and did it himself rather better than they had done it.

O.   What was the first time you conducted? Do you remember?

W.   I used to conduct as a little boy in the Westminster Abbey Choir. I would get four boys to sing Bach chorales just for fun. One would sing treble, one would sing alto, one would sing tenor—we would put it up a fourth or something so it was within everyone's range. At Clifton I conducted the house chorus in the annual singing competition. After that it wasn't until I came to Cambridge, when I was accompanist of the Cambridge University Musical Society Chorus. By playing piano with the orchestra I knew what it was like to be in the middle of an orchestra. I watched Boris Ord, and I got the chance to conduct rehearsals

when he was away. I was allowed to conduct Purcell's *Dioclesian*.*
Well, gradually from there it spread. When I went to Salisbury,
most of the works I directed were works I did for the first time,
but I felt that what I had experienced at Cambridge was suffici-
ent to see me through. You soon learn whether you are boring
people or not—you can tell from the expressions on their faces
whether they are enjoying it or not. Once when I was in the United
States, at Ogontz in New Hampshire, I met a chap called William
Owen who had a conducting fellowship. He was very gifted, but I
couldn't teach him anything. I let him stand out in front of the
singers, and he did very well indeed. I think the mere fact that he
had the chance to stand out in front of others, he learned himself
what he did which made them sing well, and what he did that
made them sing less well. I didn't teach him anything—I know
that.

O.   That's not true!

W.   You cannot teach conducting! I know that hundreds of people
have written books on conducting—some of them are up on these
shelves—I can see them as I speak. I don't think I've learned anything from them, but I've learned a great deal by watching people.

* See p. 74.

Interlude 8

Reflections on the Royal College

Lady Willcocks was interviewed on 18 June 2003 at her home in Cambridge.

RW.   When the vacancy came up at the Royal College, to my surprise David said, 'I think this is the time to go'. This was the one career move where I didn't play a major part in the decision. He had had seventeen years at King's and reckoned he had done everything he could do. Each year he had to start again with the choir—a quarter of the boys and a third of the men are new and it isn't the same choir ever. There was no other job he thought he wanted, so it was either go now or stay another fourteen years until the university retirement age. I think it was a very wise decision. The job was very different with lots of different challenges, and I was very pleased because I thought, having been married to an organist for twenty-five years, 'Hurray! We shall have those things other people have—weekends!' But oh no, after working hard all the week, what does he do at the weekends but go off and conduct! We had a lovely flat provided by the College in nearby Ennismore Gardens. It was on the first floor and looked out on a private garden which we had access to. There were lovely plane trees and we were just a hundred yards from Hyde Park and two or three hundred yards from the College.

O.   I guess by the time you moved to London the children were older. Did they come with you?

RW.   No, it happened at quite a convenient time, because our younger daughter started at Oxford that year. Our younger son had another year at school, but the following year went travelling a lot. The older two had their own homes by that time, and even our little dog had died the year before—as in so many places in London, we weren't allowed to have any dogs in Ennismore Gardens. All in all, it was a real change of gear for both of us.

O.   You said Ennismore Gardens was a flat?

RW.   It belonged to the College—the Director before David had used it—and had just one bedroom, a lovely big living room and a dining room. There was no question of the children staying with us, though they slept on the sofa sometimes. We kept our house in Cambridge as a family home.

O.   This was a big change for David, because suddenly he was an administrator.

RW.   Yes, it was a radical change because after being concerned with cathedral and chapel choirs for twenty-five years, he was for the first time out of church music. Also he had to learn how to deal with trades unions and professional associations and so on, which he turned out to be very skilful at. As all educational establish-ments were terribly short of money, a lot of his time went into securing more funds.

O.   Tell me about the knighthood—that came during this period too.

RW.   Yes, in 1977. I think it was automatic, because in fact every Director of the Royal College had been knighted. But I didn't think of it like that, I thought it was because he had done so well.

Leopold de Rothschild served as Chairman of The Bach Choir, Chairman of the Council of the Royal College of Music, and was Chairman of the College's Centenary Appeal. He has been a long-time friend of Sir David and Lady Willcocks, and was interviewed on 18 June 2003.

LR.   Reginald Jacques, who was The Bach Choir's Musical Director when I joined, became ill and they had to get a replacement at very short notice. David came and did a trial concert, and every-body liked it and eventually he accepted the position—so that was when I first met him. He realized there was a lot of spadework to do: like clearing out a nice garden border—eradicating the weeds from the planted flowers. He did it very thoroughly. I remember during the first few years in the choir he was very insistent on note values, quite correctly, and rhythm. He often used to stamp out rhythm when he got particularly cross. One elderly soprano wrote to me in exasperation one day and said, 'If David stamps once again, I'll stamp back!' But she didn't.

O.   What were his rehearsals like?

LR.   He taught us a lot about the music and the understanding of it; not necessarily by actually explaining, but by what he made us do. We would sing one thing, and we would do this and that, and it would come to life. One of the most interesting sessions I remember with him on that subject (he very rarely explained music verbally) was when he took us through *The Dream of Gerontius* and the motifs, which I still have written in my copy. He explained all the themes—committal, fear, sleep, and so on. I hadn't realized quite how Wagnerian Elgar's score is in the use of motifs—it was absolutely fascinating.

O.   When David went to the Royal College of Music, were you already on the Council?

LR.   No, in characteristic David fashion, one day I was doing my triennial voice test in his room at College and before we started, he said, 'Would you do me a favour?' Of course, I'd do any favour. He said, 'Would you join the RCM Council?' That was very nice of him and I readily accepted. It wasn't particularly interesting until the College Centenary appeared on the horizon. Over time I became much more involved in the College, and always had tremendous support from David. I was asked to take on the Chairmanship of the Appeal—this sounds very vain—actually Prince Charles suggested I should do it. I said that I would only do it if David Willcocks and David McKenna (who was also my predecessor in The Bach Choir) thought that I could do it. There was a sort of silence for a bit, and then they came back and said that, yes, they thought so. It worked very well, I think. As to what David brought the College, the main thing I would say was that he was a practising musician. As a conductor, he took concerts around and put the College on the map a bit. He also got together a good team of professors who worked with him. He could be very tough. As you know, he got the Military Cross in the War, and you don't get that for just being a shrinking violet.

O.   I believe the Prince of Wales sang with The Bach Choir?

LR.   Absolutely, he has sung with the choir many times. David sometimes can be rather ruthless. I will never forget Prince Charles was going to sing in the tercentenary of Bach's birth in 1985. The performance was the B minor Mass in the Royal Albert Hall, which was being televised. David did a deal with the television people that they would not dwell on Prince Charles more than anybody else. He didn't come to many practices, so David thought, and I think Prince Charles thought, it would be a good idea if he had some personal coaching. A group of basses went to Kensington Palace for a run-through of the B minor Mass. And a run-through it *was*, because normally, when you are practising, there are other parts to deal with, but *no*! This was just the bass part and David just went through it from start to finish. By the time we finished we were on our knees!

O.   I bet you were. So the Prince learned his part?

LR.   Yes. He was very modest, but he was OK. I used to stand next to him. Then he sang in Wells Cathedral in Handel's *Coronation Anthems*. I thought it was funny hearing him sing 'May the King live for ever'—probably talking about himself one day!

O.   What about the famous Bach Choir Christmas concerts?

LR.   We were doing a carol concert in the Royal Albert Hall, which we still do every year. This one was being televised, and we had worked with the Philip Jones Brass Ensemble. David came on to the stage, dapper as ever, upright. He didn't look around and he addressed the audience and said some customary words like, 'Good afternoon, ladies and gentlemen! Welcome to The Bach Choir's annual carol concert, and I'll ask you to stand and join the Choir and the Philip Jones Brass Ensemble in the first hymn.' He turned around, and we were all with our hearts at our mouths because there was no brass ensemble! The people at the Albert Hall had called David and had not called the ensemble. We all saw this happening. Anyway, not fazed at all, he turned around and said, 'We *were* going to be accompanied by the Philip Jones Brass Ensemble—I think I had better go and fetch them.' Of course, the audience fell about with laughter. He recovered himself very quickly.

O.   He had such an extraordinary tenure with The Bach Choir.

LR.   He just seemed to have the feel for the music so wonderfully in his grasp. He would tackle anything; nothing would worry him. He used to say, 'I can tackle any music as long as I feel a composer really *meant* what he was saying and writing.' I won't cite one particular composer who's quite popular with the public, but David didn't believe this man really believed in what he was writing. Of course David was adored by the choir, there was no doubt about it at all. They realized that he had done a lot for them, and he was always very personable with the choir. I think they were very sad when the time came for him to retire, but he gave thirty-eight years to it. I doubt he had very much more that he could give, these things happen naturally. Of course he hasn't retired at all. He retired from The Bach Choir, but there are a lot of other choirs in other parts of the world that he still enthuses. Enthusiasm is one of his great qualities.

Philippa Thomson Dutton was Sir David's personal assistant at the Royal College of Music and secretary of The Bach Choir. She was interviewed on 23 June 2003 in London.

PD.   Sir David was very, very particular; very, very precise in everything he did. He checked absolutely everything. The College really sharpened up because of Sir David, but he had all this awful business with the unions. Before, it had been more like a gentlemen's club where people used to get paid fifteen pounds or whatever to lecture, even if they were really famous, but now people were saying 'I have my rights, and I want more money'. I felt terribly sorry for him at the time, but he was very good at dealing with it. He's got a degree in economics, and I'm sure that helped. But I do think it encouraged him to go off and perform more, because all that was just so alien somehow. He would sign all the cheques. And he was always correcting things. It used to drive me a bit crackers sometimes, especially when we were putting together Bach Choir programmes. He would correct the Incorporated Society of Musicians (ISM) book and even entries in *Who's Who*. I always call him Sir David, I still have never got out of that old-fashioned way. Everybody else always calls him David, but to me he's Sir David, my boss.

O.   He wasn't an administrator closed off in an office?

PD.   Oh, no fear! I didn't think of him as an administrator; he didn't
        like the paperwork and bureaucracy. He was the Director of The
        Royal College of Music, and he was there to do music. I think he
        was a complete inspiration to the students. He saw a great deal of
        Herbert Howells, and that was a lovely and very important rela-
        tionship. You know the story of Merlin, the old wizard and wise
        adviser, and King Arthur? Howells was Merlin and David
        Willcocks was King Arthur, because Herbert Howells was the
        elder statesman, the Senior Professor Emeritus. HH would come
        and sit on a chair outside Sir David's office and wait to see him. Sir
        David would come out and say, 'Ah! Just the person I want to see',
        and they would talk about all the difficulties in the college, the bits
        of bureaucracy, people's personalities, and how best to handle it.

O.   You must have dealt with his post every day.

Figure 8.4. Four Directors of the RCM, 2005; left to right: Colin Lawson, David,
Janet Ritterman, and Michael Gough Matthews, with The Prince of Wales, centre
(photograph, Chris Christodoulou)

PD.   Sir David used to go to America every summer, and after he came
       back there would be all these fan letters, from lots and lots of
       different people. A lot of the writing seemed to slant sideways, and
       there would be all these little perfumed envelopes from all the
       girls. He'd met them at some Christian Science place I think,
       where they ate nuts, wore sandals, and made music in these
       wonderful summer camps. There were lots of fan letters.

O.   Was most of your work with The Bach Choir or the College?

PD.   The College. It was a very exciting time there. There were con-
       certs virtually every night, and he went to every single concert.
       It was the job of the Director, and even if he sat in the front row
       of the balcony signing letters, he would be at those concerts.
       His presence was very supportive. He may not always have
       enjoyed it, but he was a real friend to the students. Sir David always
       gave them his time, even to the few who were deeply irritating.
       He would see the genius in them, and I thought that was
       excellent.

O.   What about some of the royal events? Were you involved in them?

PD.   I was involved at Windsor Castle when Prince Charles came to
       sing the *Coronation Anthems* with the choir. Her Majesty The
       Queen was in the audience, and so the national anthem was sung.
       Sir David had to teach the Prince the bass part of the national
       anthem—it was so funny. We were standing ready to go on and
       Sir David said to the Prince, 'Sir, do you know the bass part?' and
       he said 'I think you'd better hum it to me.' So there was Sir David
       singing our future King the bass part of the national anthem. Sir
       David adored royalty, and they've all got such respect for him. I
       think some of the most exciting days of my life have been singing
       with The Bach Choir, when Sir David was conducting. He is so
       conscious of the rhythm; it's got that crisp sparkle, and you always
       watch the eyebrows go up and down. What is unique about that
       style is that I feel he's watching every single face when he con-
       ducts. You don't dare look away because you know he will see you
       not looking. I probably sound as if I'm a complete fan. I would
       never write to him with slanty writing and smelly notepaper, but
       I have got a great deal of respect for him, and he's made a great im-
       pression on my life.

Callum Ross was a student at the RCM and sang in The Bach Choir during Sir David's tenure. He was interviewed on 13 June 2006 at his home in Buckinghamshire.

CR.   David had a very sensible idea at College and that was, with the exception of first-study singers, that every student in their first year had to attend the RCM chorus every Wednesday morning between eleven and one o'clock. A lot of people didn't like to do this. They weren't interested in choral singing. But the reason he did this, as I learned afterwards, was because he was worried that some students who didn't have to come into college very often might otherwise not meet many people. He did it as an act of bringing people together. You would hear him at the beginning-of-year Director's Address, welcoming new students to the college and hoping that they would be very happy there and make lifelong friendships. Of course, he also believed strongly that the discipline of singing in the choir was a good skill to learn. The first work that I rehearsed under him was Britten's *War Requiem*. He's always pushed himself very, very hard and set a standard for people to emulate. He would always be first *in* and last *out* of the college. He never shirked his work, ever, and I think he overworked himself.

O.   What about as an administrator, making the transition from a practising musician to the administration of a large college like that?

CR.   I always found him marvellously well organized. I have to say that I always thought that it was something of a waste to have such musical talent sitting there behind a desk. Obviously he had to use that musical talent within the administration of the college, but it was sad that we didn't see very much of him as a practising musician. That was one reason why I founded the chamber choir with him. He seemed to enjoy his work, though. He'd get into the office in the morning and look at his desk, he'd solve the various problems there and think, 'Well, the next time that problem comes up I'll know exactly how to deal with it.' Of course, it never did— it was always something different.

O.   What is unique about David's work?

CR.   He has an innate musical talent, backed up by this wonderful ear he has, and is incredibly disciplined. He's never short-changed anyone or himself. He has always worked himself very hard. The easy option, the easy way out, is not on David's agenda. What is it that makes him unique? I suppose I can give you one example. Although I've heard many of David's recordings it was only very recently, I think within the last year, that I heard any of the famous psalm recordings that he made with King's. When I put them on, I thought, this epitomizes great choral singing. You could hear all the words, the tuning was beautiful. As you know, he was playing the accompaniments himself and the ensemble was flawless. He certainly brought choral singing at King's to a standard in *his* way that I don't think had been evident before: this tightness of ensemble, this meticulous approach to intonation and rhythm, but not at the expense of the soul of the music. David has never been somebody to be overly indulgent. If you listen to his performance of, say, *Gerontius* or *The Kingdom*, there are lots of very subtle rhythmic touches of *rubato*. His pacing of *Gerontius* is just beautiful, it flows naturally as it should do, but with a great sense of *rubato*. I think he was a master of that.

9

A Musical 'Retirement'

O.   What have you been doing since 1984?

W.   There have been many highlights for me since then. After my retirement from full-time musical employment, I've had the opportunity to undertake all kinds of enjoyable extras. I've been on a number of 'singing' cruises, to exciting places such as the West Indies, Alaska, down the Adriatic to Athens, the eastern and western Mediterranean, and from St Petersburg to the Baltic states. At these, I conduct a large choir made up from the passengers, and we have a very enjoyable time. The repertoire is generally kept simple—I usually choose simple Tudor anthems or madrigals—so nobody feels inhibited from joining in. Sometimes we've ended with a concert on the last night. We sing for about an hour each day—on some occasions we have sung to a school of whales!

O.   What about the festivals?

W.   I have very much enjoyed conducting at a number of festivals around the world. I've been to Wisconsin (Green Lake Festival, directed by Dr Douglas Morris), New Hampshire (Ogontz, a festival arranged by Professor George Kent), the International Church Music Festival (arranged by Elwyn Raymer from Nashville and Paul Leddington Wright from Coventry), and the Seychelles Music Festival, including singing in Kenya. I have particularly enjoyed bringing rarely performed British music to the attention of these gifted amateur singers and choral conductors. Their enthusiasm is so exciting to me. I have made several visits to New Zealand, where I have worked with some of Peter Godfrey's fine choirs, some of which have won international competitions—including 'Let the People Sing', organized by the BBC. I have known Peter and admired his work since our undergraduate days in Cambridge in 1945. I have also enjoyed many visits to Australia to work with a number of fine choirs and orchestras. In Canada, I have enjoyed friendships with the country's leading choral conductors, including the late Elmer Iseler, Jean Ashworth Bartle, Doreen Rao, Susan Knight, Lydia Adams, Robert Cooper, and Peter Partridge. What Jean Ashworth Bartle has done so well in Canada, Susan Digby (now Lady Eatwell) is doing in England. I was honoured to serve as co-chairman, with Yehudi Menuhin, of her Voices Foundation, which continues to spread a love of singing among children—particularly in schools where this opportunity did not exist. Since Menuhin's death, I have continued as President.

O.   I believe you have a long history with the Leith Hill Festival in England.

W.   Yes. I was President of this Festival in Dorking from 1978 to 2005, following Sir Adrian Boult (1959–77) and before him Ralph Vaughan Williams (1951–8). Vaughan Williams was the festival conductor from the beginning and for nearly fifty years thereafter. The main Festival runs over three days in April and still operates according to the basic outline laid down in 1905 when Vaughan Williams's sister, Margaret, and Evangeline Farrer founded it. It has been my great pleasure over the years to serve as an adjudicator, guest conductor, and member of the Music Committee. For the Festival's centenary celebrations in 2005 I was one of three composers commissioned to write a short competition piece. I chose Shakespeare's words from *Twelfth Night*, 'O mistress mine'.

O.   Tell me about the work of the Churchill Trust, which is another organization you have been associated with.

W.   This wonderful Trust was formed in 1965 to enable UK citizens from all walks of life to acquire knowledge and experience abroad, thereby enriching themselves and the communities in which they work. I was made a Life Member of the Churchill Fellows' Association of the Winston Churchill Memorial Trust in 1990. My duty was to evaluate the proposals of gifted musicians who would benefit from experience abroad.

O.   Have you been involved with any special charities?

W.   I am a member of several charitable committees, and started my own David Willcocks Music Trust in 1989. It primarily supports the musical training of young musicians and choristers. I have also supported the Musicians Benevolent Fund, which is the music business's own

Figure 9.1. The Queen presenting David with a life membership of the Churchill Fellows' Associaton of the Winston Churchill Memorial Trust, April 1990

charity. It supports musicians of all ages from across the UK and the whole of Ireland. The MBF helps music professionals of all ages who are struggling because of accidents, illnesses, or old age, and also aspiring professionals with educational costs. I became a member of the Council in 1974 and Chairman in 1989.

O. You had the incredible experience of conducting the first *Messiah* in English in China.

W. I was told that they had sung the work many times in Chinese, but never to anybody's knowledge had they sung it in English, and would I take it on? I said I would be delighted to conduct. I felt a bit nervous because I don't speak one word of Chinese, so I went to one or two people and asked, 'What can I do?' They said, 'Just say "Si", smile, and everything will be all right.' They said, 'Most of them speak a little English now, and the orchestra you'll be working with will all be young people, probably between the ages of eighteen and twenty-four. You'll find them very musical, very sensitive. See how you get on. You'll want to take some English singers with you to assist with the pronunciation. You'll have about thirty Chinese people and perhaps fifty or sixty English people. It should be a lovely sound.' We sang in the Forbidden City Concert Hall in Beijing, which is a lovely building. We were put in a very comfortable hotel there and were well cared for. We walked on the Great Wall, which was an unforgettable experience, and visited a number of other places. We all enjoyed it enormously.

O.   What about things closer to home?

W.   I remember once going to the annual convention of the ABCD in Cambridge. ABCD stands for the Association of British Choral Directors, and each year at the end of August they have a weekend of singing and workshops and stage a big gala concert. I was asked to lead a session in King's College Chapel. It was a very hot day but, as always, it was lovely and cool inside. We sang my choral piece, 'Sing!', which is an arrangement of Widor's famous toccata for organ to which I've added some simple choral parts. Stephen Cleobury played the organ magnificently and the choir really enjoyed the experience of singing there.

O.   What about other pieces or arrangements you've written recently?

W.   I wrote a little carol called 'Starry Night' for King's College in 2004.* My daughter Anne wrote the words, although I didn't realize that when I composed it. One of my most recent pieces is an arrangement of the plainsong carol, 'High Word of God, eternal light', which I wrote for the King's College Advent Carol Service in 2007. The carol ends with two bars of 'Amen', the first quite quiet and the second *fortissimo*. We decided to save the organ until the very last bar—it was a splendid moment when the organ entered at full volume and filled the Chapel.

O.   So your work has come full circle—back to carols and to King's College.

W.   Yes, it has. It was lovely also to honour my great friend and carol co-editor John Rutter at a splendid event held in Clare College, Cambridge, to mark his sixtieth birthday in 2005. There was a most marvellous dinner in Hall, at which John gave a very witty speech. Before that, Clare College Choir, conducted by their Director, Tim Brown, gave a wonderful short concert in the Chapel. For that I wrote a little setting of those lovely carol words, 'Lullay, my liking'. The choir sang it very nicely, I must say. And I'm pleased to say that OUP felt able to publish it, too!

* See p. 264

Interlude 9

Reflections on Retirement

Lady Willcocks was interviewed on 18 June 2003 at her home in Cambridge.

RW.   When David went to the College, they had no retiring age for the professors, so the first thing he did was initiate a policy, so anyone appointed would retire at sixty-five, which is in line with what the universities do. To everybody's surprise, he applied it to himself. He had every intention—when he was sixty-five and when he had done ten and a half years—to retire, and he did. It was just about right, because he had accomplished all he set out to do with the centenary celebration. He'd got the new library, the new opera school, and all the new accommodation for the dining rooms and kitchens, and he established a very satisfactory wage rate for the staff. So he felt happy about leaving.

O.   It was a good time, then.

RW.   Yes. It wasn't much of a retirement at first, though. For ten years he had been saying to invitations, 'I'm sorry I can't do that; ask me in 1985.' That first year back in Cambridge he worked non-stop with scarcely any breaks. After that, he calmed down a bit and gave himself a little bit more time.

O.   So you moved back to Cambridge . . .

RW.   When David retired we wondered where to live. David said, 'I'm too busy to think. We had better go home to Cambridge and sort ourselves out there', so we did. We never envisioned as a retired couple we would be living in the house where we raised our family, because it is quite large and has a large garden, but anyway back we came. At that time, my mother had a fall and was unable to be independent, so we asked her to come and live with us, which she did until her death seven years later. By then we were both quite happy in Cambridge, and it suited David, being quite handy for Heathrow and other airports, and so here we still are.

O.   You've done a lot of travelling as well since you have been back here.

RW.   Yes, without the children or dogs or guinea-pigs to look after, I was able to accompany David on his trips abroad. I would go on the ones which were longer or when we could have a bit of free time following his engagements. I have been very lucky, and I think I have been to thirty-five different countries with him and very much enjoyed it.

O.   You have sort of fallen into the role of manager as well with David—the extraordinary amount of work you do with him of printing scores on the computer. That all sort of evolved, I guess?

Figure 9.2. David at Grange Road, Cambridge

RW.   Well, he's always been very clever at getting people to help him. He has this theory that he can't work machines, which is absolute nonsense really. I wasn't familiar with computers but when we got a music program, he sort of thrust it at me and said, 'Learn how to do this', and I very much enjoyed doing that. So I do the turning on and putting the staves up, and then he puts the music in.

O.   Talk to me a little bit about David's composing, because he has, I think, written some really wonderful things in the last few years. Did that really begin when he had more time?

RW.   He has always done arrangements as needed for his various choirs, and very often at the last minute because the instruments available were different from what he expected. Then, when we came back here, a lot of our friends were getting to retirement age and in came the requests, 'David, I'm retiring; I'm having a gala concert. Please will you give me seven minutes for a tuba and three tenors and a soprano?', and he would write something appropriate. He's done a series of Shakespearean songs, which started because they were commissioned for the Toronto Children's Choir and which were subsequently published. It all starts with a specific request.

O.   I really like his Magnificat and Nunc dimittis.

RW.   That was a commission from s'Hertogenbosch, a Catholic church in Holland. We went over for the first performance and the choir was excellent.

O.   David has always had such remarkable health; he had a bad bout with his heart, but he still seems very active.

RW.   He comes from a very healthy family, very long-lived and they say there has never been a fat Willcocks; they tend to be small eaters and very healthy. He did have this one episode. It was three months after our son died, and they were not surprised to hear he had had a trauma in his life; apparently it is very often connected with something like that. He goes back for a yearly test and goes on the treadmill until steam comes out of it!

O.   Did he have surgery with it?

RW.   Yes, he had an angioplasty, which in his case was absolutely successful and I went back to the hospital when he was convalescing for a couple of days thinking they would say now he's got to take it easy. I had his diary ready for a lovely red line to go through, and his consultant said, 'Oh no, he can conduct as much as he likes. I

Figure 9.3. The three Willcocks brothers, 1994; left to right: 'Phil', Wilfrid, David

       don't want him sitting at his desk all day without taking at least half an hour's exercise.' So there we are; apparently conducting is a very healthful occupation.

O.   You have kept David in great shape and strong in mind and body all these years.

R.W.   Yes, well, he has kept himself. I do try and insist that he have three meals a day because left to himself he doesn't think about food at all. He gets weary if he forgets to eat, so I have to watch out for him. But otherwise it's been a matter of chasing after him as fast as I could. I suppose the down side of being married to David is his fans. He depends, though not entirely, to quite a degree on applause; I suppose all performers do. He is very tolerant of his fans. I come along and I have to put up with hour after hour of people saying, 'Oh, isn't he marvellous? And you must be so proud of him.' Well, yes, I am proud; but I get a bit tired of saying it, you know!

O.   I'm sure, and the telephone ringing all the time and huge bags of post.

Figure 9.4. David and Rachel on their diamond wedding anniversary, Grange Road, Cambridge, 2007 (photograph, Chris Christodoulou)

RW.   I know he writes the most lovely letters, and people often tell me they treasure letters he's written, especially in response to times of stress or something. He really is a very gifted letter writer.

Stephen Cleobury succeeded Philip Ledger as Director of Music at King's College, Cambridge. He was interviewed on 18 September 2003 in Cambridge.

SC.   I think that I first met David when I came up to Cambridge as Organ Student at St John's College in 1967. He was extremely generous and welcoming towards me and made it very clear that I'd be most welcome to come up to the organ loft in King's for services if I wished to, and indeed I did do that sometimes on

Sunday afternoons, because evensong at King's is at half past three and evensong at St John's is at half past six. I subsequently became the accompanist to the CUMS Chorus which rehearsed in those days on a Friday evening at quarter past eight, and so I count myself doubly fortunate in that not only did I have a chance of working under George Guest at St John's and observing and learning from his methods, but also had first-hand experience of David's methods through the CUMS connection. Sometimes the two choirs combined together to sing evensong and that afforded a further opportunity. The early impressions I gained of David were of a consummate musician and a generous and warm-hearted person.

Philip Ledger succeeded David in 1974 and was here until 1982. If I think back to my experience of coming here then, I'd probably use the word 'terrifying!'—that wouldn't be putting it too strongly, because I hadn't been a student at King's as both Philip and David had been. It's a place with an enormous reputation, and about which people have many opinions of their own as to how matters ought to be conducted; people have great expectations, and that makes it a very demanding job. But I can only say that David has been an absolutely perfect predecessor to have. Sometimes a predecessor has not conducted himself sensibly in relation to his successor, but David has always been the soul of discretion, and I've never felt that he has been breathing down my neck. He's been always marvellously encouraging and very interested in what's going on, but has never sought to interfere or say 'Well, you know, this is how we used to do it then.' Since he's been retired—despite his world travels, which still continue apace—he's been home a little bit more, and so I've seen a bit more of him in the last few years.

O.   Of course, David was here in that wonderful period when recording was just coming into its own, and it must have been an interesting time when so many things had not been recorded.

SC. Yes, that's right. The coming of the LP coincided with those times,* and there was all this repertoire waiting to be recorded.

---

* See footnote on p. 146.

There are many fine recordings. In my own mind David's *Nelson Mass* stands out particularly, along with the Vaughan Williams G minor Mass, which is a notoriously treacherous work, from all sorts of points of view, not least intonation and blend—two areas in which David is almost unsurpassed. But economically things were brighter then. Today the economic climate is much tougher; when we look at plans for recording, we're faced with the fact that most things have already been recorded, or if they haven't, there's usually a reason for it.

O.   What about David's personality when conducting? I think it's great when a conductor can get a choir to reflect his personality.

SC.   I would want to put that slightly differently, because my own feeling is that it's not so much that it's great when they can, but that it's inevitable that they do. Some people are more able at achieving what they want to achieve than others and they're the ones that become successful. It's inevitable that as soon as somebody stands on the rostrum and starts to conduct how their face looks, how their gestures look—all that immediately has an effect on how people are going to sing. So if you think of David's way with amateur singers—the infectious enthusiasm and that playful sense of fun and so on, coming out of every pore of his being—all that cannot help but communicate itself to people. He also has a great ability to deal with different situations. You don't stand up in front of a professional orchestra and do that stuff, but it's fine with a group of amateur singers. He has an enormous ability to be able to switch from one style to another.

O.   Do you have any special stories of David?

SC.   I remember a few years ago I asked David if he'd like to conduct the annual Founder's Day Concert here in the Chapel, which he, in fact, initiated. The idea was to provide an opportunity for former members of the choir to have a nice nostalgic visit back to King's and take part in a concert. It always took place on the first Saturday in December, so the weather could be quite rough, and this particular year I think there was already snow on the ground and it was a very foggy evening. I mean so foggy that you could barely see from one side of the front court to the other. After the concert we always go over to the hall and have dinner, and I think I had decided that my chief responsibility was to escort Rachel Willcocks

across from the Chapel to the hall. We got over there and some
time elapsed and still no David—he'd obviously got talking to people, as he does—so we were peering out of the hall and you could
just see figures across the other side. Rachel said, 'Oh there's somebody *running*, that'll be David!' It was the same when we had a concert to mark his eightieth birthday in the Chapel, when the King's
Choir was joined by the chorus and orchestra of the RCM and he
conducted two of his favourite pieces, the Haydn *Nelson Mass* and
Fauré's Requiem. At the end there were many curtain calls, and on
the last one he ran up the aisle as if to say 'I may be eighty but I can
still run.' The thing that inspires those of us who love him is his
irrepressible energy and enthusiasm for everything he does and that
was expressed in the energy of that running.

O.   I think that's also true in the people he cares about. He's so giving
       of his time and energy.

SC.   Yes. There's the energy and vitality that's plain for everybody to
       see, but there's also a side of him which not everybody knows
       about, a side which is generous, warm, and supportive.

O.   And very loyal, I find.

SC.   Yes. There's a kind of 'integrity' about the way he approaches issues
       and he won't be deflected from what he believes to be right and
       just in a situation.

Anne Willcocks was interviewed on 26 October 2006 in Cambridge.

O.   You had the wonderful experience of writing the text for the carol
       'Starry Night', which your father wrote for King's in 2004.

AW.   That's right. It came about because I was here one summer's day
       and Dad was saying he had this carol to write but he really could-
       n't think of any words. He asked if I would look for a text, so I
       went to the library and I looked up a lot of different religious
       poems. By the next day I'd collated quite a few for him and, just
       for a laugh, I wrote one myself. I copied these out and he reduced
       them to two: one was an excerpt of something by Milton and the
       other was mine! I hadn't told Dad who they were by, and my
       brother Jonny said firmly I shouldn't tell him because he thought

this was very amusing. Dad looked at them and he didn't say much. Finally he said, 'I can hear this one'. It was mine; it was my words. Then he said, 'But it's not long enough'. He furrowed his brow and the next morning I came down and said, 'Dad, you know those words for the carol that you liked? I've found it has another verse', because overnight I'd written another verse for it! He said, 'Ah yes—that's longer, that's better, but it's still not quite long enough'. Then I had an inspiration, which was to add a bit of Latin after each verse, as well as 'Alleluia'. My Latin is rather rusty, so I wasn't quite sure I'd got it right. He was already busy writing—he went straight off and started composing it and before you knew it, there was this beautiful carol. I went back to Oxford and got the Latin checked with a classicist there. It was only about two or three weeks later, when he was putting the final touches to it, that Dad said, 'Is there a problem with copyright with those words you found for me?' I said, 'No, there's no problem'. He said, 'Are you sure? Where did you get them from?' I said, 'I wrote them'. He said, 'What do you mean, you wrote them?' I said, 'I wrote them!' First of all he was rather surprised, but then rather pleased. It was only after the carol was really finished that I owned up as to who had written the words!

Simon Carrington was a Choral Scholar at King's College, Cambridge and hosted Sir David and Lady Willcocks at Yale University in February 2005 as a guest conductor of Yale's three main choruses. He was interviewed on 25 February 2005 at Yale University.

SC.   There is a special discipline in David's type of choir training, and I watched it yesterday here at Yale, still going strong: absolute precision of rhythm, constant questioning of intonation, and always those gimlet eyes—bright, bright eyes. I said to my chamber choir here at Yale, 'When he conducts you, he's going to be looking at your eyes. He wants to see intensity and enthusiasm, he doesn't just want to hear you sing.' That tremendous energy and intensity are always there. It is so exciting and thrilling to see in his eighty-sixth

year it's still going strong. He stood Wednesday night from seven
o'clock until ten o'clock, three hours without stopping. I said,
'Don't you want your stool, David,' and he said, 'No, no, I'll be
fine.' Once he is up on stage with the choirs he's in absolute
tip-top form. It's inspiring to watch and it rubs off on the students.
I was transfixed . . . all his famous gestures with the arms going
up and down alternately and that intense sign he gives with
his left hand when he feels the music is dragging for any reason.
Suddenly that hand pops up to encourage the singers to
ever-greater efforts; that really rang a bell with me. David has
this skill which sometimes I fear I may not have, of having tremendous vibrancy on the platform but without getting everybody so agitated that they couldn't relax and give a wonderful
performance.

O.   This affects pitch, don't you think?

SC.   I often tell my students that one of David's classic remarks is, 'That
note isn't actually flat, but it *might* be flat!' Working in America I
found that there has been a long tradition—easing a little now—
to encourage what I think of as rather loose voices with too much
vibrato. This can send the pitch below the actual written note, and
I've worked hard ever since I came here to try to encourage the
idea of keeping the voices in line so that it's absolutely in tune, and
David would be comfortable! I've worked a lot since I've been
here with DW's face in the back of my mind, looking and waiting,
with this little sign he gives to get the pitch up. He was doing it
the other night. Working with David there is always so much
energy, which can be construed as a certain tenseness, whereas we
are always taught here that conductors must project relaxation and
deep breathing.

O.   I wish you would talk about the King's Singers a bit.

SC.   We were beginning to consider the idea of whether we could make
this as a living. David was clear, and said many times, that he didn't
think we 'had a hope in hell' because the market wasn't there, really,
nor were we set up to do it. When the King's Singers celebrated
its twentieth anniversary, we invited a lot of the people who had
supported us over the years and took a trip down the River
Thames on a fancy boat with dinner and so on. Various people
made speeches, including David, and he told this story against him-

self, but it was a perfectly reasonable assumption that we wouldn't succeed!

O.   What about David and his work with large amateur choirs?

SC.   As everybody knows, David is very, very good with amateur singers, who can almost always do better than they think they can. That's one of his great skills, and I've tried to emulate him in that regard. This has helped me in this country, to be honest, and I often feel him there with or behind me. I often conduct really large choirs, community choirs, youth choirs, All-State choirs, and so on. David's spirit was with me: he can be extremely demanding and intolerant of people not being prepared to give of their best and yet full of encouragement where it's deserved. I've told Willcocks stories myself when I can't get singers to watch, and tried some of his tricks. He's a very strong influence, and I think in many ways he's influenced lots of choral directors in that way. He's just now been on a cruise where the singers were of modest ability, probably not even balanced, and yet he would have expected them to do their very best rather than just to take it casually because they happened to be on a boat! I think that's what's driven me too. I have always had this need to 'reach for the highest standard' and to lift the participants two or three pips above where they expect to be!

O.   What about David as a conducting teacher? I said to him, 'I consider you a teacher', and he answered, 'I didn't teach you anything'.

SC.   We conducting teachers sometimes joke about David's conducting! It's very much in the English school, whereas here at Yale we need to teach very clear patterns. That's never been important to him—it's not necessary. You observe and you absorb and you think about the music and what's required, and then you extract it, basically. I agree with him to a point and do try to concentrate on that, though, at the same time, we're almost obliged to make sure that students come out with some kind of elegance of gesture. As everybody says, a banana can conduct; a banana can beat time. With David it's much more to do with the fact that he makes people aware that he's listening all the time, reacting to what they're doing, absolutely. That's a hard one to teach as such— maybe he's right: you can't teach it. The individual has to want to do it, and has to let everything rub off on them, and then go out and do.

Susan Digby OBE (Lady Eatwell) founded the Voices Foundation with Yehudi Menuhin and Sir David, who continues to serve as President. She was interviewed on 24 January 2004 at her home in London.

SD.   I grew up in the Far East as well as in London, but I returned here for my education from quite a young age, so for me David Willcocks really was the pioneer, the ultimate figure in the choral world. His early recordings became staple, they became bread and butter. In 1980 I managed to persuade him to come and watch me conduct a children's choir at the Hong Kong Academy for Performing Arts. I was very active in children's choir training and also in education at all levels from pre-school to tertiary. That became an obsession—how singing can develop the whole child and how musical activity, using singing as a medium for music education, develops the whole child. I was absolutely terrified when the great David Willcocks came to observe me at the Academy! He watched my work and said, 'You have a real gift, and I think you should seriously pursue this'. I applied for a Winston Churchill Memorial Fellowship and was successful. This was thanks to him. I embarked on this study around the world of not just children's choirs, but systems of music education that were chorally based. I examined why it was that certain communities had very, very good children's choirs, and why certain communities and societies had a strong singing culture. I examined the whole sociological and historical elements and influences, and it was central to what has happened since in my life. When I eventually came back to the United Kingdom in 1992, I had quite a good overview of what was happening in the world and examples of good practice, and where the real inspiration was, as far as I was concerned. I also knew what I wanted to do back here for *this* country. So with David Willcocks I started the Voices Foundation, and that was really a distillation of all I had learned. I was very fortunate with my network, so I gathered support very fast. The Voices Foundation took off, and twelve years later we have worked with three-quarters of a million children, and trained around ten thousand teachers. I think what we do is sometimes misunderstood because we are not choral animateurs; we are dealing with *curriculum* music. Without David it would never have happened. My choral discipline and what I am able to give as a choir director comes from him. That whole choral discipline is his legacy, really, and that is what I am now passing on. I owe Sir David a huge amount, which it is not possible to repay. How do you repay something like that?

Jonathan Willcocks was interviewed on 20 June 2003 in London.

JW.   I think the first time David and I shared a concert was at the Green Lake Festival in Wisconsin, which was a festival where David had been conducting for about ten years, run by Doug Morris. In one season they decided to do a choral concert entitled 'Fathers and Sons'. It was a programme with music by J. S. Bach and C. P. E. Bach, by Mozart and his father Leopold, and a work by David and a work by me. The original idea was that David would conduct all the fathers' pieces so he had his own music and a piece by J. S. Bach, but would have to put up with Leopold Mozart, who was obviously much less of a composer than Wolfgang. I would conduct my piece and I'd have C. P. E. Bach, but I'd have a work by the real Mozart. It was a lovely concept actually, the idea of fathers and sons. As it happened, I seem to remember that in the end I conducted Leopold Mozart and C. P. E. Bach! David actually pinched my Mozart piece, but it was great fun! The particular pleasure of Green Lake, for the choral works that I rehearsed and conducted, David acted as my accompanist, so I was able to tap my stick at him and tell him to play in time which was rather fun.

O.   Have you consulted him often?

JW.   The first time I really consulted him was when, aged twenty-two, I was short-listed to audition for the role of musical director of the Portsmouth Choral Union, and the audition was to take a rehearsal for forty-five minutes on the *St Matthew Passion*. 'If you wanted to impress judges, which bits would you choose to rehearse, and what would you do?' 'How can I best show what I can do?' A distinguished panel of people would be sitting at the back trying to assess how I would make out as musical director. He suggested choruses and told me to run it through absolutely boringly and then you can make improvements. The difference between where you start and where you'll get to will be really striking. The last thing you want in an audition is for it to go wonderfully well the first time, because then you can't improve it. He suggested also some of the short energetic choruses which the chorus enjoy—the crowd scenes in the first half. I have also consulted him regularly in choosing soloists to engage, because he has great experience. Latterly, because I'm now closely involved with young singers coming out of the major conservatoires, he's asked me for recommendations for concerts he's doing. So it works both ways.

O.   Do you think having David as a father has helped or hindered your career?

JW.   David would probably be the first to say that he's always been very aware and cautious, and even apprehensive, about any suggestion of trying to do things that would help my career, because of the dangers of being accused of nepotism. A lot of people have asked me if it isn't very difficult being in the same sort of business— being the son of someone who's as well known as David. It's never worried me in the slightest. I know what I can do, I'm confident in what I can do, and it's never concerned me that I'm somehow living in the shadow of anybody. I don't feel that I am at all. There may have been occasions where I've been given a chance to com- pete—to show what I can do *once*—because of who my father is, but no one ever asks you again unless you can cut the mustard.

O.   You have this incredible bond with him.

JW.   Certainly I saw hugely more of him than my sisters and brother did. I've worked closely with him in all sorts of ways, and whenever he picks up the phone we always talk about music. If my sisters phone him, he hasn't got very obvious 'common country' to communicate with them.

O.   What about his influence in your composing? Probably less so?

JW.   Yes, to a certain extent. Early on I used to show him things that I'd written, partly just to show him what I'd done, and partly to ask for his advice. He was very helpful in some ways—he wouldn't criticize it as such, but he would suggest 'I think this would work a bit better. Try rewriting the tenor part like this,' or 'I think it would work better if you voice this section like this.' I wouldn't always agree, but I valued his advice very much, because he's hugely experienced, knowing so readily what will work well. We always spoke of technical matters—he'd say, 'I think you might have over-scored that bit orchestrally', those sorts of issues. He's never said to me what he really thinks about my music. He's never said 'I think that's the best piece you've ever written' or expressed a view on an emotional level. Again, it doesn't worry me at all. My mother's a bit the same. Both my parents have taken considerable pleasure out of the fact that my music is now pretty widely heard, although David's never been terribly interested in going to other people's concerts. At home he will very, very rarely, if he has an evening free, put on music. It's the last thing he would do, partly because he can't relax and listen to music, except critically. He can't just enjoy it. He'll always think 'Gosh, the altos are a bit coarse in that movement', or 'I didn't much like the way they managed that cadence'. He can't enjoy music purely for pleasure. But there are literally hundreds of thousands of people across the world, people who have actually sung with him, who feel that they've got personal touch with David as a musician and felt what he has to give. These people feel they own part of him, have a genuine affection for him, and feel that he's touched them musically.

John Rutter CBE was interviewed on 24 June 2003 in Duxford, near Cambridge.

O.   What are your thoughts about David as a conductor?

JR.   I would put David absolutely at the top of the tree in terms of his fidelity to a composer's vision and intentions, and his respect for composers. I think this may, perhaps, come from the fact that he has a strong creative streak himself. He has always been rather modest about his own writing, but nonetheless he knows how to do it. I think, therefore, he can spot the ability to do it in other composers, and knows what they want. He has one of the most unerring senses of correct tempo of any conductor I've come across, applied almost to any composer. Although he wouldn't think of himself as somebody who's embraced the 'period performance' movement, nonetheless, the tempos that you will find in a Willcocks Bach or Handel performance, I think, are absolutely spot-on, and remain so even in an era where there's been a lot of experimentation with tempos among period instrument people. But he has a very sure sense of the flow of music and that in a way comes before all else, because if the tempo's not right, you have to work far, far harder to make a piece of music work. In his case he hits the right tempo, so in a sense you're letting the composer speak.

O.   What about David's impact on choral singing from his recordings?

JR.   The recordings do stand as a monument. I was playing recordings of choirs past and present to my then eighteen-year-old son Christopher, who was just on the point of joining Clare Choir. I remember playing one made in, I think, 1962 or thereabouts, called *On Christmas Night*, which was the one with the Rubens painting on the old LP sleeve. Christopher was quite captivated by it and he said 'There's an atmosphere, there's a magic which is not there today.' That's not to say that today's choir is less good, it's just that I think they're not aiming for the same thing. If I had to encapsulate the difference between King's College Choir then and now, I suppose really it's a reflection of changes in choral taste generally. I think the ideal then was that a choir should sound like angels, disembodied angels, and that the blend should be perfect, and it should be like an angelic visitation. When we hear even just a little piece that David loved to perform, Harold Darke's 'In the bleak midwinter', for instance, it seems to hover in the air. Time stands still and it's something that comes to you from elsewhere. King's College Choir now, like most other choirs today, sounds like a group of human beings performing a piece here and now, a group of humans all with slightly different feelings and vocal timbres and different personalities who nonetheless are forming a choir, but are having a conversation with you, the listener, as equals. They are earthlings, as are we, and they're singing to us as one group of human beings to another, and so there's more informality, I think. There's not the same sense of *illusion* that this is a group of angels that have just appeared from heaven, and are singing something perfect. I think that we like our choirs to sound more real, more earthy, these days, and I think David, probably, if he were conducting King's Choir now, would be going along with that because his ideas have changed as the years have gone by. But that ideal of perfection was something that, once you had heard it, became unforgettable and troubling, in a way, because you were always going to say to yourself 'I can't get my choir to sound like that'. But at the same time it gave one a goal. The importance of the King's sound in the Willcocks era can't be over-estimated, because of its influence on everybody else in choral music, including the influence upon those who reacted against it and said 'I really don't care for that—I want something that sounds more earthy, more real.' There are plenty of conductors who do hold that viewpoint, but nobody could ignore King's College Choir. It just had that sort of centrality and importance in the world of choral music. I personally loved it, as a sound, and I equally enjoy earthier-sounding choirs, but at the same time, for certain sorts of repertoire that kind of perfection, ethereality, is something that is absolutely right.

Q.   What else about David's impact and influence?

JR.   Just at the mundane level, in the pre-Willcocks era, even the choirs which were broadcast and recorded routinely went flat in *a cappella* pieces. One just accepted that—choirs went flat. Of course nowa-days nobody accepts that, and King's College Choir was one of the first that would stay on pitch, simple as that! Of course sometimes that was carried a little far—David did like terribly sharp major thirds, which was probably in reaction to a prevailing flatness among choirs, so he always wanted the thirds even sharper than piano major thirds, and you can hear that on some of the record-ings. I think he probably wouldn't want that now, because there's not the same paranoia about losing pitch that there was then. King's then and King's now—I enjoy them both, but I think it absolutely mustn't be forgotten how important David's achieve-ment was in the context of what was happening in choral singing at that time. I'm not sure how widely that's recognized in the choral world. Things move on, and rightly so, but it's important to acknowledge a debt, an absolutely huge debt, to David for his care for all the specifics of choral singing: the diction, the rhythm, the pitch, the blend, the vowels. That raises a whole other issue, of what sort of pronunciation you want from your choir both in Latin and, particularly, in one's vernacular. I have a theory that choirs sing about a generation behind the way that they speak. Speech in England has become more casual and diphthongized and things like double consonants have just disappeared—nobody articulates those any more—and we're now hearing, with today's choirs, something like the way people spoke twenty or twenty-five years ago, while in David's time what we heard when the choir sang in the 1960s was something like the speech of the 1930s and 1940s. If you listen to some of those wonderful old British films of the period of *Brief Encounter*, there is very clipped diction. There's something of that in the Willcocks King's Choir: we would say 'Alleluia', they would sing 'Elleluia'! That's rather charming, but I think David would now be the first to smile at that and say 'That has dated a bit, hasn't it?' because the mode of speech has changed.

O.   You know David so well as a person and friend. Anything you would like to share?

JR.   I think I should mention, as somebody who's been on the receiving end of it, my gratitude for David's immense loyalty to those he believes in, or likes, or feels have been helpful to him, because that's something which I've had ample proof of over the years. It was a long time ago now that we met. We don't now meet as often as we once did, but from time to time I learn how he still remembers me. I think it's probably no secret when I was given the Lambeth Doctorate of Music that it was absolutely on his personal recommendation, and he wrote the citation—I recognized the style! This was very inspiring for me, and is one of the inspiring things about him, because that quality of loyalty is not all that common in the musical world among those who've achieved eminence. They sometimes choose to forget the people they knew years ago and feel that 'well, we've moved on since then', but he's shown in a number of ways, in recent years, that he still remembers that shy young undergraduate who was awkward and lacking in confidence back in the mid-1960s. He's got space for me in his life and is from time to time able to do me a good turn and remember me. That's a very inspiring quality. And he is somebody who has always wanted to put back into the musical community more than he has received at every sort of level, who's always willing to sit on a dull committee, who's always willing to lend his name to an appeal, to be patron of this or that, always willing to go out and conduct a *Messiah* in some amateur backwoods place, and who's always willing to encourage younger musicians, and who is always interested and welcoming. That generosity of spirit is something from which a lot of people have benefited over the years. So, long may he continue, speaking of which, of course, there he is at an advanced age quite undiminished, which gives me great hope!

O.   All of us!

Acknowledgements

We are grateful to all those who kindly provided the photographs that have been used throughout the book and in particular to the following for permission to reproduce them.

Clifton College: Figures 2.2 and 2.3

Chris Christodoulou Photography: Figures 8.4, 9.4, copyright © Chris Christodoulou

The Duke of Cornwall's Light Infantry Museum: Figure 3.3, copyright © DCLI Museum

Getty Images: Figure 4.3, © Kurt Hutton/Picture Post/Getty Images

Illustrated London News/Mary Evans Picture Library: Figure 8.2

King's College, Cambridge: Figures 4.1, 6.1, and 6.2, copyright © John Edward Leigh, and Figure 6.5

Maggie Heywood: jacket photographs

Janet Lewison: Figure 7.2, copyright © Janet Lewison 1969

The Royal College of Music: Figure 8.1

General Index

Index of Musical Works